Remembrances

*A fond
look back
on life,
love,
craziness,
and
joy ...*

Remembrances – VCWC Anthology

Hardbound: 978-0-9828549-5-2 ISBN

Chairman/Editor: Carol Malone

Reading Assistants: Jann Correll   Joan E. Day
                       Sheli Ellsworth   Garette Lampert
                       Rhonda Noda   Barbara Piszczek
                       Peter Pohl   Shelba Robison
                       John Shehorn   Marc Tapper

Editing Proofreaders: Pat Caloia   Greg Elliot
                       Rhonda Noda   Victor Noda
                       Duncan Smith   Lee Wade

Layout and design: Carol Malone and Barbara Piszczek
Cover Photo: Courtesy of pixaboy.com

VCWC Press
P. O. Box 3373
Thousand Oaks, CA 91359
venturacountywriters@yahoo.com

From the President...

Ventura County Writers Club introduces *Remembrances*, our fifth anthology. *Remembrances* follows four previous anthologies: *Out of Thin Air, Quintessence, Windows,* and *Serendipity*. This book is for everyone who has written a poem, short story, essay, memoir, non-fiction, or fiction book using life experiences and special memories to enhance and bring originality to their works. These thought provoking memories remind us that humanity is not perfect, that life lessons teach us to be diligent in kindness and forgiveness, and to know that living each day is to keep learning about being human.

Thank you to the Anthology Chair Carol Malone and the many people who assisted her in the journey of assembling the creative written works that make up this beautiful anthology. We want to send a special thank you to all the writers who shared their poems, short stories, and essays for use in *Remembrances*. We are thrilled to share the works from our short story contests and poetry contests from 2012 and 2013. Your experiences will continue to teach us and inspire us in our daily living.

The Ventura County Writers Club invites you to learn about us on www.VenturaCountyWriters.com.

For each memory made there is an original experience to be shared. What have you written today?

Rhonda Noda

President 2014-2015
Ventura County Writers Club

From the Editor...

Memories. Nostalgia. Longing. Reminiscing. Whatever you call that thing we do as humans when we gaze into our past to see what happened to ourselves and to others, falls under the title of *Remembrances*. I know when I stop and take a moment to gaze back upon the sum total of my life; I look past the faults, the foibles, and the frustrations. If I went through something that at the time I thought would certainly kill me, like cancer, I can now look back and forgive myself for not realizing the growth potential it afforded me or the empathy I gained because of that horrific experience. What I also remember are the good times. *When we think of the past it's the beautiful things we pick out. We want to believe it was all like that.* — Margaret Atwood, *The Handmaid's Tale*

I began this journey of discovery with my co-chair at the time, Glenn Turner. I want to thank Glenn for his valuable input in selecting the pieces we've featured. When we read through the submissions of the club members, it wasn't long before a clear theme presented itself. VCWC writers wanted to remember everything from a beloved puppy, to a favorite horse adventure, to their heart-tugging memories of growing up at home with their weird and wacky family, to the stark contrast of war and the pain of losing a loved one, and everything else in between.

Each author in *Remembrances* seemed to find strength and comfort from walking into the past, from reaching into their conscious memories of a precious or perilous time in their lives, and they've shared it in this volume for all the world to learn from.

I felt compelled to open and close the anthology with a poem and a story by two great ladies who are no longer with us in this earthly existence, but have passed on to that great writer's group in the sky: Poetess Joyce LaMers and Author Marjorie Moore—the open and closing acts for our book. It is with great pleasure that we remember them in this compilation.

Part way through the process of gathering stories, poem, and essays; Glenn had to bow out because he moved from the area. The challenge of making this a quality book fell to me. I felt the weight of this responsibility upon my shoulders like Atlas holding up the world, and reached out to members of the club and the board for their much appreciated assistance. There aren't words enough in the English language to express my heart-felt *thanks* to all those last minute submission readers and those who have proof-read to catch those pesky grammatical issues we're all guilty of as writers.

A big warm thanks goes to Janet Correll, Sheli Ellsworth, Garette Lampert, Rhonda Noda, Barbara Piszczek, Peter Pohl, John Shehorn, Marc Tapper, and Glenn E. Turner, who read countless hours for me. And a special thanks to Shelba Robison, Barbara Piszczek, and her good friend, Joan E. Day for their poetry expertise. I couldn't have done it without their help. *"I'm not a poet and I know it."* – Carol Malone

No compilation of writing would be complete without our dedicated proofreaders, those individuals with their fine tooth combs and very large magnifying glasses. My special thanks go to Pat Caloia, Greg Elliot, Rhonda Noda, Victor Noda, Duncan Smith, and Lee Wade for whipping out their tools of the trade to help make this compilation as perfect as possible.

And a world of thanks goes to those contest winners and featured member writers who took the time to edit and polish their pieces for all of us to enjoy over the years ahead of us.

No matter how much heartache, triumph, or mediocrity you go through in your life right now, today—it will be remembered by someone. Make that *memory*, that *remembrance* something special for another anthology compilation at some future date.

Remember dear readers: *The best way to see the future is to remember the past.* Zoe, from *Kiss at Pine Lake,* Hallmark Movie. May the faith and triumph over adversity spoken of within the pages of this anthology give you pleasure for many years to come. This is my hope.

Thanks,

Carol

Carol Malone, Anthology Chair

Table of Contents

Memorable Member Short Prose Selections –

Memorable Member Poetry Selections –

Memorable Photos – Of Ventura County

Theme Poem for Our 2015 Anthology.
With much gratitude
to Poet, Joyce LaMers

★ *2013 Poetry Third Place Winner – Pending by Joyce LaMers*

– Joyce passed away in 2014. We will hold you in fond remembrance, dear Joyce, who was named a Ventura Country Literary Treasure. She was treasured by us.

You left before our conversation ended
There are matters I intended to bring up,
questions to ask, or answer. You
should have waited, given us time
to check for what was missing,
find the pieces, tie loose ends.

Now gusts of words unspoken
swirl through emptiness of rooms,
rattle silence, cloud the light.
Tense in the dark, I listen
for an unfilled shoe to drop.

About the author: Joyce LaMers was a celebrated light verse poet, born in Billings, Montana, and who lived much of her adult life in Southern California. She wrote of her experience of being human; combining wit and humor. Her later work was often her perspective on aging and death, as in her poem, "Why Must I Die Before My Wake?"

~ Written by Juliet LaMers-Noble, daughter

This has been a hell of a journey. Yes, I saw movies and heard stories of what it would be like, but I had no idea what it would be like for me. It progressed slowly and then, after about a year or so, for her safety and everyone's quality of life, we had to take the big step. We? Our kids, Sharon's best friend, Diane, me, and the caregiver. We found a memory care setting that we all liked, including Sharon. It was the best we could find given our resources and wanting Sharon close enough for regular visiting.

During all this time, some people did not know what was happening. When our paths crossed they would ask, "Where is Sharon?" That seemingly innocent question was at the heart of it, at least for me. As Sharon changed, I, too, wondered: Where is my wife? Is my wife the woman who sits quietly in the brown chair in front of me, who has been my life partner for over forty-three years, who occasionally talks to me – is that my wife? It looks a lot like her. Everyone told me that this setting was for the best. Still, I couldn't shake the part inside me that felt like I was giving up, like I was deserting her.

I went to visit her every day. As they warned me, she was often different from one day to another. Sometimes, even from when I arrived, until a few minutes later.

"Who are you?" Sharon asked as I walked up to her.

"I am your husband, Marv." I smiled. "May I sit down?"

"You are my husband?"

I nodded.

"Okay, I think that would be okay."

The visits were different each day and yet they were the same. I usually spent about an hour with her, unless it was one of the days she did not wish to see me at all, or a day she got angry. Sometimes, when I was leaving and we'd had a good visit, I would ask if I could kiss her on her forehead. Sometimes she said yes. Some days she was more interested in a game of Dominoes, or putting icing on a cupcake, or watching some reality show on TV, or visiting with a friend who ate at the same table as she did.

I was pleasantly surprised, once, when she was unusually talkative. "Was I a good wife?"

I held back the tears and managed to answer. "Yes, you were."

"I'm glad. You seem like a nice man."

"May I hold your hand?" I asked, pushing my luck.

She nodded. I reached for her hand. "You like to hold my hand, don't you?"

"Yes, I do." I answered.

"Do you love me?"

"Yes, I do."

"Were we married a long time?"

"Yes," I said.

"Are you going to stay for lunch?"

"I think you already had lunch."

"No, I didn't."

"Okay," I agreed.

"Do you like sandwiches?" she asked.

"Yes, I do."

"What's your name?"

"Marv. I'm your husband."

"Are you really? Are you teasing me?" Her voice got louder. "I don't like when you tease me. I don't want to talk to you. I don't know you!"

The first month was the hardest for me. I saw what people warned me about: she didn't recognize me, she was easily distracted, her mood changed quickly, she asked the same question more than once, and she was quick to get angry.

And so it went.

Frankly, for the first weeks, I was feeling pretty low, pretty alone. One day, after she had been in the care facility for about a month, I received a letter at home. It came in a thick envelope. The return address was Sharon's friend, Diane who lived about four hundred miles away in northern California. I walked back into the house and opened the letter. Inside was a sheet of paper, wrapped around a second, thicker envelope.

The note was brief.

> Dear Marv,
>
> When Sharon was first told what was happening, she asked me to help her write a letter. She wanted me to give it to you later, when you needed it and when she could no longer talk to you.
>
> From our phone conversations, I think that time is now. I hope someday, someone loves me as much as Sharon loves you.
>
> Diane

The inner envelope was the color of lavender. I gasped when I saw what was written, in Sharon's handwriting, on the outside: *My Dearest Marv.*

I sat down and slowly opened the inner envelope. My heart was beating as if I had run a race. This was like opening the ultimate "Dear John" letter. I was impatient to read it, but yet, I did everything slowly, to prolong this moment. There were three pages inside. I have read that letter many times, but the first time, I almost couldn't hold it still—my eyes were full of tears. It took me a while to get through it.

Dearest, dearest Marv,

First, Sweetheart, I want to say I'm sorry. Sorry that I've left you. Sorry that I'm not there to be with you in this hard time. Maybe magically, while I'm writing this letter and you're reading it, we can be together. Can you feel my hand on your face, my eyes looking at you, my heart going out to you?

If you are reading this letter that means you and I are no longer able to connect. As I write this, I know how I would feel if I could not reach and connect with you. Very alone. You must feel the same. Sorry.

I want to thank you, again, for all the times we laughed together and we cried together. From the depths of my soul, with all the love I could possibly have for you, I tell you that I am sad. Sad that you, my wonderful husband, do not have a full relationship—with sharing of bodies and feelings, like we used to have. The person who you visit, the person who uses my name and my face is not me. Actually, she's more like a long lost identical twin. If you are looking for me, I'm here in this letter, in your memories and in your feelings.

Isn't it ironic: my "today," in some months or years, will be your "today?"

Thank you for all I know that you are doing to help me to be as comfortable as possible. If your visits appear to make my life better, that's good. If not, don't make yourself crazy.

Marv, the main reason for this letter is I want you to be free to make for yourself the best life you can. That person who looks like me and even uses my name, she's not me and she doesn't know you and love you the way I do now.

Consider this a love letter from your real wife.

You do whatever you need to do to give yourself a life that I would want for you. It may also include your visiting that woman who looks like me. I don't care what you do with money, time, activities, or with the house. Knowing you, I do hope that you soon may have a good friend and maybe a special relationship with someone. At this point, sweetheart, there is no such thing as cheating on me or disrespecting me. On the contrary, nothing would be honoring my love for you more than for you to arrange the most satisfying life you can.

That thought—that you will take care of yourself as I would want you to, were I there—has given me peace in this period of time when I recognize that my aliveness and my relationship with you is slipping away. As we promised a long time ago, I want to love, honor and cherish you. So, here are your orders, from the real me to the real you:

1. *When you are with or planning to be with the Sharon look-alike, ask yourself, "What would the real Sharon want?"*
2. *Remember that I feel and felt lucky to have your love.*
3. *Most important, promise me you will take care of my husband.*
   Sharon
   P.S. If you don't follow these orders, I'll come back and haunt you!

I was not able to read the letter all the way through. Here was my Sharon, the real Sharon. Many times I had to look up, try to dry my eyes, and take a breath. I looked around the room, everything was still; the earthquake was inside me. What a weird and wonderful letter. Just like her!

There was another irony to this letter: Sharon is the one I could go to, who understood me best, no matter how crazy or confused I was. And where is she? She stepped out ... permanently!

Visits were often unpredictable and sometimes frustrating. Once, after she had been there for a few months, I was very excited with what I thought was a great idea. I came in that day with a special plan. As I approached her, she looked up.

"Hello, what's your name?

"Marv, I'm your husband." I sat down. "See what I have here?"

"A big book?"

"A special big book: a photo album of our family! I thought we might want to look at, together."

"Marv, I'm kind of busy. This is my friend, Sam," she gestured to a man standing nearby I had seen before. Apparently, they ate at the same table.

"He wants me take to a walk with him. Maybe you can come back another time." She stood up, walked toward Sam.

"Sharon, I brought this in special. Can't you just take a few minutes and try to look at a few pictures of your own family?" I spoke in desperation and frustration, and regretted it immediately.

"I gotta go." She took Sam's arm and they walked off toward the garden.

That was a bad day for me. I was still holding on, hoping.

5

Several months later, Sharon's friend Diane and I were talking on the phone, as we did a few times a month.

"Marv, it's been almost a year since Sharon went into the Memory Care Center. Would you say, considering everything, that that's a good place for her?"

"Well, I guess so," I answered.

"From what you tell me, she seems pretty much at home there. You agree?"

"Well, she seems more at ease with this whole thing than I am." I laughed at my unintended revelation.

"That's kind of what I thought. Sharon's doing okay."

Two days later, just before dinner time, FedEx delivered a package, with Diane's return address. My hand shook as I opened the thin package. Inside was a DVD. How dumb of me; I never even thought to ask if the letter was all that Sharon had left. I was impatient to see what was on the DVD. At the same time, I wanted to delay having what I knew, in my heart, was going to be a connection with Sharon.

The note was brief per Sharon's instructions. I slowly walked to the DVD player, put in the disc, walked back to the couch, sat down and pressed PLAY. There was Sharon, smiling. "Hello, Sweetheart." I lost it. I found the PAUSE button and pressed it. I cried. There she was, right there! She knew me! My Sharon, the real Sharon, after all these months, knew me! I took a few deep breaths before I was ready to press PLAY again.

She continued, "You remember, Marv, that our religious tradition recommends that when someone close to you dies, you're encouraged to mourn hard, to allow yourself to experience the loss at first, but then, when it approaches a year, it's time to try to get back to your life. Marv, I think what has happened between us is like a death. Other than in your memories, and in your heart, I am gone." She paused, took a deep breath, smiled.

"Honey, it's time. I know you. You like to hold on to things. I bet you still have your old computer, up on the shelf in your office, which you're planning to update someday. Honey, down deep you know you can't bring it back. Let go of it. No reason to hold on to it. Do the same with the Sharon I was. Marv, we had a good life. Now, Sweetheart, it's time to say goodbye. And, please remember my wish: if a time comes when it looks like I'm not enjoying my life and you think I would just as soon 'leave,' don't stand in the way, please. Okay?

"Marv, this is the last time you will see or hear from me. There are no more surprises. It is time for me ... and you, my love ... to say goodbye ... like we never really had a chance to before. So, I'm saying goodbye, to you, here, now, in this video." She smiled briefly and started to cry. I did, too.

The DVD played on, her face was there, both of us crying ... together. After a few minutes, she spoke one last time. "Marv, say the words." She looked at me quietly.

My mouth wouldn't work, but I knew she was right. Finally, I spoke to my real Sharon and said the words, "Goodbye, my love, my sweetheart." I took a deep breath and exhaled. She looked at me and her image on the screen faded.

I didn't sleep well that night. I cried more than I had for months. If you had watched me that night and the next morning, you'd think I was crazy. I cried and then I smiled and then I cried and then I smiled.

Sharon knew me better than I knew myself.

The next day, I was sitting near Sharon. We were watching television. On this day, Sharon allowed me to hold her hand. Then one of the attendants came around and announced, "Time for the painting group, everybody." Sharon got up and started to walk away with the others.

I stood up, called her name and walked after her. She turned around. "I may be late tomorrow," I said. "There is something I need to take to the Electronics Recycling Center."

She turned, "That's okay. I have a busy day tomorrow. You've been coming for a long time, right?"

I nodded.

Sharon stepped toward me and whispered in my ear. "It's okay if you don't come tomorrow." She kissed me on my cheek, turned and walked off.

I blew her a kiss.

Don't rush to leave our bed, my wife
Don't rush to go away.
I want to feel your warmth
Before I start each day.
Stay with me, my love

     With all we are we touch each morn:
     Our hands, our mouths, our eyes.
     Your sound, your warmth, your skin
     For me, a paradise.
     Lie with me, my love

The day is full, much work to do
Sometimes I feel alone.
Each eve to you I come
For you, my dear, are home.
Lie with me, my love

     Don't rush to leave this life, my wife
     It's you I want to touch.
     A hundred years of nights
     Would never be too much.
     Stay with me, my love

~~*

About the Author. Shlomo Kreitzer—Retired psychologist, cancer survivor, witness to life in eight decades and husband for twenty-eight years, Dr. Shlomo Kreitzer's writing explores life within and between people. Under his nom de plume, Doctor Shlomo, he writes stories with a message. Recognized three times in VCWC contests, Shlomo has expanded his writing to include humor and serious poetry. His motto remains, "Being alive, relationships, and honesty are precious; cherish them."

If I were a blue bird, I would chirp with delight.

If I were a bat, I would soar through the night.

If I were an apple tree, I would have branches

and graceful leaves.

If I were a sweater, I would have long sleeves.

If I were the ocean, I would be the sea.

But the only thing I want to be is me.

~~*

About the Author: Hannah Buch lives in Simi Valley, CA. She is fourteen and will be entering Santa Susana High School in the Fall of 2015 to pursue film studies. Hannah likes to read poetry, short stories, and mysteries. In her spare time, she likes to play the flute and spend time with family and friends.

In one of my quiet times, as I sat on the family room sofa, I closed my eyes and thought back on my early years to see just how far back I could remember. The earliest was three or four years old—there were only snippets, scenes really, of occurrences—putting the ice tray from my toy kitchen set out on the neighbor's picket fence overnight in the winter time to find it frozen in the morning. There were times when Mother would fry up a platter of French fries and we'd lie, tummy down, on her bed by the window while we ate the fries and watched a gathering thunderstorm's glowing yellow branches of electricity light up the night sky. Then we'd listen for the rumble and house-jarring boom of thunder that would follow. In East Texas severe thunderstorms are common. She explained what caused these events and the power and beauty of Mother Nature's ways.

There was the time Mother said she was going to make soup. I couldn't see how. There were only potatoes and an onion on the kitchen counter. She picked me up and set me by the sink so I could see what she was doing. She peeled the potatoes and showed me the different steps needed to make potato onion soup. I was *amazed*—you really can make soup from something hard like potatoes!

The time I remember most vividly was the surprise I'd worked on for a long time, and was so proud of, that turned out to be not such a good thing at all. Daddy was the Assistant Manager of the Tyler Theatre. Whenever Mother went to the theatre she'd take me along. We'd go almost every time there was a new feature. I got to see movies, news reels and short subjects. One of the specials I saw was on wood craft. The man had sanded a piece of wood down. First he used rough sandpaper then smooth sandpaper until the wood was "as smooth as a baby's cheek." *Ah-ha*, I thought *Daddy's got sandpaper in his tool box.* I had watched Daddy do repairs and make things so I knew what to do. Where to find a piece of wood? I couldn't ask Mother or Daddy 'cause if I did it wouldn't be a surprise. I searched all around the backyard, in my toy box, and around the house until I found the perfect piece—the windowsill of the window by the back door. It was close to my kitchen set where I played a lot so I wouldn't be noticed.

I don't know how long I worked … at the time it seemed like forever. Finally after I'd worn a nice groove the length of my hand, as wide as two fingers across and one finger width deep I was finished with my project. The curtain had covered the area so I knew it would be a complete surprise when I unveiled my prized work of art.

I waited until Mother had finished the dishes and was ready to go to the living room to read her book—that's when I knew the time was right…

"Mommy, here, give me your hand I want to show you something." I could hardly contain myself nor could I keep myself from giggling.

"What have you got?" She took my hand and let herself be led.

"It's in here. Remember the short that was at the Tyler about the man who had a wood shop and made things?"

Apprehension crept into her voice, "Yes…"

"Well, I have a surprise for you!" With a grand gesture I'd seen used in the movies I pulled the curtain back with one hand, held the other arm out to full length, bowed and said ♪ "Ta Da." ♫

Mother's eyes opened the widest I'd ever seen; she gasped and covered her mouth with her hand. "Oh, Lari, no, you didn't."

"What…?"

I dropped my outstretched arm, turned to look at my smooth piece of work for flaws. "What's wrong with it?" I ran my hand over the exposed wood centered perfectly on the white painted windowsill. "Here feel, I used Daddy's sandpaper, I've been working on it for a long time, feel, see how smooth it is. Just like the man in the short said, "Smooooooth as a baby's cheek." Happily I asked, "Won't Daddy be surprised?"

"He certainly will be!" Mother said as she slowly shook her head from side to side.

That was the last time I *fashioned* anything with sandpaper.

There were many other early discoveries I thought of on that day of reverie in the family room. I smiled a lot, chuckled, and even laughed out loud some. Other memories brought tears or just a shake of the head. Now that I'm aging and on the other end of life's continuum I've started to make unexpected and different kinds of discoveries.

Ah, but that is another story for another time.

~~*

About the Author: Lari Newton writes memoirs, creative non-fiction, and personal essays. She has a happy nature, loves life, and…finds adventure wherever she goes. Lari's daughter wanted to know whether she'd written any of these experiences down, and if not, encouraged her to do so with, "Please don't just keep them in your head." It was in response to that request that Lari began a written legacy for her only child. In 2010 she joined the VCWC. She's been published in *The Write Stuff, Serendipity, Writer's Digest,* and a winner of that magazine's "Your Story" #40 contest. February 2013, she was the opening speaker for the VCWC meeting. For the past four years she has been leader of the VCWC Memoir Workshop.

In the Middle East
they call the desert wind a khamsín.
There, it swirls the sand into dense clouds
that can blind those trapped in their midst.
> *When my husband and I were new lovers*
> *We got caught in one as we walked*
> *in a suburb of Tel Aviv.*
We held hands,
taking turns leading
and protecting each other from the wind,
our eyes stinging, throats burning,
as one familiar landmark after another
was obliterated by thick brown clouds.
When we finally reached the safety
of our ulpan,*
the night watchman,
an unshaven old guy
with scary blue eyes and tawny skin,
whom everyone called crazy David,
greeted us with a knowing grin
and offered us Jaffa oranges.
> *We quickly peeled their fragrant skins,*
> *sharing the moist sections,*
> *their piquant juice*
> *perfectly quenching our thirst.*

*A school in Israel, usually with dormitory facilities, where new immigrants study Hebrew and learn about Israeli culture.

~~*

About the Author. Bonnie Goldenberg has been writing poetry for over thirty years. Her poems have been published in several literary journals, as well as in *Serendipity,* the VCWC's 2012 anthology. She is currently working on a memoir based on her parents' letters from World War II, tentatively titled, *Love, A. My Father's Letters from World War II: A Jewish Soldier in Nazi Germany.* Defying stereotypes about "retirement," she and her husband, a former Amgen employee, have recently launched a biotech startup, Golden Biotech, in Newbury Park. If it succeeds, she plans it to be the subject of her next book! She has lived in Thousand Oaks for almost twenty-three years with her husband and son, who is a graduate of USC and the London School of Economics. She is originally from New York, where she was a labor lawyer, legal writer, and editor.

I didn't know the importance of my brother's letters until second grade, after too many days of celery soup. The US Army needed Paul and our house filled with sadness when he shipped out.

Mama and I walked to town each week to check the mail. We opened the blue envelope addressed to us in Soledad, California, USA, and out came a money order from Paul. We cashed twenty dollars right there in the post office.

I watched Mama's dark-skinned forehead wrinkle into thought. "Four months behind on rent, but no, we'll go to the Purity Store," Mama said. Inside we selected our goods – a fifty-pound sack of flour, two dollars and fifty cents, a fifty-pound sack of beans, a can of lard, potatoes, five cans of tomato sauce, and some canned milk. We needed everything.

We walked over to the cold milk, thirty-four cents a gallon, and got corn flakes, too. Mama liked to cook with onion and garlic. She wanted *fideo*, rice, and little stars. Mama liked star-shaped pasta for her *sopa*. My mouth watered, my stomach growled, and I wanted to jump up and down like my little sister, Lita. My mind raced forward to our next meal. It couldn't get any better. Then Mama reached for a bottle of Nesbitt orange soda.

"It stays here, what we do in town," Mama said. "You know what I mean."

"Yes, Mama." No one else needed to know.

Mama's last selection, Twinkies. I felt a smile down to my toes.

Before we called the taxi Mama and I sat down to share the soda, something we never had in our house. We sat with our backs to the stores, we looked out over the tracks and the bare mustard twigs. We weren't like the people walking by, but we sat there with our bags of food and our orange soda as if we were.

We were from Anthony, New Mexico. We were citizens. Dad said we were proud people. "We take care of ourselves." And we didn't call Mexico home because it wasn't. All my older brothers and sisters – Paul, Sally, Molly, and Chila – spoke English, and so did I.

After savoring the sweetness that filled us up, Mama said, "*Vaya* Monchi, go buy a stamp at the post office. You'll write Paul a letter and tell him we are all fine, okay *mija*?" She handed me three cents.

Then Mama paid the taxi to carry us and everything home.

I enjoyed a week of corn flakes for breakfast. Tacos, *sopa,* and enough of everything. The last thing I ever wanted to remember were the days of soup. But our twenty dollars lasted only so long. January turned to celery soup. Even soup with *don* Tomaso's potatoes tasted like celery.

February's celery soup days made school turn into blah, blah, blur. That's when the warden's son, John came up to me at school and said, "poor little Indian girl, want to cry?"

* * *

"Mama, some kid called me Indian," I said.

"Who would say that?" She stopped washing dishes, dried her hands.

I looked up at her face. "A kid."

Mama looked old. Even Mama's braid looked old, pinned up at the back of her head in a bun.

"Don't worry. You don't have any Indian." Her dark eyes were steady on me.

"Sally? And Chila?"

"We have laundry to hang."

"Okay."

"Don't ask again. There are no Indians here."

That ended that.

* * *

Paul's next letter came in March. Life turned normal again, for a while. I played with my cousin Amparo, but never said a word.

"Mama, the relief truck," my sister Chila said one day. People in camp with coupons walked away along the dirt paths and gravel road, with cheese, margarine or butter, canned meats, coffee and sugar.

"No hand-outs for us, Cheta," Apá's voice commanded. "Work is a few weeks away."

"Apá, it's not a hand-out, they're called commodities," my sister begged Dad, but he'd have nothing to do with the relief truck.

Our hunger embarrassed us. I told no one, not even my oldest sister, Sally. Like Mama, Sally always fed anyone who came through her door, lucky for me. When she saw I ate only half and wanted to take the rest home, she started wrapping extra food to send with me. "For Mama," she'd say.

My brother, Tony, ran off every afternoon. I missed the way he tousled my short hair, the way he made me the catcher in baseball, the way he always had a reason to chase after me in a game of tag or a fake you-did-it-fight. I loved the way he had eyes watching over me and protected me even when he was away at work.

I didn't feel lost in the middle of such a big family like just another sister.

"Look, Monchi." His eyes sparkled. He juggled stones in the air, or asked me riddles. We played jacks together sometimes. I was part of the stories he strummed on his guitar, part of his laughter, the laughter he lost during the celery soup days.

* * *

In March, fieldwork started. Apá brought home a dozen little chicks.

"Here," he said to Mama. "From Archuleta's Farm … on credit." Too cold for them outside. Mama brought in a basket and we put them in our kitchen. They grew fast.

"Hi, *Apá*." Sally greeted Dad. She came to our house with her thick hair covered in a bandana like maybe she'd worked or went looking for work. She had her toddler, Anastasio with her, put him down, then handed a bag of flour to Mama.

"Monchi," she called to me. She patted the kitchen bench for me to sit with her.

"Have any books with you? Bring one over. Read to me later, *mija*."

Mama cooed over Anastasio, Sally's third child. Brought him to Apá. "Say hello, *Papito*."

"We drove around to the fields today," Sally said.

"What are people saying?"

Dad and Mama both wanted to hear news. "Who prepared fields for planting, who worked on the irrigation ditches?"

"Any barn doors open? Did you see any tractors? Did you go as far as Salinas?" Dad listened for word about work in the valley.

A terrible commotion interrupted the answer. The chicks had gotten out of the basket. Peeps in the kitchen, loud, stifled, screeches and scuffles, the sounds of bones being crushed under Anastasio's feet. More than half the dozen lay in motionless puffs by the time Sally grabbed my little nephew.

The air filled with our loss. It was a quiet, wordless loss because there was nothing we could do about it, like the heavy silence we felt when Paul left.

~~*

About the Author. Lori Anaya's new novel is set in the Salinas Valley of California during the late 1940s, a mixture of historical fiction and magic. A storyteller at heart, Anaya draws on over thirty years' experience teaching young English learners. She lives in Port Hueneme where she now pursues volume two of a trilogy about a gifted young girl from a mixed-race heritage.

I open the door, and there's something on the floor.

It's mushy and gooshy and feels like it's squishy.

And now I can't remember it any more.

It's bumpy and lumpy and looks like it's slumping,

And now I'm stuck to the floor.

It's hard to get up, and I'm getting a cold.

I'm hoping someone gets this gunk off the floor.

I'm getting the jitters, and there's a knock on the door

Finally a person to get me off this rugged old floor.

~~*

About the Author: Maya Porche is a Simi Valley native and lives with her parents, sister, two dogs, three bunnies and a cockatiel. Maya enjoys sports, especially soccer, volleyball and horseback riding. Maya hopes to become a veterinarian and seeks out books featuring animals. Maya loves drawing, painting and expressing her creativity.

Horse Original art work
by Maya Porche

I regularly flew to London on business. My expense account allowed for
a stay at the London Park Lane Hotel, my favorite, across from Hyde Park
and a short walk to Harrods. Not far in the other direction was
Buckingham Palace.

A cold, fog-filled October evening greeted me on my latest trip.
Though exhausted, I felt the need to get some air and stretch my legs, move
my arthritic bones. Exiting the hotel, I turned right instead of my usual left
towards Knightsbridge and the big store.

The fog got thicker the further I wandered. I must have been walking
for ten minutes, perhaps more. I turned up one side street, then another,
thinking I knew my way, that I was blessed with an acute sense of direction.
I realized suddenly that the neighborhood was unknown to me. I could not
see clearly through the fog.

I walked, one step in front of the other, scarcely able to make out what
lay ahead.

How did I get here, so far from my hotel room? "I should have
dropped bread crumbs along my path," I murmured to myself. Then an
electric light above a door, diffused though it was by the fog, beckoned me.
Advancing closer, I was able to read a sign in a grimy side window:

Peering into this window, I could see another small light, emanating
from a candle flickering inside a room of dusty book shelves and cobwebs.
I am normally attracted to used book shops, but something about this
establishment was disquieting.

Despite the interior's uninviting appearance, the cold chill on the street
persuaded me to enter. I did so in the hope of finding a warm chair, a cup
of coffee, or even tea, and directions back to my hotel.

Once inside, I closed the door and moved toward the light resting
upon a grime-encrusted reception table near the back wall. The cold, damp
room made my arthritic bones tremble—not much better than outside. The
air tasted stale. I choked. My eyes burned.

A small sign requested striking a nearby service bell. I did so.

From behind a curtain came a small, hunch-backed man, no more than five feet tall, wearing what, in the poor light, resembled a czarist-era tunic and pantaloons. The tunic covered him from nearly his chin to his thigh. It was white with maroon striping at the cuffs and around the bottom. A braided rope acted as a belt at the waist, gathering up the tunic. It too was a dark red color. The pantaloons were black with a white herring-bone design. I could not see his shoes.

Some unseen force drew my focus to his large, coal-black eyes which seemed out of proportion to his weasely, ill-formed head. The flickering of the candle flame was reflected in his wide-open eyes. These huge orbs bulged, unsynchronized, looked at me and then looked past me, at what, I don't know.

The little creature raised a hand to point, causing the sleeve of the tunic to fall away. A thin arm was revealed, from which hung a withered hand with long fingers, and black nails.

He pointed to the darkened stacks to the right. Glancing in that

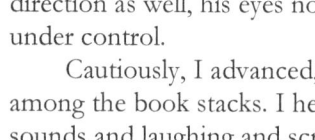

direction as well, his eyes now seemed under control.

Cautiously, I advanced, moving among the book stacks. I heard distant sounds and laughing and screaming and running, as though I was hearing from afar a child's school at recess, and I heard the horns of steamboats and trains and ancient automobiles.

As I proceeded, the screams of playing swelled into screams of pain and fear. The laughter amplified until they were roars gone mad. All were mixing, merging and increasing in intensity the deeper into the unholy shadows I walked.

The books showed signs of chewed-through spine bottoms—so dusty and dirty that the titles were beyond recognition.

I took my handkerchief from my back pocket and, after wiping ancient grime from the edges of some of these ill-maintained shelves, I started recognizing lettering on the books. A few were machine–printed in old font styles, most were hand calligraphies.

Many titles were in languages unfamiliar to me. I assumed ancient Greek and Latin, for some. Lying about in disarray between and among the books were documents of parchment with what I guessed were Runic or cuneiform symbols.

On the spines of some now-cleaned books, I could make out German that said Kafka, Dante in Italian, and Cervantes in Spanish. Sounds of screeching and scratching and galloping horses seemed to run right through me. I swung around to see the horses making those sounds, but I could see only the dust and grime that filled the milieu.

At the back of the aisle were shelves of books by British, and occasionally American, authors—Maugham, James, Joyce, Stevenson, Shakespeare, Milton, Kipling, London, Wells, Doyle, Dickens, Bronte, Austen, Ballentyne. Too many to count, the books overflowed their shelves. I could not possibly examine them all.

Hearing what sounded like the clashing of steel against steel, I stopped in front of a Robert Louis Stevenson title, *The Black Arrow*. I lifted the book from its place, and as I did, my hands burned with such pain, I dropped it to the floor and screamed in agony. As the pain subsided, a glow, intense as sunlight, radiated from the book on the floor. I shielded my eyes from the powerful glare.

When I again could see, I was astonished to find myself reclining in a field of grass. The air was clear and fresh and the temperature mild. I stood up and just as I did, a horse and rider swiftly rode by barely avoiding me. Quickly following, another came about to catch up to the first. They passed into the forest beyond.

As the two vanished into the forest, a troop of iron-clad mounted warriors rode rapidly towards me from the same direction. On their helmets they wore white plumage, and each horse was bedecked with white and black coverings which I thought must impede their stride, as did the men in their armor suits. The riders were perhaps ten or twelve in number. I was too dazed to make an accurate count.

The first in the line stopped and addressed me.

"Yo, what manner of foe are ye? I recognize not yer dress. Are ye a citizen of yon city? Declare ye'self. Be ye for Lancaster or for York?"

I did not know what to answer.

"Fair sir," I said, "I am disoriented and my head is bruised."

"Perhaps I'll run ye through right here and worry no further! What do they call ye?"

Not knowing what to respond, I just stated my true first name. "I am Neal." I offered with no apology.

"Neal? Ellis O'Neal!" shouted the leader. And with that he dismounted and removed his helmet and gauntlets revealing himself to be a youth of no more than twenty years. "Here stands the leader of the Black Arrow Fellowship, himself! The honor is mine, sir! But why are you disguised in such strange garb?"

I still wore a business suit, minus the necktie.

He continued, not waiting for my answer, "I am Richard Shelton. My friends, and sometimes my enemies, call me Dick. You were my dead father's ally, I know. How badly are ye hurt? Come with us and I'll search out care for your wounds. We are on our way to do battle with the

Lancaster bunch in yon Shoreby town. I hope to revenge my father's death, murdered as he was at the hands of the foul knight Sir Daniel Brackley and his henchmen. But nay, you yourself have mighty grievances against that man."

I wanted no part of this fight or to venture farther into the muddle I was in. "Fair sir," I said. "Thank you for your kindness. You go on to your fortune. I will care for myself."

"Thank thee, Sir Ellis." And with that, young Dick donned his ancient helmet, then, with the aid of a mounted man on each side, laboriously climbed on his horse, adjusted himself and his metal suit in position, and rode off with his troop toward the town.

I stood watching the horses disappear into the forest. All was silent. Then I heard an irritable voice screaming. It sounded as if the clamor was coming from within a tunnel.

I looked around but could see no one. Then, in the blue sky, there appeared an image—a human head as big as a harvest moon, though it was somewhat of a thin face with a large drooping moustache and piercing eyes. It was the author, Robert Louis Stevenson himself. And he was yelling at me.

"What the devil are you doing in my story?" he cried. "I didn't write you in! Who in the name of—? Who are you? What are you?"

The talking head had murder in its eyes, I could tell.

"I don't know what I'm doing here, sir. One minute I'm in an old book shop and the next minute I was here." I tried to explain.

"Get out, or I'll write you a terrible end! I promise you," yelled the talking giant head.

I started to run backwards, keeping my eyes fixed on Stevenson's monstrous image. I lost my footing, and fell into a bottomless abyss. I kept floating downward so slowly until I passed out.

I awoke back at the book shop, sitting on the floor in the dirt and musty air. I arose and made my way to the front counter.

The strange little man stood there, pointing me back to the stacks.

A sense of unbearable confusion pervaded my spirit. The impulse to run incited every synapse and sinew of my being—but to where, in what direction should I have gone?

I wanted to ignore the little man's mute instruction, turned in panic, and ran out the door. The fog, thicker than before, frustrated my ambition.

Running with no plan or sense, I collided with a bobby, an English cop. He thought me mad when, out of breath, I tried to explain where I'd been. He walked the few feet I had traveled when I collided with him. He explained that I must have eaten something undesirable on the plane because we were standing right in front of Buckingham Palace—and everyone was home.

The bobby politely escorted me back to my hotel where I spent a restless night attempting to sleep. I wondered if I had been dreaming in the book store, or had gone through some sort of time portal. Never-the-less, I needed to get some sleep. I had a business meeting the next morning.

~~*

About the Author. Before retiring, Neal Shapiro operated an electronic printing/publishing consultancy, advising companies on their document creation needs. He has had a dual career over the past forty-two year that has seen the merger of the two crafts he knows well, data processing and publishing. Neal has a BFA in man-machine interface design from California Institute of the Arts, Valencia, and a MS in Technology Management from the School of Business and Management at Pepperdine University. Neal has a daughter and a grandson in Long Beach, CA, and he lives with his adult son in Ventura.

At the Harbor – Photo Courtesy of Wendell Ward

She lies in the middle of the street
kicking feet
flailing arms
a dying insect on its back trying to recover life

> *"Oh God you have forsaken me and my children*
> *I cry but do you listen? Do you care, God?*
> *I would damn you but for fear*
> *you would damn me first.*
> *I am old and lost and you do not care.*
> *I am poor and do not eat.*
> *My clothes are torn and ragged.*
> *My love for you is greater*
> *than your love for me."*

While shaking the plastic cup,
at those rushing past in the shadows
her eyes screaming, "Please"

> *Sobbing, striking at demons around*
> *she stops looking at those around*
> *then struggles to her feet,*
> *a torn month old newspaper of a person*
> *hunched and like a matter of fact*
> *goes to a nearby diner*
> *orders a cup of coffee, cream, two sugars*

"How ya doin, Mildred?" the waitress asks.

"Not bad. Eighteen bucks
but gotta tell ya the damn street's
cold tonight killin' my back for real
maybe I'll go work over by Western"

> *sipping coffee, shivering, sobbing*
> *brushing her disheveled hair away*
> *"ashes to ashes, dust to dust"*
> *rocking a non-baby in her arms*
> *"the child shall pierce your heart"*
> *caressing sorrow stroking sadness*
> *"where else would I go"*
> *the tears streaming across her lips*
> *muttering her life story again.*

About the Author. Robert Geweniger is not fond of his name. Robert means bright star, but Geweniger means unimportant. He thinks of himself as a bright star at the edge of the universe. In a sense, he's been writing his entire life, primarily as a radio announcer and newsperson at small stations in the Midwest. He began writing short stories and poetry when he retired. He earned a B.A. in English and studied Communication Arts at the University of Maryland. A year ago, he became a grandfather, a career path he never previously considered. Now he is writing poems about the new girl in his life. His poem, "She Lies in the Middle," began with the memory of a woman sitting in the middle of a street in London. Sometimes he just wants to give it all up and become a handsome billionaire.

Ocean Foliage - Photo courtesy of Gregg Miller, VCWC Photography Chair

"I think it is all a matter of love;
the more you love a memory the stronger and
stranger it becomes"
~Vladimir Nabokov

Facing Nolan Ryan, An adapted excerpt from the novel "Unexpected Hero" by John Shehorn

Hank Waite was driving to the grocery store and casually mentioned to his young passenger that Little League sign-ups were next Saturday. He continued nonchalantly, "If you promise to manage your game, Mom and I will let you play baseball this season."

Brock rocked back and forth in his seat with excitement, pumping his fist and yelling, "All right, yeah!"

"Calm down, Heavy Waite. Let's not wreak the car." Hank was glad Mattie wasn't with them because his wife absolutely abhorred that silly nickname. Yet it so aptly described his young son who looked more like a young teenager than a ten year old. Brock was already nearing Mattie's height of five foot seven. The boy's dark thick black hair matched his own, but his eyes must come from his mother. They were a bright sky blue color. But it was his son's unusual muscular physique that had always been a source of parental concern.

A thirteen pound baby, Hank realized early on his son would be an outlier—far outside the normal limits for his weight, size and strength. After months of research and lengthy discussions with her doctors, Hank concluded his son's abnormal size was due to an experimental stem cell treatment his wife received for her infertility problems. Despite the doctor's negativity on her chances of pregnancy, Mattie had delivered a healthy and enormous baby boy. And what a son Brock had turned out to be. He was smart, compassionate and already at ten nearly a giant, at least for his age.

For years they had hidden Brock's size by pretending he was much older. Only recently they realized hiding his remarkable physical gifts had resulted in their son missing out on so many childhood activities, especially in sports. Today, Hank had finally given his son the good news. He would be allowed to play baseball, and he felt a part of Brock's excitement.

Sharing his love of baseball with Brock was natural. Like his father, Hank had been a Dodger fan his entire life. He marveled at how quickly Brock had learned the subtleties of the game. Brock certainly enjoyed their frequent summer evenings at Dodger Stadium, and he often sat with Hank to watch the blue crew on television.

Brock learned to admire the complex duel between pitcher and hitter. How a pitcher would apply his mastery of pace and location to confound a batter who had spent his lifetime dedicated to the art of hitting. It was the ultimate showcase of two masters of the game, which the pitcher usually dominated. Baseball had a tradition and purity that the recent steroid abuse had tarnished, but Hank knew the game had survived scandals, vices, and corruption in the past. The game would endure. His fears had almost cost his son the opportunity to play a game they both loved.

His son took a deep breath, trying to calm down, and then boldly promised, "Dad, I'll keep my batting average at no more than four hundred and fifty points, and I'll hit only one homer each game. Can I really play?"

Hank glanced over, shook his head slowly and warned, "Sure you can throw and catch great, but don't be so cocky. Hitting a baseball is much harder than it looks. You know only the very best hitters can get one hit in three tries. Hitting has too many variables. I can't even remember ever taking you to the batting cages to practice your hitting."

"What batting cages?" Brock asked.

Hank slowed and made a sudden U-turn.

"Dad, what are you doing? Where are we going?"

"Okay, Heavy Waite, time to show me what you've got. I want to see you hit a baseball."

The batting cages used to be a popular haunt for the youth of Malibu. Hank remembered spending some memorable long afternoons there with his high school buddies.

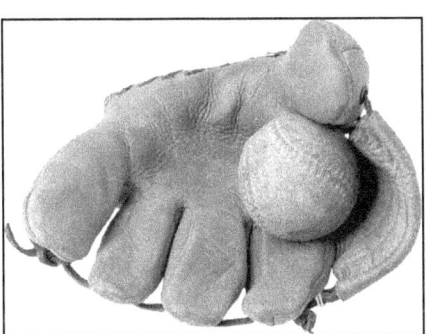

The chain link and netted enclosure occupied the back corner lot near a big box home improvement store about a mile south of the Malibu City Center. As Hank turned into the lot, the batting cages looked so much smaller than he remembered. The chain linked fence was rusted in places and sagging; the netting was patched and frayed. Still there were quite a few cars parked in the lot, and he recognized the tell-tale ping of metal bats in the distance. He parked his blue minivan, and led his still smiling son into the small office located in front of the dilapidated enclosure.

At the counter, sat a tall, gangly teenager wearing a backwards Dodger cap. The clerk ignored them. Chomping loudly on a huge wad of gum, all his attention was riveted on a comic book. Every bit of space in the tiny room was stuffed with racks of old baseball bats and stacks of dirty, scuffed batting helmets. The air smelled of leather and the distinctive aroma of chalk.

The teenage clerk wore a high school baseball jersey apparently to indicate his expertise in the game. They walked around the narrow aisles looking for a helmet that would fit Brock's rather large head. Hank noted the excitement still etched on his son's face. Brock finally selected a blue helmet that seemed to fit. Then they headed to the front counter.

Without glancing up from his comic book, the young teenager finally spoke, "Take any of the bats along the wall. Remember to wear a helmet, and you'll need to buy tokens."

Hank laid a ten dollar bill on the glass counter. The teenage counted out five tokens and finally looked up. He seemed somewhat thin and pale for a baseball star. The kid sized up Brock then delivered in a monotonous tone his instructions to Hank, "Twenty balls per token. I suggest your kid stay in the middle lanes where the pitches are calibrated for Pony League talent. The more to the right, the faster they get."

The dour teenager turned his attention to Brock, his voice suddenly rising in intensity and authority. "You stay away from the Nolan Ryan machine. It's only for the pros. As advertised, its pitches exceed ninety-five miles per hour, and it means it. Last week a guy on my high school team wasn't paying attention and got a nasty black eye from a foul ball."

"Which one do you use?" Brock asked.

Hank saw the teenager smile noting it was not friendly. The teenager seemed to puff up his chest and haughtily explained, "I play on the varsity high school team, so I only practice using the two lanes on the right. I bet ya I'm the only guy in town who can hit the Nolan Ryan fastball. Last week, I hit all but three balls which is probably the world record."

Brock lifted a few of the older wooden bats, taking a few practice swings. The teenager wasn't finished applying his intimidating brand of coaching and ordered a bit too loudly, "No. You should use an aluminum bat. You're only in middle school. It'll be much easier for you to swing."

The clerk would never believe Brock was only ten. Hank wondered if Brock had noticed the patronizing tone in the teenager's strident voice.

Hank wasn't surprised when Brock spurned the teenager's advice and grabbed the largest wooden bat in the entire bin at thirty-nine ounces. As he exited the smelly room, Brock commented in a calm voice, "My dad says wood is best. Only the pros use lumber."

Hank smiled at the teenager to clear the tension, but the surly clerk was already engrossed in his comic book. So much for customer service. Hank turned and followed his son out the door.

Brock stopped to evaluate the long row of pitching machines ejecting a torrent of baseballs in a steady rhythm. Most of the cages were occupied on the left side. A father was tenderly helping a tiny tot in the first lane try to hit a baseball from a tee. The small crowd of mothers and fathers were standing by the fence cheering enthusiastically for their kids and applauding after every hit even the foul balls. Three tier aluminum bleachers lined the outside of the fence where a group of older people sat also clapping their support. The batting machines on the right were vacant.

It was bright and sunny, the perfect day to be outside, and Hank enjoyed the moment watching his son pause to watch the others. Hank really loved baseball: its emphasis on statistics, its traditions, and the storied legends of Babe Ruth and other ancient heroes. His own father had taught him how to throw and catch, and now he would finally be passing that legacy to another generation. He remembered his father commenting on the masterful pitching of Nolan Ryan and his incredible speed sometimes clocked at a hundred miles per hour.

Brock seemed to have made his decision and walked to the right. "Dad, let's start up the Nolan Ryan machine so I can watch the pitches."

Hank walked through the chain link gate behind Brock, ready to insert a token. He watched Brock step up to the batter's box. He couldn't help himself and issued a stern warning, "Careful, son. These machines are like the real thing, sometimes a little wild. You better warm up first."

Hank clearly remembered his own experience with the dangerous Nolan Ryan machine. It was almost twenty years ago, but he could still recall its scary velocity and the embarrassment of not being able to hit the infamous pitching machine even with his father's coaching and encouragement. Hank carefully laid the five tokens on top of the metal controller wondering why Brock seemed compelled to try this particular machine. Certainly the teenage clerk had goaded him on, but his son usually ignored the teasing of older kids.

Hank walked quickly outside the enclosure, closed the gate, and turned to hang on the chain link fence to watch his son warm up. He felt sweat on his forehead, took a big breath and rubbed his neck. Twenty years is a long time to recall a failure so vividly. Now he had led his son into the same situation, and he felt foolish for bringing him here.

In many ways Hank thought baseball was a reflection of life. It rewarded the precious few who had integrity, struggled to foster their talent and had the courage not to give up. It heaped scorn and harsh lessons on those who cheated, gambled or gave up. Maybe that's why his Nolan Ryan failure was stuck so indelibly in his memory. He so wanted to play high school baseball, but after his struggles at the batting cages, he decided not to go out for the team. Hank had few regrets in his life and realized this one still lingered and bothered him.

Hank shook off his lethargy to focus on his son. Brock was a picture of total concentration. Even in his oversized Dodger tee-shirt, his muscular physique was evident, especially when he stretched and unleashed a series of powerful swings. His tee-shirt bunched and it almost ripped apart with his powerful stoke.

His son had finished warming up. Brock deposited a token into the slot and hurried back to address the machine. He tapped the brightly painted home plate with his bat. Hank noticed his own sweaty palms, and fought back his nerves. His son, on the other hand, seemed very much at ease settling into his stance.

27

Would his son also fail in facing Nolan Ryan?

Hank watched his son carefully study the mechanical arm cycle, how it captured the first baseball then with a sudden explosion of force rocketed the ball towards him, trailing up high and away. The second ball hissed past him head high, but Brock did not flinch or swing. The third pitch was slightly higher making a loud thump as the ball missed the heavy backstop pad on the fence causing Hank to jump back startled. Another was slightly inside, but Brock stayed glued to his stance watching it barely miss his head. Brock took another practice swing. Another pitch was a bit outside, but again well over his son's head. The machine continued its rotation until it completed its twenty ball cycle. Brock took several mighty cuts through the air then turned to his father, "Dad, can they calibrate these machines? The pitches are coming in way too high for me."

Hank expelled a deep breath. He chuckled, "Most of the hitters who use this lane are probably six feet or taller, so they're set perfectly for them."

"Dad, can you also ask the guy to fix the speed?"

"What do you mean?"

"These pitches aren't fast enough. He said they were ninety-five miles per hour and these aren't that fast."

Hank did not want to argue with his son who seemed so happy to be here, so he headed back to the office. The sallow looking teenager with the attitude was still behind the counter focused on his comic book and ignoring customers.

"Hey. Can you calibrate the pitching machine to pitch lower in the strike zone?"

Without looking up the teenager replied, "Sure. But the machines on the left should be just fine for your kid."

"My son likes fast pitches. What can I say? Humor me and adjust the machine."

The kid seemed angry at having to get off his stool, and he grumbled an epithet not appropriate for an adult. He stomped around the building and appeared to notice Brock standing near the token feeder in the Nolan Ryan pitching lane. The teenager yelled, "Hey kid, get out of there."

Brock ignored the command and replied, "This machine is pitching over my head and is not that fast. Can you fix it?"

The teenager started to argue, seemed on the verge of losing his temper, but then smiled in a nasty way. "It's your funeral," he mumbled. He said it softly, but loud enough for both Hank and Brock to hear.

Hank watched the brooding teenager enter a side gate that allowed him entry to a separate wire tunnel that protected him. The teenager crouched down and adjusted some dials on the back of the Nolan Ryan pitching machine. He seemed pleased with himself because he grinned widely and shouted, "Try it now!"

Hank watched his son drop in another token. He confidently strode over to the batter's box, touching the home plate to position his stance. The machine started its automatic delivery of blazing heat.

Whomp! The ball sailed a little inside, but the pitch was right at Brock's belt line.

"Yeah, that's better, thanks!" he shouted to the teenager who now smiled back.

Hank watched the teenager take a seat on the plastic chair behind the pitching machine. He placed his hands behind his head, tilted the chair back to observe his son who let the next pitch go past him not even taking the bat off his shoulder.

"Come-on kid, at least take a cut!" taunted the teenager laughing.

Hank realized the kid had dialed the machine to its maximum velocity and wanted Brock to fail.

"Lean in and just let the bat do the work. You can do it," Hank encouraged.

The next pitch was down the middle, and Hank swore he could hear the sizzle as the baseball accelerated towards Brock. The crack of the wooden bat was loud, and the ball came whistling straight back at the pitching machine in a wicked line drive. The teenager instinctively flinched, tumbled backwards, and landed hard on his back. He lay spread eagled on the black asphalt.

Brock struck the next ball more sweetly, and it arched deep and far back into the back netting. The following line drive was to the left with the next two hit solidly into center. Two more were struck hard and whistled into right center on a solid line, hitting the back of the enclosure.

The following pitch was inside and Brock laid down a perfect bunt to protect himself. The next few swings deposited the balls well back into the back netting. The resounding deep crack of the wooden bat echoed loudly across the enclosure. All the kids who were hitting stopped and even the spectators paused to watch Brock's awesome display of power hitting. It was a rare thing to see someone try to hit the Nolan Ryan pitch. It was rarer still to see someone who could actually hit it. Hank was not surprised by his son's power, but how could he be so consistent?

Two more prodigious swings launched two baseballs high into the back of the cage where they stuck in the netting. The last ball was hit so hard that it went through the back netting just missing a parked pick-up truck.

Brock looked back at him. He was grinning from ear to ear.

"There are limited variables,' Brock said. "If you watch the seams, you can pick up on the spin. Each pitch is coming at the same speed, so it is a simple matter of physics and hand-eye coordination." Brock twirled the bat around like a baton obviously enjoying the broad smile on his dad's face.

Hank roared with laughter. His nerves and any past regrets disappeared in a burst of pride.

The teenager was still sitting on the ground with his mouth gaping open. Hank shouted, "Hey, thanks for helping us out. We're done for the day. I counted eighteen straight hits. Is that the new world record?"

Driving home Hank became serious. "You really could see the seams?"

Brock looked back at his dad puzzled. "What do you mean? How else can you know the ball's angle of trajectory?"

"Oh nothing, I think four hundred would be a good batting average this year, but no more than one homer every two games, fair enough?"

"Okay, Dad. Thanks for bringing me here and letting me play."

"I think I'm the one who should say thanks." Hank started the car and turned for home.

~~*

About the Author. John Shehorn wrote his first action and adventure novel, *Unexpected Hero,* to honor our armed forces and the sacrifice of their families. It retells the true story of four courageous American heroes who shaped our nation—Chamberlain, York, Doolittle, and Sorenson. The book also creates a fictional hero to illustrate that the battle to protect our constitutional freedoms against religious intolerance and global terrorism continues. John and his wife live in the Conejo Valley.

"Remembrance restores possibility to the past, making what happened incomplete and completing what never was.
Remembrance is neither what happened nor what did not happen but, rather, their potentialization,
their becoming possible once again."
~ Giorgio Agamben,
Potentialities: Collected Essays in Philosophy

A Dog's Tale by Margaret Morris

(As communicated to a human friend)

You humans don't give us enough credit. I understand a lot of things about you because you're so like us, really just a different kind of the same thing. For example, you have a greeting ritual when you meet someone new and so do we. You shake hands and we sniff rears.

I hope I'm not being dogmatic, but my way's more informative. You can tell some things about a stranger from a handshake, I suppose, but not much. But with one sniff I know forever this individual's identity no matter how he disguises it, better than a fingerprint when the wind is right. I know what he ate last, whether he's top dog or underdog, or if a she, whether she's interested or you needn't waste the time. You human fellows have to take your chances.

Like you, we form packs and mark our territory. Again the dog's way is better. Our marking lets our friends know we visited, and lets outsiders know it's our territory they're coming on, so they'd better give us proper deference. You people use flags, religious symbols, and gang graffiti for the same purpose, of course, but that's so impersonal.

But some things about humans just baffle me. Take Clara, my human. I mean, I love her, don't get me wrong, she gives me food, takes me for fun walks, tells me what a special doggie I am. And she's taken care of me ever since I can remember, since way back last year when I was barely more than a shelter puppy.

But she has no concept of danger. She lets complete strangers come into the house to fix the TV, I mean, grown men. How does she know they won't kill her and take all her stuff? I try to warn her by growling a little and warn them as well they better not try anything. So far she's been lucky and they haven't hurt her or the baby.

The baby—sure I was jealous of her at first, but I got it pretty quick this was a pack member, Clara's equivalent of a puppy. Humans and dogs alike understand the vulnerability and helplessness of the young and give them some slack. I understand now it's my duty to protect the baby, too.

Maybe a month ago, my life changed abruptly. I knew something was up. Clara's parents came to the door for Clara. I'd met them a few times so I figured they were okay. Clara was all hyped up, happy as I have seen her and then teary a little, but through smiles.

They all left in one car and I was put out in the yard a really long time that day, which I hated. I'm a pack animal, for Pete's sake, and I get lonely and bored without company or something fun to do. Sure, I could pass the time digging up the petunias, but how long does that take?

When Clara's parents left her and the baby off at the house and she let me in, she had this other person with her, a person who smelled dangerous.

He was already inside the house, so I couldn't keep him out. I barked to show he'd better watch out and when he tried to reach out toward me, I backed up and growled.

"It's okay, Reginald," Clara said. "Brandon won't hurt you."

Oh, about my name. Not a very good choice on Clara's part. The vet Clara takes me to says I'm part Labrador, but who isn't these days. He says Labradors are sweet natured, love everybody. But the rest of me is something a little feisty he thought, maybe Rottweiler or maybe something else. Okay, I'm a mutt. So Reginald may be a tad highfalutin for a handle.

No way I was going to take Clara's word for how dangerous this Brandon was. Not only did he smell male to the max, but he was big, wearing hard boots and a camouflage sort of outfit, like he was fixing to sneak up on someone. The guy could do in all of us without turning a hair. And then, to prove herself completely insane, Clara hands the baby to him! That's when I really started in.

Brandon laughed at me, cradling little Bessie in his arms. "Fine thing. I can't even cuddle my own kid. What a welcome!" Then he opened the blanket a bit and started to talk to her. "What a little beauty, you are. And so chubby. You know, I think you look a bit like your grandpa, bald and fat."

His voice was soft and friendly, and both he and Clara were laughing, but I wasn't convinced he was okay. I was still letting him know with soft growls when he turned to Clara and said, "Maybe we could do without Reginald for a while?"

And then I'm out and he's still in. Was she crazy?

Well, I didn't go quietly, but I was beginning to see barking and growling was not a good strategy. I came in meekly when they let me. Brandon gave me my dinner, a pretty obvious ploy to win me over. I wasn't going to fall for it, but a fellow's got to eat. The rest of the evening I lay down between the baby and Brandon, keeping an eye on him.

Later, I got my chance. He went into the bathroom, I heard the shower running and then he emerged in the doorway, all wet, and naked so he couldn't be hiding any weapons. I was ready for him. I stood there barking and snarling, trying to tell Clara it was her chance to escape while he was trapped. I swore he wouldn't't get past me.

"Clara," he yelled. "Reginald won't let me out of the bathroom!"

32

Instead of being grateful for the rescue, Clara started to laugh. Then she scolded me and told me, "Come."

Well, come I did. She's got me trained unfortunately, but I didn't like it. Brandon escaped from the bathroom, of course.

The woman had no sense. She actually let him sleep with her. That meant at some point she'd be asleep and even more helpless and he'd be right there. I wouldn't let them out of my sight.

When they woke up in the morning, they talked. I listened, but I'm not so good at words. But tone of voice I get real well. Theirs were low, kind of relaxed. I saw she looked at him in a way I know, her eyes brimming over with a soft beauty you could almost feel, like the sun's warming.

I'm just a dog. I don't know much, but I know love. She looked at me like that a lot, so I know.

Suddenly, a great sadness overcame me. I'd been replaced. I'd done my duty best I knew how. Now she was looking to him to watch out for her. He was the new alpha, the new pack leader, and I'd been demoted.

They continued to talk. I'm not that great at understanding stuff outside my direct experience, but I knew something terrible made him very sad. Something about another place, one Clara mentioned from time to time, Afghanistan. He'd lost some friends there and seen some awful stuff. I got that it was not a good place to be.

Well, like I said, I'm part Labrador so I couldn't entirely help myself. When I saw tears fill this big guy's eyes and spill over, I knew he now belonged to my pack, and I knew my duty. I walked up to him and licked his face to show my sympathy. I even let him embrace me from the side, something we dogs don't really relate to—no hands you know. But people do it, Clara, for example, so I make allowances.

It's not so bad being an ordinary pack member instead of the alpha. Brandon played with me a lot in the next month or so, more than Clara used to. He was far better at throwing a ball for me to retrieve than Clara who doesn't really have the arm for it, and he seemed to enjoy it more. It's nice having another person around to take me for walks and help guard Clara and Bessie and our territory.

I think he felt the same. He told me, "Reginald, old boy, it's good you're a hyper paranoid freak of a watch dog. That way I'll know when I'm gone, someone will be looking out for the family. There's a lot of bad stuff out there." Then he added, "Only don't bite the mailman. I don't want to get sued."

I was surprised that I really missed him when suddenly he left. He didn't want to go. I could see that. He seemed really happy here. Clara came unglued and cried a lot.

I don't know—why do people do that? Leave their pack members to go someplace they don't want to go?

About the Author. Author Margaret Morris, a native Angelino, holds degrees from two California universities. Her wide-ranging interests spurred her to publish articles, essays, book and theater reviews, and a number of poems. She taught English and History in public schools. Morris's last four years have been focused on writing a novel, *The Gardener*, a contemporary story laced with dark humor, biting dialogue and stunning reversals. It tells of the powerful friendship between Mark McMann, a twenty-seven year old Ventura man, and Norma Armstrong, a retired botany professor, the gardener of the title.

Old HWY 1 near Emma Wood Beach – Photo Courtesy of Wendell Ward

Poetry should ... should
strike the reader
as a wording of his own highest thoughts,
and appear almost a remembrance.
~ John Keats

Love
Love wears a silk pink dress with satin rose slippers
Love glides in the cherry-violet clouds brimming with the
sunset, her long hair waving in the breeze, dress skimming the sky
Love lives in a golden pavilion by the calm, soothing ocean
with her boyfriend,
Watching the peaceful waves tossing themselves against the
gullible sand, white foam bubbling at their lips as the sun
drowns itself among them.
Love's friends are Affection and Fondness.
Love has no enemies, her heart is filled with tranquility.
Love loves herself into dreams.

Hatred
Hatred wears dark black robes.
Hatred stomps along the highway, suicide
 bubbling in his mind.
Hatred lives in a torn, tattered shack, the
victim of his uncontrollable, repulsive
angry temper which no one can stand.
Letting his fire blow out of his mouth, care
never to be available.
Hatred's friends are Abhorrence and Loathe.
the ones who share his greed for
heartlessness and malice.
Hatred's enemies are the ones who long for
the sun in a storm or pounding rain showers
and cackling lightning partnered with
booming thunder.
Hatred shows no knowledge of the warmth
around him.

~~*

About the Author. Elana Luo is a teen writer from Newbury
Park, California. She enjoys writing about deep thoughts
and creating descriptive pieces, but she keeps things light
through her love of dancing, laughing, and adventuring.
Her writing reflects her young perspective of life, but
there is much more for her to explore!

When I think of my grandmother, I remember the smell of burning chicken feathers.

Growing up, the holiday celebrations took place at my grandparents' apartment in The Bronx. No matter what else was on the menu, there was always soup, made from fresh chickens bought from the live poultry market. Grandma would take me with her when I got home from school to help her pick out the plumpest chickens, the ones most suitable for a holiday or a *shabbos* dinner. Grandma knew I didn't like to see the butcher slaughter the birds, so she sent me around the corner to the bakery for a cupcake while she attended to business. By the time I returned, all that remained was the smell of burned feathers and the heavy brown bag she stuffed in her shopping cart.

The shop owners fussed over me. Shapiro the butcher—not Mr. Shapiro, just Shapiro the butcher, like Rubinstein the grocer, or Katz the hardware man—wiped his hands and came out from behind the counter to pinch my cheek. I frowned and moved closer to Grandma. I thought I was too old to be treated like a baby in a carriage. Worse, I wondered if the blood splattered all over his apron came from the chickens Grandma had just bought from him.

"What a big boy you're getting to be, Martin," Shapiro said, reaching once again for my cheek. I kept him away by bending to tie my shoelace, which didn't need re-tying. But Shapiro looked like he was more interested in Grandma than me. They spoke mostly in Yiddish, but I could understand a lot of the language from listening at home.

"I don't see you so much, Mrs. Feingold. Is everything all right? Maybe you don't like chicken so much anymore?" He moved closer—close enough to put his hand on her shoulder, close enough so I couldn't hear what he was saying. She looked over to me, not so much asking me to rescue her, but to assure me she was in charge.

"Shapiro," she said. "You're turning into a dirty old man."

"Maybe so, but don't forget even dirty old men need love once in a while."

Grandma laughed, then put both her hands on the butcher's shoulders and pushed him away. "Goodbye, Shapiro. Maybe we'll see you next week."

"*Zeit gezunt*, Mrs. Feingold. Be well."

Free of him, she took my hand and pulled me from the market. Out on the sidewalk, she took a deep breath and said aloud, this time in clear English, "Disgusting man," and turned us toward the fruit and vegetable stand on the next street. I wondered whether her reaction to Shapiro had anything to do with his dirty apron.

The family observed the Passover *seder* ritual as an excuse for everyone to get together for a big meal and catch up on news. Before all the aunts

and uncles and cousins arrived, my father and brother Jules moved the living room furniture against the walls and set up the main table in the middle of the room. They allowed me to help carry the folding chairs to the table and put them in place. I was proud to be included in the work, feeling like I was now one of the men of the family, but Jules made sure to put me in my place. "Hurry up, punk, we haven't got all day."

My father came to my defense. "Jules, don't talk to your brother that way." But his half-hearted reprimands never did much good, and as soon as Pop turned his back, Jules gave me a sharp poke in the arm to remind me who was the boss.

Grandpa Avram ran the *seder* according to his own plan. He let Uncle Danny give the blessings over the *matzoh* and the wine. With that part of the ritual behind us, he went through reading the Passover story from the *Haggadah* as fast as possible, with only passing reference to the prescribed format. The family all followed along in their own books as best they could.

"Grandma, how much coffee did you have to drink to get all these?" Jules asked, probably remembering that Maxwell House gave out a free *Haggadah* in the grocery stores with each can of coffee purchased.

Grandma laughed. "A lot of years, a lot of coffee, a lot of *Haggadahs*. When they're free, you don't argue."

I was the youngest boy who could read Hebrew so it fell to me to recite the traditional Four Questions. *"Ma nish-ta-nah ha-lai-lah-ha-zeh* ... Why is this night different from all other nights?"

Why, indeed? If they had asked me, the response wouldn't match their expectations. This night was different because I had to wear a starched white shirt and the tie my mother put on for me.

"It's too tight," I complained.

My mom sighed. "You're growing so fast. All your clothes are getting too small for you."

This night was different because I had to shine my shoes and comb my hair before I was allowed to mix with the rest of the family. And the night was different because Passover was the only time of the year I was allowed to drink wine, even if it was diluted four-to-one with seltzer.

Seltzer came from the Seltzer Man. His name was Feldman, but no one ever called him anything but Seltzer Man. Once a week he carried a wood tray of a dozen of the heavy siphon bottles up five flights of steps to make his delivery and collect his payment. For the holidays, he came early so he could get a sample of Grandma's *gefülte* fish or a handful of the macaroons she baked especially for Passover.

"*Gut yomtov*," he and Grandma wished each other.

He always dressed the same—baggy wool pants, a pin-striped gray vest from some old suit over a plaid flannel shirt, and a gray fedora hat tilted back on his head. He leaned against the refrigerator to catch his breath. "Why do so many of my customers live in buildings without elevators?" he asked, talking to the ceiling as if to God.

"Rest a while," Grandma said. "Here, have some *gefülte* fish. I made it fresh." She gave him a patty on a small plate and handed him a fork. "Would you like some horseradish with it?"

"No. Thank you, Mrs. Feingold. I love horseradish, but I can't eat like I could eat twenty-five years ago, you know what I mean?" he said, holding his hand to his chest for emphasis.

"I know, I know. My Avram also has this problem. If it wasn't for Tums...." They both laughed.

"This fish is wonderful, Mrs. Feingold. It makes *schlepping* up all these steps worthwhile."

Grandma smiled with pleasure from the compliment. Everyone we knew loved her cooking, but she was happy to get confirmation and reassurance.

"Thank you," she said. "You look tired. You should get someone to help you with the deliveries. "

"When your grandson gets older, maybe he can help me," Seltzer Man said. He rubbed my head with his rough hand. "Such a nice boy. You're very lucky, Mrs. Feingold." He was messing up my hair, and I knew my mother would take one look and drag me into the bathroom to comb it again. Seltzer Man wasn't doing me a favor.

"Yes, Martin is a wonderful child. We're so proud of him."

Child? Even Grandma was still calling me a child? "I have to help getting the chairs out of the closet," I said and left the kitchen.

When I finished reciting the Four Questions, the family applauded. My parents glowed with pride. Even Jules looked happy with me. Grandpa handed me a dollar bill for doing so well, but as usual, my mother took the money for safekeeping. "You'll lose it," she said, though once she got her hands on the cash, I knew I'd never see it again.

At the part in the *seder* when we broke for the meal, my mother and my aunts got up to help Grandma with the serving, first bringing out the *gefülte* fish, then the chicken soup, each bowl with two half-submerged matzo balls surrounded by globules of fat floating on the surface. I remembered Shapiro and his bloody apron, but finished the bowl anyway. By the time they served the pot roast and the potatoes and green beans, I was too full to eat anything else.

As the meal went on, crumbs and scraps of food covered the tables, made worse when Uncle Danny spilled a glass of wine. He apologized, but Grandma eased his embarrassment.

"Don't worry," she said. "The stain will come out when I wash it." The table linens in her house always smelled from bleach. "You want to eat from filth?" she said, when my father joked about it. Then she scanned the room, her lips pressed tight and her eyes glaring, challenging Pop or anyone else in the family to argue with her. No one was so brave.

Uncle David, flushed with a few glasses of wine, told a dirty joke, bringing peals of laughter, subsiding only when Grandma reminded the adults there were children in the room—their children, she emphasized. When she went back to the kitchen, Uncle Joey told another joke, more risqué than the first. Aunt Sophie laughed the loudest, a staccato cackle.

"Oh, Joey, that's so funny," she shouted, and cackled even more. Soon the laughter became less about the jokes and more about Sophie's response.

Pop joined in the ribbing. "Sophie, when you laugh you sound like a chicken, but don't stop. We need the eggs." The family groaned from the tired old joke, but Sophie cackled even more.

The cousins pretended we didn't understand what was going on, afraid that if we let on, the jokes would stop. We were happy that it would still be a while before our parents knew how much we did know.

The laughter stopped when two brothers-in-law started arguing. What had been quiet fuming between the two turned loud enough for all of us to hear. "I lent you money last year and you still didn't give it back. You're a *gonif*, a thief," Uncle Irving said.

Uncle Louis' face reddened and shouted back, "I'm a *gonif*? You're a Shylock."

Aunt Irma sobbed in shame. Grandpa drummed his fingers on the table. It was the tipoff he was getting angry. At times like this, he let Grandma be the peacemaker. Soon, it got quiet, the adults nervously shifting in their chairs, embarrassed that things had gone too far.

"*Nu*, it's over?" she asked. "You're finished spoiling the day for Papa and me? It's a *shanda* to argue like this on a holiday. It's a sin." The guilt was spread around like chicken fat on a piece of *matzoh*. When she was satisfied she had made her point, she set another tray of pot roast on the table. "Eat, everyone, before it gets cold."

Things returned to normal. Aunt Rose announced, "Harold made Honor Roll in school for the third straight time. We're so proud of him."

"God bless him," said Grandma.

"*Mazel Tov*," chipped in Aunt Irma, now dry-eyed and ready to put the embarrassment behind her.

The anointed prodigy assumed a smug look on his face. I turned to insults to hide my jealousy. "You're such a jerk, Harold," I said, to the laughter of the other cousins sitting apart from the main table. Harold pouted, which was my invitation to pile it on. "Sissy," I said with a sneer. "You throw a ball like a girl." For us, that had to be the ultimate insult.

Harold whined, "Mom, Marty called me a sissy."

Aunt Rose flashed an annoyed look at my mother, who glared at me, reached across to my table, and twisted my ear. She had a way of talking with minimum lip movement when she was angry so that I was the only one close enough to hear her. She started the usual lecture about embarrassing her in front of the family, about how I was turning into a good-for-nothing, and how, if I didn't behave myself for the rest of the night, she would make me sorry I ever started up with Harold.

The room conversation turned to politics, as it often did. Everyone spoke in campaign slogans. "Eisenhower was a good general," Uncle Danny said, "but the working man needs Stevenson."

Aunt Rose added, "What we really need is another Roosevelt." The others nodded approval.

My mother never liked these discussions. They always ended up more heated than friendly. As a young woman, she had once told us, she rolled bandages in support of the republic in Spain, stood silent vigil in front of the White House to beg for action to end the concentration camps in Europe, and handed out leaflets condemning the British in Palestine. Her leftist credentials were impeccable, so it wasn't that she disagreed with her in-laws, but that they didn't go far enough.

"Roosevelt's big mistake was dropping Henry Wallace from the ticket. Truman wasn't much of a bargain," she said.

"Wallace wouldn't have stood up to the Russians like Truman did," Uncle David said. "He wouldn't have been so quick to recognize Israel, either."

"Wallace? He's a communist," Uncle Danny said. "You aren't a communist, are you, Gloria?"

She glared at him. "Wallace was a wonderful Vice President. He's a progressive. He isn't a communist." Her eyes narrowed. "And neither am I." For the rest of the evening she sat without speaking.

Once we got home, Mom made sure my father got the brunt of her feelings, not just about Uncle Danny, but her analysis of the shortcomings of his family.

"Your sister Anna has put on so much weight, she's asking for a heart attack," she said.

Pop answered with a grunt, but she didn't wait for his reaction.

"Your brother Joey keeps bragging about how much money he makes."

Another grunt.

"And your brother Danny is a miserable ...."

My father nodded in agreement, but cut her off. "He means well."

"He means well? He insults your wife in front of everyone, and all you can say is he means well? You should have said something. Why would you let him talk to me that way?"

"Did you want me to get into a fistfight? Can't we get through one holiday without you arguing with the family or trying to save the world?"

"Not *the* family, *your* family. My family doesn't act that way. And what about your parents? What happened to the drive and ambition they brought from Russia? Your mother could have been something, somebody with a purpose. Instead, she makes chicken soup."

"She makes good chicken soup." He slammed the bathroom door behind him.

"Don't get lost in there," she said. "I have to get ready for bed."

It became quiet in our apartment. Later, my brother and I heard our parents' bed squeaking.

"The argument must be over," Jules said.

~~*

About the Author. Victor H. Prushan's writing experience includes a business-related book, *No-Nonsense Marketing*, published by John Wiley and Sons in 1997. After retirement from business, he switched to fiction, including short stories and a novel in progress. His writing inspiration, he says, comes from life experiences and the people and events around him. Vic grew up in New York, graduated from the U.S. Naval Academy, and later earned an MBA degree from Northeastern University in Boston. He is a former naval officer and a retired marketing executive and consultant. When he isn't writing, he plays golf, takes travel photos and pictures of family and surrounding, and reads. For reading pleasure he indulges in spy novels—Alan Fust, John le Carre, Daniel Silva, and David Ignatius take up most of his iPad capacity— and crime novels, especially from Michael Connelly. When he's in the mood for serious material, he focuses on 19th and 20th Century history from authors like Doris Kearns Goodwin and David McCullough. His advice to any writer is to get in the habit of writing every day. He lives with his wife Florence in Thousand Oaks, California, near their three sons and their families.

I loved it because it was an astonishing display of vibrant colors. I loved how it felt to my fingers when I touched it. It felt like, or I felt like, I would be safe from harm as long as I kept it in my grasp. It smelled like fresh cherry blossoms with a hint of peach fragrance. I could hear no sound except my own breathing, but when I listened a little harder, I felt the soft vibration of a tiny bit of magic. I loved it so much that I would never let it go. I loved it once, and I still do.

~~*

About the Author. Seamus Morrison is a junior at the Oak Grove School in Ojai. At the age of ten he had to learn to walk and talk again after brain surgery to remove a malignant tumor called Medulloblastoma. He underwent radiation, a year and a half of chemo and intensive physical therapy. Seamus is a sea creature enthusiast and aspires to protect the ocean. On weekends, you can find him talking to guests about the animals at the Santa Barbara Natural History Museum Sea Center and he volunteers at the Monterey Bay Aquarium in their Teen Conservation Leader Program. He is passionate about ocean conservation, has organized beach cleanups and is on a mission to educate people about ways to reduce our use of plastic. Seamus is a pretty good pianist and enjoys composing classical music, especially during math class. He loves Joseph Campbell, Edward Abbey, Chopin, Erik Satie, Beethoven, John Steinbeck, nudibranchs, cetaceans, and his cat, Danny Boy.

To look backward for a while is to refresh the eye, to restore it, and to render it the more fit for its prime function of looking forward.
~Margaret Fairless Barber

Sara flounced out of the grocery store. Joe had just said, "Hi, Sara," and she'd been speechless. How had he even recognized her without her face or hair done? Of course, she wanted him to recognize her. She was interested in him, but he hadn't asked her out after their first date and was barely saying "Hi" when they saw each other.

Maybe he was so stunned at how bad she looked he wanted to make sure it was her. Guys. Who knew what they were thinking? She sure didn't—she could barely keep up with her own thoughts. Besides, he didn't look as hot as he usually did, although there was no hiding his boyish good looks.

She wanted a guy to love her, maybe one that was slightly on the naughty side. They seemed much more interesting than the boring ones she ate lunch with, and she thought Joe could be a little wild.

Once home, Sara thought she'd fix her hair and face, then saunter past his house. Maybe he'd notice her, and they could talk. She could wear her cerise blouse that revealed her curves and cleavage. But then she'd have to change her nail polish color, and would he even be home yet?

Sara impulsively dialed his number and then held her breath. What had she done? What would she say? Should she hang up? Too late as she heard him say, "Hi."

"Hi, Joe, this is Sara. What were you doing in the store so early? I thought you were a late night, party guy."

"Getting some milk for breakfast. How about you?"

"I'm making something for Tammy's party this afternoon. I didn't expect to see anyone, so I came right out of the shower."

He snickered. "That's what it looked like—sorta like a drowned ... uh, cat."

Her feelings were hurt, but she decided to ignore it rather than invite other criticism. She was having a hard enough time dealing with her changing body and facial hair, without hearing someone else's judgment. "Are you going to the party?"

"No, Tammy isn't speaking to me after the last time I took her out."

"What happened?"

"She said I tried to get her drunk and take advantage of her." Joe laughed again. "As if I have to get a gal drunk. Hey, want to go out tomorrow?"

Sara gasped softly. She knew he was popular, but had no idea he was so crude. Was this the adventure she'd been waiting for?

"No, I'll see you some time at Senior Bingo," she said and hung up.

~~*

About the Author. Sunny Glessner loves rainbows, finds travel irresistible and has

never been asked to leave a country ... so far. She treasures her friends from all over the world and loves being a grandparent. She also revels in ethnic cooking, parties and reading in bed. Recently Sunny won the Simi Valley Acorn Flash Fiction contest. Her short stories and essays have also appeared in the *Cup of Comfort* series as well as *Reflections: A Collection of Memoirs* and E-zines "Eye on the Lake" and "Persimmon Tree".

Top of the Pier – Courtesy of Dallas Clemmons

The Shell for the Soul by Maya Fay Allyn, a.k.a. Manisha Patel

The heart beating
Only with a machine's ministrations
The feet made of lead
Heavy with life's burdens
The strings break
The promise of freedom
Drags the soul clear through the soles
Into the very heart of Earth
It roams free of its burdens
Leaving an empty shell
To roam
Lifeless
Desolate
Empty

Until some entity takes notice
And fills the void
Bringing light into a shell
Where only dark clouds hung

The soul stops
Sensing the new visitor
Like a cat
Slinks up
Eyes the renovated space
And takes back residence

But a body is a space
For only one tenant
Who is to say
Who deserves the spot
The first one there
Or the one that made something of it?

~~*

About the Author: Maya Fay Allyn has not looked back since moving from the Midwest to the West Coast. She lives in Los Angeles where she works in the private sector as an Analyst. She focuses on writing contemporary and fantasy YA novels, psychological thrillers for adults, and when the whim moves her, poetry. Besides writing, Maya enjoys cloud watching and the subtle joy of doing absolutely nothing. More so is the intense need and love of surrounding herself with books. There are few pleasures better than sinking into a great story!

"Clara Jean, why don't you visit your sister this afternoon?" Mama's voice rings from the parlor.

"Because she's busy, Mama."

"Your sister always has time for you."

"Not since she had her baby. The little one takes all of her time and attention and all she ever talks about is her baby weight and how Russell don't help her none."

"Russell's a good man. Your sister is lucky to have him."

For a moment, I think I've won. That I'd exhausted Mama's stubborn quest to get me "out of the house" hoping I'd find my own Russell. Then Mama's voice chimes again, "San Francisco's got a herd of eligible bachelors, but you gotta get out to meet 'em. None of em' knockin' on our door unless you fancy up and leave this house!"

"Fancy up! Have you seen those bloodsuckers? Losers, the lot of 'em. Lookin' to git rich the lazy man's way. Niners. Wish I'd never laid eyes on this place." Papa, a would-be forty-niner, died within a month of our arrival. He was panning for gold on a hot July day.

"We's here now. Make the best of it."

I've lost this round, but fortunately, I have plenty of work, so I'm too busy for Mama's socializin'. My sewin' business is boomin', my reticule fat with coins and gold dust. I'll buy my way out of this devil's paradise after next winter. No family tie is gonna keep me harnessed to this hell hole. Preachers and prostitutes be damned. I'm goin' back to my sweet Virginia where people still know what polite society is.

"Clara, could you go get us some venison for stew? Them turnips and onions need somethin'."

"Yes, Mama." Mr. Carlisle's market is just around the corner. I make about ten trips a week there since Mama never plans very far in advance.

"We live in the city now, we don't need that canning nonsense with a store next door," she says. I pin on my dark hat and grab my shawl. I slip out planning to be back by the time the stove needs shovelin'.

At the market, I wait for Mama's meat. The old grocer is gone for several minutes. Wasn't thinkin' I'd see anyone in the small store, never did. Then Elizabeth Tallwaite breezes in.

"Clara Jean. Haven't seen you in a month of Sundays! Has your mama been sick? She wasn't at church last week."

"My, Lizzy, don't you look nice." I've learned to distract the church people, so I don't have to explain why I ain't been sittin' on them hard pews. In truth, I can't stand to sit there and listen to some preacher tell me how it's my job to get married and have young'uns. My hips belong to me. I'll decide if they are for breedin' or not.

"Oh, thank you! My new gentleman friend is comin' to call this day. I want to look nice."

"Well, I'm sure he'll appreciate the effort." *I'll be out of here in a minute.* Just as I finish my thought, Mr. Carlisle returns. I place the nickel on the counter and turn to leave.

"Clara Jean." Lizzy's voice trills like a lark.

"Yes."

"Would you care to join some of us for a sail around the bay this Friday?" My gentleman friend knows a captain and made special arrangements.

I'd rather have my head shaved. "Oh, what a dear you are. When are you setting afloat?"

"Around ten in the morning."

"Let me consult with Mother. I usually accompany her on Fridays."

"Excellent. I hope you can make it. Eli Halbeck will be there ... he'd love to see you. He's so handsome these days."

Lizzy is always trying to match someone up. "Good to see you, Lizzy." I hold my head higher than usual walking out the door. *Elizabeth Tallwaite has nothing on me.*

By the time I reach home, Mama is scraping turnips and carrots for the stew. "What's the meat look like? The last batch was a little bitter."

"I haven't seen it. 'Twas already wrapped, didn't want to bother Mr. Carlisle more than I had to."

"He's gettin' old. Last time I don't even think he recognized me," Mama said, shaking her graying head.

"Saw Lizzy. She asked me why you twernt at church Sunday."

"Lizzy is such a sweet girl. You know there's a gentleman caller in her life."

"She mentioned as much. Tried to match me up with that Eli Halbeck on Friday."

"Is there a party? Clara Jean you have to go to parties."

"Not a party. Just a sail around the bay."

"A sail around the bay ... you've never sailed. You must go. What a generous invite."

"I knew I shouldn't have told you. I don't need Lizzy's suitor service. I need to go back to Virginia and find myself a real gentleman."

"Clara Jean, you never know what Cupid has in store for ya."

"Cupid. Honestly Mama. You think Lizzy is Cupid? She *is* getting a little girth on her ... probably should snag a man before she weighs more than a milk cow."

"That is no way to treat someone who invited you on an outing."

"Maybe this stew could use some of the dried rosemary?" I move toward the spice shelf. "I love the scent of it cooking."

"Perhaps it could."

My distraction habit works on Mama as well.

We finish eating the stew I sit in front of the stove for warmth. I have a basket of mending and Mama sits with the Bible open on her lap. The night air is chilly, but the fire warm. I weave small stitches across the mending gourd and dream about my sweet Virginia.

"Wear the chestnut dress." Mama's words seem spoken more to the fire than to me.

"For what?" I feign ignorance.

"The outing. The sailboat trip."

"I think the chestnut dress is tight."

"Wear it with your nice straw hat. It frames your face and will keep the sun off ya."

"Why should I have to sail with those pew polishers? If God intended fer us to be on the water he'd have given us webbed feet."

"He did give us the sense to stay dry. You're goin' if no other reason than to be polite."

It's over. I'd lost. Why hadn't I kept my big mouth shut?

A frosty coolness settles in our small house. I refuse to acknowledge Mama's demands and she refuses to acknowledge my resistance. I awake Friday morning to the reddish brown dress pressed and hanging from the kitchen doorway.

I figure I can get dressed, leave the house and return in a few hours and Mama would never be the wiser. Except that damn Elizabeth Tallwaite would surely mention my absence to Mama on Sunday. Reluctantly, I dress and plop the dark straw hat on my head and tie its sash. I might have to go on Lizzy's excursion, but I don't have to like it. No one can make me like it.

I hail a coach to take me to the wharf and trudge along the boardwalk trying to ignore the fish smell while looking for Lizzy's auburn hair. She spots me before I see her and her new beau.

"Clara Jean, Clara Jean!" Again, the chirp of Lizzy's voice annoys my senses.

Waving my arm, I head in her direction.

"Clara Jean Trumbull, this is my friend Leo Philips."

"My pleasure, Miss Trumbull."

"And mine, Mr. Philips." *Who are you kidding?* Lizzy's gentleman caller is old enough to be her father. Niners! They find a few nuggets and think new boots and a waistcoat will buy 'em a wife.

"Come on Clara, we're over here. See the captain with the blue shirt."

I stomp across the nasty ground and follow Lizzy to a smaller pier. I see Eli Halbeck standing near the man with a blue shirt. The pocks on Eli's face have cleared, but he still looks like a boy dressed in his father's clothes. He stands and walks to the front of the craft and helps me aboard. The step is steeper than I would have liked, but Eli has a firm grip so I step down without falling. Lizzy and I sit on the bench next to each other and look out at the busy port.

Four more young people from the church have joined us and I'm forced to relive the shaky boarding of the boat again and again. Finally, we are seated and the captain who looks to be about a decade older than most of us orders his first mate to untie the craft and shove off. The mate and the captain hoist the smaller sails and maneuver us out of the congested harbor. Larger sails are raised, the boat picks up speed.

Suddenly, the fishy stench of the boardwalk is gone. A crisp, fresh breeze blows my hat off, and it flops around, bound by the ties under my chin. The boat seems to lift and skims across the water. I am no longer a seamstress on the east side, but the guest of the sea. We all gasp as the boat slows to bounce over a rough wave. Sea lions bark along the beaches and the reedy grasses that jam the coves. We bring the boom around, catch another breeze and fly some more. I'd never really thought about how wonderful it would be to soar over the ocean like a bird looking down at fish and seaweed. I feel free for the first time since I arrived at this God forsaken place.

"What do you think?" Lizzy says, holding her own bonnet in place.

"That this is better than a train. No smell, no stuffy compartments."

"Yes, I suppose it is wonderful. My hair is getting into an awful mess, though."

"I feel like a bird. Like I can fly." The boat slows and we lap peacefully next to a pod of dolphins. I so envy them. No churches or bonnets. Just soothing water skimming over their smooth bodies.

Suddenly, a huge rush of water bursts from the surface. I feel panicky then the captain shouts, "It's a humpback! A beauty!"

"A what?" I shout to Eli.

"A whale, a humpback."

The enormous animal throws itself back into the water. It is bigger than a railroad car and powerful. I'd never imagined anything so breathtaking. And what keeps it from turning the boat over?

The captain says that humpbacks are one of over a dozen species of whales that roam the Pacific. I was familiar with whale oil, but I'd never envisioned the amount of effort it must take to obtain the fuel. The animal is massive, I feel so small and powerless next to it. I sit looking toward the horizon, hoping for another glimpse of the huge creature. When I can't sit anymore, I climb up and stand on the narrow bench.

"Will it come back?" I ask the captain.

"I reckon we'll see it again. The whales seem as curious about us as we are about them."

I stand waiting. Just as I am about to sit, the boat steadily lifts with a large wave then suddenly plummets leaving me several inches off of the bench in midair. I reach for the ropes tethered on the gunwale, but before I can grab one, water comes at me fast and hard with the force of a blizzard.

I need to right myself and spit out the seawater in my mouth. I don't know if I'm the only one or if all of us have been pitched to our death. The skirt on my gown is like an anchor. I can swim, but not in a dress. I reach down and rip the stitches I'd so carefully needled less than a year ago. I hold my breath and tear enough away so I can tread water more easily. I see the boat not twenty feet away and move towards it.

Eli throws off his father's coat and dives in the water swimming toward me. Once we meet, he shouts for the captain to move the rope ladder and we swim together, finally reaching the vessel. I grab the rope ladder and cling to it. Eli yells at me to climb while he wrings the water out of what is left of my skirt. As I clamber in, Lizzy is holding her shawl out and wraps me in it. "Oh my! Oh my! Are you sound? Will you ever forgive me?" There are tears in her eyes. Here I am, a drowned rat with everyone looking at my knickers. No hat, half a dress and feeling such a fool.

"I'm fine. Wet, but fine."

"We must get you home and into some dry clothes," Lizzy says.

The ride back to the wharf dries me out some and I feel the captain glance over my way and see a smile out of the corner of my eye. Some nerve, it was his fault we drifted so close to the whale. By the time we reach shore, I'm only half-drowned. Lizzy and her beau escort me home and I try not to think about how embarrassed I feel. It doesn't matter anyway. I'll be leaving San Francisco as soon as my purse is full. No whales where I'm going ... or arrogant captains.

Mama is shocked at the sight of me. I duck upstairs while Lizzy explains the whole shameful situation. I hear Mama laugh as she closes the door.

"Clara Jean, dear, how about some warm soup?" Mama's voice travels up the stairs.

"Yes, that sounds good." I wish I were sippin' it on a ship bound for the East though.

By the time I finish the broth, I'm more than a little tired. The warmth of my bed is a welcome relief compared to the cold ocean water I'd experienced a few hours before. I drift off to sleep trying to bury the image of my soakin' self deep in the recesses of my mind—forgetting the whale, the captain and the perfect Elizabeth Tallwaite.

"Deeear, Miss Lizzy is here!" Mama's voice echoes off the bedroom door.

Why can't those two let me be? Didn't Lizzy get enough of the sight of me yesterday?

"I'll be right down Mama."

I take my time hoping that Lizzy might give up and leave, but luck is not to be had.

"How are you? I feel so bad. I just had to come and see with my own two eyes that you are well." Lizzy sips tea from Mama's best teacup and seems truly contrite.

"I'm fine, Lizzy. I'll just remember to stay in my seat next time." *Like I would do it again!*

The girl doesn't stay long and I am quite relieved when she takes her leave. Later that day, I answer a knock on the door and find Eli standing there, hat in hand.

"Clara, I had to stop by and tell you how truly sorry I am. I should have stopped you."

"Eli, thank you for coming by, but I'm fine—really."

"You'll let me know if I can do anything for you or your mama."

"How nice of you. But we are all right, surely." I begin to close the door fearing that he expects an invite to tea. Fortunately, he takes the hint and leaves me to my privacy.

Mama sends me back to the store early in the evening and this time I am more careful. I wait down the street a piece to make sure no Lizzy Tallwaite or anyone else who'd heard about my spill is around. When I return home, I'm surprised to hear voices in the parlor. "Clara Jean, Captain Strauss has come to check on your condition."

Captain Strauss! My condition! Why I never. The captain stands as I step around the corner. "Clara Jean, the captain here was just telling me why he came to California."

"Afternoon, Miss Clara. I'm glad you're feeling well."

Well. I wasn't sick. Haven't you people ever seen someone wet before? "Thank you Captain," I say, smiling.

"Now, tell us. Why did you come to California?" Mama says.

The captain looks down at the floor for a moment and then speaks. "I guess the same as everybody else. I wanted riches."

"And did you get your riches?" I say. I don't think the captain is rich, or even close to it.

"Well, I guess you could say I did. I may have come here lookin' fer gold, but what I found was worth much more."

51

"What did you find Captain Strauss?" Mama says.

"I found this brand new state and the biggest trees in the world. Sequoias. Giants of the forest. Huge reminders that God is greater than us all."

"You didn't stay here cause of some big trees?" I say.

"No, but the tallest mountains in the country are worth staying for. The Sierras rise to almost 15,000 feet high. The lowest point in North America, Death Valley, is nothing to ignore either."

A glint comes to his eyes. He is more handsome than I remember.

"The best farmland, the brightest sunshine, beaches and sea ports unlike any I'd ever seen. Glaciers, deserts and forests. The gold in California isn't the dust panned in the streams, it's the abundance of Mother Nature in all of her splendor—the whales, the dolphins, the bears. A place that hasn't been spoiled. Unlimited possibilities. To a man who isn't afraid of work, California is a king's ransom."

The captain seems younger and suddenly taller now as he sits up in the chair. He isn't the same man who smirked on the boat.

"What about the boat? How did you come to own a boat?" I ask.

"Hundreds of 'em just abandoned. Importers got the gold fever and left 'em to ruin. My eureka moment had nothing to do with prospectin', but the rescue of the *Kathleen*. We take passengers down to San Diego and Pueblo de Los Angeles, then carry another fare back. It's safer than horseback and stagecoach. Sometimes I drop anchor at one of the islands ... had a fare to the Mission San Buenaventura once. The rail will be going down there soon enough, but for now I can get people down there and back faster than anything else."

"Do you often spot whales?"

"More often than not. Always see dolphins and sea lions."

The beauty of the ocean comes alive in the man's blue eyes. He doesn't stay much longer, but invites me and Mama to come down to the wharf again, even recounts stories about he himself fallin' overboard. I don't feel as embarrassed as I did before.

I go to church with Mama on Sunday. Lizzy can't wait to sashay up to me on Leo's arm. "Clara Jean, you are looking well. I hope you'll forgive me for your accident."

"I'm as well as ever. I may even go for another sailing adventure. Your Captain Strauss invited me again to sail on his boat."

"Which boat? He has several you know," Leo says, earnestly interested. "Now that he has the dry good business, he doesn't sail as much."

"Oh, I didn't know that." Captain Strauss was a man full of surprises.

I return to the wharf later that day. I hear the captain before I see him. With his sleeves rolled up, I notice that he is fit, not afraid of hard work. He is confident and strong, not desperate and dirty like the niners. I wave in his direction and he speaks to his first mate and steps off the boat to meet me.

"Miss Clara Jean, are you here for another swimming lesson?" His smile breaks into a set of straight white teeth.

"Captain, I figure you might need some lookin' after, seein' as you too have been known to fall overboard." His laughter rings off the bow, at once I feel comfortable. We sail out in a smaller boat called a yawl, and I observe a pelican diving for food. Something about the captain makes me feel like anything is possible. Like dreams do come true. His spirit is infectious. I find out that his given name is Jonas and his mother was a dressmaker in Bavaria. He is kind enough to escort me home.

Mama invites him to dinner. He and I walk down to Mr. Carlisle's store. I feel comfortable beside him. He takes his coat off and puts it on my shoulders. We walk in rhythm, slowly, my arm linked in his. I almost pray to run in to Elizabeth Tallwaite.

This evening, I can't help but wonder if the captain's California is the same one I know. *There is an energy here*, one that I have found annoying up until the present, but there are also opportunities and at least one gentleman.

Captain Strauss and his brother are particularly successful. He asks me to come and work at his shop or at least sew for them in my home. He claims that his brother's waist-overall production needs the oversight of a woman, that there is more work than his brother can handle. He says that the garments are quite sturdy, practical to a fault almost.

Perhaps I will take him up on his offer, call on his brother Levi. Maybe California is the land of opportunity.

About the Author. Sheli Ellsworth is an award winning author, humorist and journalist. She currently writes for the *Ventura Breeze*. BeachHouse Books published her first two books, *The Psychoanalysis of Everyday Life: sometimes I pee when I laugh* and *Confessions of a Pet Au Pair: the ABCs of pet ailments including traditional and homeopathic care*. She published the colorful interactive children's book *My Winter Holiday by Noah* co authored by Sheldon Brown and is currently publishing *Henry, the Helicopter*, a children's book she illustrated. You can also find her writing in *Quintessence, Windows,* and *Serendipity*.

I lose everything as it's meant to be.
Turquoise pawn slides from my wrist,
silk scarf from my neck.

Monsoons in New Mexico are short
as life. In the arroyos
tadpoles grow instantly to frogs.

Then everything desert.

How fortunate
I am each dawn to wake up alive.

About the Author. Glenna Luschei's latest book is *The Sky is Shooting Blue Arrows* from the University of New Mexico Press. She has published Solo Press books and magazines for fifty years and will now be publishing translations. She spends her time between North Carolina, New Mexico, and San Luis Obispo, California, where she was inducted as Poet Laureate of City and County in the year 2000. She received the D.H. Lawrence and Helene Wurlitzer Fellowships in Taos, New Mexico, where she still conducts summer workshops.

Seeking to forget makes exile all the longer; the secret of redemption
lies in remembrance.
~ Richard von Weizsaecker

"It's a beautiful day for a funeral, don't you think, dear?" The white haired lady, adorned in a well-worn black lace outfit, addressed herself to the other elderly woman, similarly adorned, sitting beside her on the graveyard bench.

"Yes," the other replied. "It rather reminds me of last year. Do you remember the name of that charming family last fall, the one with the three little boys? I can't remember. My memory fails me so often; sometimes I wonder when it's all going to end … Gladys, are you listening to me?"

"Sorry, Edna, it's this yarn. The color is too dark for me to see the knots." Gladys stared down at her knitting as her old and worn hands tried desperately to untangle a section of the yarn.

Edna sighed and straightened the black hat that sat crookedly on the well-brushed nest of grey hair atop her head.

"You should know by now what black yarn does to your eyes," she said to Gladys.

"I know, but it's the only yarn worth knitting, since we never go to any social occasions except funerals these days," Gladys said, still struggling with the knot, "Do you think the vicar will stay for the reception?"

Edna thought for a moment, then answered, "I doubt it. He's usually busy getting ready for the next funeral, what with so many deaths lately."

"True," said Gladys.

They sat for a moment in silence, Gladys trying to untangle her yarn and Edna straightening her hat. Suddenly, a black clad procession in the distance caught Edna's eye.

"Gladys," she said, "Look! There they go. Shall we join them?"

"We must." Gladys tucked her knitting away into her purse, and the two stood up and slowly ambled over to the group surrounding the freshly dug grave. They stayed far in the back throughout the ceremony.

Afterwards, the group, including the two old ladies, adjourned to the parish hall where a hearty meal of potluck foods brought by various families was being served. Scalloped potatoes crammed with melted cheese, roast beef practically swimming in the meat juice surrounding it, cooked vegetables steaming hot, freshly baked Irish soda bread with homemade butter on the side—all these dishes and more greeted the mourners.

Gladys and Edna found two seats by the fireplace and sat down to warm themselves. Gladys took out her knitting again and continued unknotting the yarn. Edna had been watching the people around her, following the plates of food in their hands with her eyes as the mourners walked around the room.

"I'm off to get myself a plate," she declared to Gladys, standing up, "would you like me to bring one for you?"

Gladys shook her head but Edna insisted, "I'll bring one for you just in case you get peckish." And off she went toward the food tables.

"Excuse me, ma'am," Gladys looked up at the young lady who spoke to her, "may I take this seat?" She gestured to the chair on the other side of Gladys.

"Of course, my dear!" Gladys moved a tad so that she could slightly face the young woman.

"What a beautiful day for a funeral," Gladys remarked, having unknotted the yarn finally and continuing to knit, "Don't you think? Of course it's a terribly sad occasion, but I've seen many worse days for a funeral."

"I suppose so," remarked the young woman, "but then again I don't go to enough funerals to know what kind of a day would be best. I can't think of anyone who does."

"I do," said Gladys quietly, looking down at her knitting.

"Oh! I'm so sorry," apologized the young lady, putting a hand on Gladys' shoulder, "it must be hard to watch so many of your loved ones pass away. It's hard for me now and this is my first funeral. How often do you attend funerals?"

"Oh, about a dozen a month," replied Gladys, sighing, "but then again, the Good Lord takes them so much more often nowadays than he used to. The important thing is to look on it as a blessing rather than a sorrow. If you have this in mind, then funerals can be quite rewarding." She smiled up at the young lady.

Meanwhile, Edna was moving through the food line at a very slow rate, making sure to give her and Gladys' plates each a double helping of every dish. A gentleman beside her in line chuckled to himself, watching the thin old lady trying to juggle the heaping plates of food while reaching for the polished silverware and linen napkins.

"Quite the appetite!" he remarked with a laugh. Edna stared back at him with cold distain.

"True mourning empties the soul as well as the body of all sustenance. One who has the stomach to mourn must also have the stomach to eat."

With that she turned her heel on the wide-eyed man and marched over to the fireplace, grasping the plates of food as the trophies of her victory.

She returned to her seat beside Gladys, who was still talking earnestly with the young lady, and threw herself into her plate of food. When she had emptied her own plate she stared for a minute at Gladys', which lay untouched on the table beside her. Edna glanced over at Gladys, who was still talking, and then dove into her plate as well. Gladys obliviously continued her conversation with the young woman.

"Forgive me for asking," said the young lady, "but I don't recognize either of you. Then again, I am not familiar with all my uncle's friends. How did you know my uncle?"

Just as Gladys was about to answer, Edna began to cough furiously.

"Are you all right, dear?" asked Gladys with concern.

Having regained her breath, Edna answered, "Yes, thank you. They really must be more careful preparing these vegetables. We wouldn't want two funerals in one day!" She laughed and continued eating.

"Not that we really mind going to two funerals a day," Gladys continued speaking to the young woman, "Why sometime we even —"

"Have you seen my other glove, Gladys?" Edna interrupted, "I seem to have misplaced it. Perhaps it's over by the silverware. Go and search for me, will you?"

Gladys smiled at the young woman, put her knitting away, and went to search for the glove.

"Can I help you, ma'am?" asked one of the men passing by the silverware table where Gladys was searching.

"Oh, no thank you," she replied, smiling, "simply searching for a glove."

"I'm sorry," he continued, "but who are —"

"Found it!" Gladys interrupted him, holding up a worn black glove and smiling triumphantly, "Thank you so much, dear." She bustled off quickly.

"Gladys," Edna called to her in a harsh whisper, "Gladys! Look! The vicar is here!"

"Oh!" remarked Gladys, coming to Edna's side and peering through the crowded room. "Has he caught sight of us yet?"

"I can't be sure," said Edna hesitantly, "but he's been glancing our way and now he's talking to who I presume is the widow. And that one gentleman you were approached by is now counting the silver. We had better go."

The two old ladies grabbed their purses and hurried out of the parish hall, avoiding all eye contact and pretending to be deaf to the shouts that came from behind them.

"That was close, Edna, you had best be more careful next time."

"Me, be more careful!" Edna said in exasperation, "You are the one who always talks too much. One of these days you'll give us away!"

"But it did pay off," Gladys said, emptying her purse on the graveyard bench they had come to. Three silver spoons, one expensive silk handkerchief, and two hand crocheted lace doilies came tumbling out alongside her knitting. "And you got four good meals out of that one!" she remarked.

"Gladys, I can't believe you!" Edna said sternly, "Only three spoons! You are losing your touch."

"I was under pressure." Gladys replied indignantly, "Besides, it took me quite a while to get that handkerchief. And look, this one isn't even that tear stained."

"Tomorrow I expect better," Edna said, sitting down on the bench to straighten her hat.

"Yes," Gladys said, sitting down with her knitting, "I've heard that it promises to be another beautiful day."

~~*

About the Author. Zoe Katharine Fowles Appleby. As a child, Zoe was raised on books, from Edward Gorey to Nancy Drew. That is one reason why Thomas Aquinas College, with its Great Books Program, was the perfect choice for her. Luckily it is located in Santa Paula, CA, the same town where her loving parents and talented younger brother live. She is in the process of earning a liberal arts degree, with emphasis on Philosophy and Theology. Her love for literature and poetry has led her  to form a poetry group on campus as well as attend the 2015 Catholic Literary Conference at USC. Outside of school, Zoe enjoys water polo, river rafting, art museums, beaches, and the many adventures Southern California has to offer.

Being apart makes it easy not to try
But I suspect you'll come back
And I won't be strong enough to leave
And not wanting to cry alone
I'll help you pretend
We're not pretending anymore.

~~*

About the Author. Lee Wade holds a degree in Classics from the University of Southern California. She's authored award-winning fiction and drama, has published poetry, essays and articles, and is an eagle-eyed editor through DreamLight Press (writersdesk126@gmail.com). Passionate about encouraging reading and creative writing, Lee's volunteered in the Conejo Valley Unified School District for almost a decade helping youngsters read and create stories. She lives in Southern California with her husband.

Flute-playing Mermaid – Courtesy of Wendell Ward

She awakes to the sound of a helicopter circling overhead. She cannot just rollover and ignore the incessant sound of this phenomenon of urban life. The light from the copter illuminates the room. She sits up, shivers and looks around. She reaches for her robe, stands and slips into it. Without turning on a light, she moves quietly through her ground floor duplex into the front hallway to check the door. It's locked. She moves into the kitchen to check the back door. It too is locked. The sound of the helicopter fades as she walks with confidence to the French doors of the living room and turns the door knob. It opens unexpectedly.

She looks down, unsure by this breach of security, and quickly locks it. The bolt slams into the lock ringing out like a gun shot. She vows to be more careful. Retracing her steps to her bedroom, she enters, takes off her robe, and leans over to turn on the light.

"Don't do that," a surly voice whispers. She freezes. She is grabbed violently by her hair, "If you make a sound, I'll kill you."

She gasps and shakes in fear.

The intruder lets go of her hair, puts his arm across her shoulders and presses the barrel of a pistol against her temple. She feels her body tensing with fear, but senses she must keep herself calm if she is to survive. He is breathing fast and it scares her.

She remembers reading in some magazine article some hints to survive a crime, but she is so terrified that she can't remember what they were. She instinctively knows that she needs to keep her wits about her and takes a deep calming breath.

Her assailant relaxes his grip, and she notices his breathing is slowing and is less intense. He pulls the cold steel away.

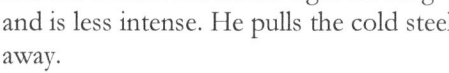

She stands, but turns away from him, saying a silent prayer. His voice is harsh when he tells her to turn around. Slowly turning, she feels her knees shaking, so she grabs the edge of the bed to steady herself. Her whole body is wracked with fear and she loses her equilibrium. To keep from falling, she sits hard on the edge of the bed. Pulling herself together she looks up and studies the man standing before her. His gun is pointed directly at her face.

He's younger than she had imagined, about her age, maybe twenty-four or twenty-five. Maybe it's his raspy voice that sounds old. He's not tall, but he's not short either. His hair is shaggy, clothes disheveled, and he is dirty.

"What are yah lookin' at?" he snarls. Before she can muster an answer, he leans over and turns on the light next to the bed. Then he moves over to the window, looking upward toward the sky. He moves back toward her, waving the gun around in a nervous manner. He points it at her and using his head, gestures to the hallway. Not sure what he wants, she just continues to take deep breaths without moving from the bed.

He grabs her arm and drags her into the hallway. Putting the gun in her back, he pushes her painfully in the back, forcing her into the living room.

"You should really keep all your doors locked," he says. He shoves her into a chair and walks over to the French doors. He turns the door handle, realizing it's locked. He laughs and turns back to look at her.

"Shutting the barn door after the horse is out or is it in? You're not very smart." He grins. "But, I don't suppose you expected company."

She responds angrily, "Certainly not uninvited ones." He whips around and points the gun at her again. Her anger overcomes her fear and she looks him squarely in the eye. He boldly returns the stare.

Then he asks, "Do you have anything to eat?"

She starts to stand, but catches herself and stays seated. Using the gun he waves it around and says, "It's okay, I won't hurt you. Make me some breakfast."

She stands, goes into the kitchen and turns on the light. He follows her and sits at the table in the small nook. He watches her open the fridge pulling out eggs, bacon, and butter. She finds comfort in the activity and soon the smells of bacon and coffee brewing fills the small kitchen. He smiles, probably enjoying the comfort of long forgotten rituals.

"What's your name," he asks.

"Kelsey, and yours?" she inquires breaking two eggs into the frying pan.

He picks up the gun and waves it around for a moment and says, "Roy, my name is Roy." Then he laughs and points the gun at her. "It sounds like we're at a meeting. But I don't suppose you know anything about that."

With an edge to her voice she responds, "You make a lot of assumptions about people, don't you?" She loads a plate with fried eggs, bacon and toast and places it in front of him. He takes a bite of food and lets out a grunt of pleasure. Then he quickly takes another bite. She pours him a mug of coffee and asks, "Milk?" He shakes his head no, and continues to eat.

When every crumb is gone, he takes a large drink of coffee, sets the mug down, sits back and says, "Yeah, I know a lot about people. There are those that have and then there's the rest of us."

"Oh, and what category do you put me in?" Kelsey asks, clearing the dirty dishes and placing them into the sink. Roy stands, shrugs his shoulders, and turns to go into the other room.

Kelsey, needing to keep busy, rinses the dishes and stacks them on the counter.

"Hey, bitch! Get in here!" he yells.

The nastiness in his voice sends a chill through her body. She quickly wipes her hands and moves into the living room. He is sprawled in the big overstuffed chair that used to belong to her dad. For a brief moment, she feels like she is walking into one of those domestic moments of fantasy that she occasionally day-dreams about. But, watching him wave the gun around, jolts her back to reality. She sits on the sofa across from him and asks, "Why did you break into my house?"

Pointing his finger at her like a naughty child, he says, "No, no, no. I didn't break in, the door was unlocked."

She is outraged. "Oh, so I'm responsible for your invasion into my house, because I forgot to lock the door?" Standing, she says, "Well the party's over, you get the hell outta my house."

He leans forward re-aiming the gun at her. "I'm not quite ready to do that, Miss Uppity. I'll leave when I am good and ready. You don't seem to understand, as long as I have this gun, it will be my decision to stay or go, not yours." Suddenly, the sound of the helicopter patrolling the skies is heard again.

Roy stands and goes to the French doors. He looks up at the sky and then walks back to the chair and sits. He picks up the television remote, turns it on, and starts flipping channels. Kelsey's fear has turned to anger. She watches Roy find a channel and settle in for some late night viewing. She sneers at him. "You comfy?"

He ignores her and raises the volume. The helicopter comes closer and Kelsey watches it light up her backyard. She looks at Roy who surprisingly begins to nod and doze off in the chair. The sound of the helicopter overhead is mesmerizing. She sees his gun has fallen out of his hand and rests tantalizing close between his leg and the arm rest.

She moves slowly toward Roy and the beckoning gun. Quietly, inch by inch, she creeps forward. A smile passes across her face because she realizes Roy is snoring. He has fallen sound asleep.

She reaches down and carefully picks up the gun. He shifts his weight slightly, but does not wake up. She steps back and examines it. She has never held a hand gun. It's heavier than she expected and she wonders if it is loaded. She puts her hand on the trigger and for the first time since the evening ordeal began, she feels a sense of control.

Roy is asleep, snoring obnoxiously. She points the gun at his mid-section and slowly pulls the trigger. The shot is louder than expected and she jumps, startled. She puts both hands together on the gun and empties it into the midsection of the sleeping, now dying man. She slowly puts the gun down on the chair, walks into her bedroom, and dials 911.

~~*

About the Author. Katherine L. Todd has a bachelor's degree from University of San Francisco and film training from UCLA's Motion Picture and T.V. Production Program. Her short film *The Celebration*, won multiple awards including a gold medal in the New York Film Festival. She was president of Burnt Meringue and independent film company. And has a solid business background in a major food corporation. She has written five screenplays and several short stories.

Wagon Wheel Hotel - Courtesy of Wendell Ward

For us, the best time is always yesterday.
Engrave this quote in Our Store!
~ Tatyana Tolstaya

Debbie slid into the armless desk chair on a gloomy Monday morning at the unemployment office, stuffed her lunch bag and purse into the bottom drawer, and flicked on the table-top fan to agitate the musty weekend air. She had arrived early, hoping Mr. MacKenzie would notice her promptness when he walked past her cubicle to his private office at the end of the aisle.

"Good morning, Ms. Johnson."

"Good morning, Mr. MacKenzie." It worked. Debbie grinned and began gathering the pencils and pads of paper she would need for the morning's assignment—workshop leader for Experience Counts, a group of unemployed senior citizens looking for work. Debbie's job was to convince them that experience really does count, even more than youth and beauty and a willingness to start at the bottom and work for pennies. It was a daunting task for the youthful public servant with large green eyes, spiky red hair and a figure sculpted from a dozen summers surfing the California coast.

Debbie never slept well on Sunday nights, fighting the queasiness that preceded the weekly assignment. Several months ago, she worked up the courage to tell Mr. MacKenzie she would gladly accept any extra duties in place of the senior job search program, but the year's budget cuts and hiring freezes kept the rookie social worker at the bottom of the totem pole, pulling Monday morning job club duty longer than the normal rotation of responsibilities.

Debbie glanced at the time on her computer screen and took a moment to sit back and gaze at the beach pictures she had pinned to the gray, fabric partition between her cubicle and the next. Someday, she and fiancé Brad would travel to far-away beaches, but with his part time job teaching accounting at the local college and her entry-level wages with the county, real vacations would have to wait.

"Hey, Deb, ready for the knitting circle?" Lucy teased. Lucy was the claims specialist who had just arrived at her desk across the aisle.

"Morning, Lucy. I guess so. But to tell you the truth, I don't know how much longer I can do this. I'm feeling sicker and sicker every Sunday night. They stare at me like I'm a joke—a twenty-five year-old joke. And you want to hear something weird? Last night I actually had a dream about these people. I dreamt they didn't show up this morning because they all got jobs and Experience Counts was canceled for good."

"I think your dream is having a dream, girlfriend."

"I guess so." And with a final glance at the time, the reluctant group leader gathered her coffee mug and other supplies and headed for the staff lunch room doubling as a meeting space for the job club.

Flicking on the light and opening the blinds, Debbie placed Friday afternoon's smelly pizza box in the trash, put up a pot of coffee, and wrote Experience Counts in big, red letters on the white board above the sink. The sky was still gray when she poured herself a cup of decaf and sat down at the head of the table.

"Anyone home?" tweeted sixty-five year old Sadie Leibowitz, gently knocking on the open door jam.

"Good morning, Mrs. Leibowitz. Thank goodness you're here. I was worried no one would show up today." Debbie lied.

"Good morning, darling," Sadie cooed in the Brooklyn dialect of her youth. "Such a gloomy morning like you've never seen."

"But it's always like this in June. How long have you lived in California?"

"Let me see. This coming April will be twelve, no thirteen years. Morty, may he rest in peace, and I moved out here thirteen years ago—the land of sunshine and tofu. We ran a nice, little dry cleaning shop in the Valley for many years, but when people couldn't afford to get their clothes professionally laundered anymore, we lost everything. It was one thing after another. Right after the store closed, we got a letter stating that the rent would be going up on our space at the Friendly Valley Senior Mobile Home Estates. Then on top of everything, Morty got sick and I spent every last dime on Morty's medications. If he had lived, it would have killed him to see me schlepping all over town, looking for work."

Debbie reached out to pat the woman's hand and noticed her thin skin barely covered her bones and veins. "Did Brad ever call you about the accounting job at the college bookstore?"

"Yes, dear. But that job requires a degree, and my only credentials are from the University of Morty and all the years I kept the books for the shop. I've been on dozens of interviews and no one is interested in hiring Nana Sadie to do their bookkeeping."

"Where the heck is everybody?" Joseph Miller said, an unemployed construction worker, pulling out a chair from the table, turning it around, and straddling it like a horse.

"Good morning, Mr. Miller," Sadie said.

"Yeah," he grunted back. "So are we going to get started or what?"

"In just a minute, Mr. Miller." The young group leader nervously pulled a tissue out of the box to wipe her sweaty palms and was relieved to see Myra Robinson sashay into the room. Myra had lost her retail position in a high-end clothing boutique in Beverly Hills as the weak economy devoured jobs in all sectors of the labor market.

"Good morning, Mrs. Robinson. Please take your seat and we'll get started," Debbie said.

"Good morning," Sadie said to the stunningly tall African-American woman in a camel hair Chanel suit with contrasting piping.

"You look beautiful today, as always," Debbie said.

"Thank you, dear. I picked this up in Paris on my last trip abroad with Charles, before he dumped me for his assistant."

"I'm so sorry," Debbie consoled.

"Oh brother," Joseph muttered.

To complete the group, fifty-five year-old Maria Ortiz entered the room, along with sixty-six year-old Frank Allen. Maria had lost her job as a front desk manager in an exclusive hotel when it was sold to a national chain, and Frank had been laid off from his information technology position with a pharmaceutical company that began off-shoring its technology development department.

"Welcome, Ms. Ortiz and Mr. Allen. We're just getting started."

"It's about time. I've got a very important meeting this afternoon," Joseph said.

"Do you have a job interview?" Sadie asked.

"Nah. I'm meeting some lady at the bank about my mortgage. The wife wants me to see if we can refinance or something to bring down the payments. Sheesh."

Joseph lowered his eyes and the room grew silent, each person enveloped in personal pain like the thick overcast that smothered the coast. Debbie glanced up and down the table, feeling the suffocating weight of her responsibility and coming close to tears. She picked up the black, ceramic coffee mug and took a sip of coffee, attempting to hide her face for a few moments. A Christmas gift from her mom, the mug was inscribed in gold paint with the question: What would you attempt to do, if you knew you would not fail? Debbie used the mug each day, but never thought about the anonymous quotation until now, so she read it again, this time out loud.

"Hey, what are you saying there? Are we going to get started or what?" Joseph grumbled.

She read the quotation again. And in that moment, as the reluctant leader of five troubled souls gathered around a kitchen table on a gloomy Monday morning, the novice social worker summoned her strength and decided to trash the lesson on resumes. Instead, she would springboard off the coffee cup.

"Okay, this morning we're going to discuss something different." She pushed the mug toward the center of the table, sloshing a little coffee over the side. "What would you attempt to do if you knew you would not fail? Who wants to go first?"

The pattern was broken.

"What do you mean, dear?" Sadie asked.

"You're not trying to play some kind of weird, psycho-shrink games with us, are you, cutie?" Joseph asked.

66

Debbie ignored his comment and instead looked toward the technology guy. "How about starting us off, Mr. Allen."

"Okay, I'll give it a shot. If I knew I would not fail, I'd take every cent out of the bank to start my own IT company in the field of mobile application design. That's where the money's at today—apps of all types for hand-held, mobile devices. That's exactly what I'd do, if I knew I wouldn't fail."

The group looked up. Even Joseph seemed interested.

"That's exciting," Debbie said. "How about you, Ms. Ortiz?"

"That's easy. Although I enjoyed working with the hotel guests, I always wanted to be a nurse. Make a real difference in people's lives. Maybe specialize in oncology. But do you think I'm too old to go back to college?"

"Not at all. Brad tells me all the time about older adults taking classes to learn new job skills. I think you'd be a wonderful nurse. Who's next? Mrs. Robinson?"

"Hmmmm. Let's see," she paused for a moment to think and then continued, "If I were absolutely certain I wouldn't fail, I'd be a travel agent or maybe work for the airlines."

"You mean the lady who does all the pat-downs at the airport?" Joseph asked.

"No. Of course not. I'd be in customer service or sales. I could make reservations or maybe sell advertising space in the airlines' on-board magazines."

"That's great. I'll bet there's an airline somewhere in the world that would love to hire someone with your travel expertise," Debbie said.

By now, the group was sitting forward in their seats, wondering who would speak next.

"Okay, Mr. Miller," Debbie said. Her nervousness had disappeared, replaced by calm, confident leadership as she danced in rhythm with her students' dreams. "Your turn. What would you love to do if you knew you could not fail?"

"That's easy. I know what I'd do, and there's no way I would fail."

"What's that? Myra asked.

"If I had the chance, I'd join the union and work in the studios. I hear there's a new Jurassic Park movie in the works. You know they're gonna need a lot of hands to build them sets and stuff. Make a bundle building sets for the movies."

The group clapped their hands in support of the construction worker.

"Hey, you gonna be on the red carpet or something when that movie wins an Academy Award?" Frank asked.

Joseph joined the group in laughter.

"Okay, who haven't we heard from yet? Mrs. Leibowitz, I don't think we've heard from you," Debbie said.

"Well, if you really want to know," teased the diminutive bookkeeper in the pink polyester pant suit.

"Yes, Sadie. Of course we want to know," Myra said.

"Well, I didn't have the time to cook very often when I was working at the cleaners, but once in a while, I'd love to make truffles."

"Really?" Debbie asked.

"Yes, dear. I'd spend an entire Sunday morning in my kitchen, over a steaming copper kettle of molten, bittersweet chocolate, carefully adding it to simmering cream, flavored with vanilla beans and just a little bit of brandy—the good stuff that Morty kept in the liquor cabinet. The aroma of the mixture would fill our little mobile home from end to end, and I felt as though I were in heaven."

The kitchen conference room fell silent.

Sadie continued, "Then I'd let the mixture cool until I could scoop out little balls of truffles and roll them in slivered toasted almonds or cocoa or shredded coconut, just like this." Sadie took the eraser off the top of her pencil and rolled it between her hands. "You need to work quickly or else they melt back into liquid. I used to give them away for holiday gifts. But if I could, I would package them in fancy little boxes with gold foil liners and sell them to candy shops in West Hollywood or Santa Monica or Beverly Hills. That's what I would do, if I knew I wouldn't fail."

"My god, Sadie. You're not an accounting clerk at all. You're a candy maker." Debbie patted Sadie's hand.

"Like Willy Wonka?" Joseph asked.

"No, not like Willy Wonka, more like the chocolatiers on the Champs D'Elysee in Paris. Small batches of beautifully decorated confections. Handmade. The finest ingredients. Very expensive," Myra said.

"My goodness, dear. I'm just a nana, not a choco-tilly-a, or whatever you said."

"But Sadie, think about it," Myra encouraged. "I know all the boutique managers on Rodeo Drive. What if I asked them to put out some of your truffles on little silver platters for the customers to nibble as samples—with your business card conveniently close by, of course?"

"And I know the housekeeping manager at a hotel in Santa Monica. Maybe they would buy your candies to put in the rooms at night when they turn down the beds," Maria added.

"Hey, I can take some down to the union hall. Would give me a good reason to go down and talk to the guys," Joseph said.

"And once your business is up and running, you'll definitely need a mobile app so that people can find you easily and buy your truffles online," Frank added.

Debbie's eyes welled with tears, but this time she didn't try to hide the emotion.

"What's wrong, dear?" Sadie asked.

"Nothing. Just allergies," said the young woman who had just grown into her profession.

"I have an idea," Myra said, peeking out the window to see that the sun had broken through the fog. "Let's get out of this young girl's pretty red hair for a while, grab some coffee and start writing down a few ideas to sell Sadie's Truffles."

"Hey, that ain't a bad name—Sadie's Truffles," Joseph said proud of his contribution.

As Experience Counts left the room, Debbie sat back for a few minutes to take in everything that had just happened, enjoying the irony of the big red letters on the white board over the kitchen sink and savoring her new found confidence. There would be other days for resume lessons. Today was for helping these good people draw strength from a renewed sense of optimism about the future and support from each other. Heady stuff for a young social worker.

Mr. MacKenzie entered the kitchen and broke Debbie's reverie. "Excuse me, Ms. Johnson, I saw your group all walk out together. A little Mutiny on the Bounty this morning?"

The manager snickered.

"Uh, no, sir. It wasn't like that at all."

"Well, it doesn't really matter. I have some good news for you. They're downsizing the South Central office and someone named Gloria will be transferring in by Friday. She'll be assigned to the Monday morning job club beginning next week, so you're off the hook, kiddo," he said and left the room.

Debbie sat motionless for a moment, then sprinted toward the door, "Mr. MacKenzie, wait…."

~~*

About the Author. Karen Gorback has a Ph.D. in education and thirty-five years' experience as a teacher, counselor and administrator. Her short stories have placed in a number of VCWC's contests, and her one-act plays were produced in several years for the New Works Festival at College of the Canyons in Santa Clarita, CA. Her debut novel, *Freshman Mom* (bn.com and amazon.com) is a contemporary, fast-paced story  about a divorced mother's difficult decision to return to college. The book was honored as a finalist in the 2014 Readers' Favorite Book Awards and won the 2015 Regional Excellence Book Award in the Adult Fiction category for the Western Region of the United States.

Dreamtide by Antony Villalobos

Nighttime, nighttime,
Time to go to sleep.
Nighttime, nighttime,
Time for all to dream.

Where're you gonna go? Whatcha gonna see?
Whatcha gonna play? Who you gonna be?
'Cause nighttime, nighttime, you can be,
Anything you want to dream.
Nighttime...
Dreamtime...
Sleeptime.

The Picture by Antony Villalobos

Chapter One – Point of Two

Mrs. Flubdub stood from behind her desk, her glasses teeter-tottered on the bridge of her nose. "Five more minutes. Please finish up your artwork."

The fourth grade classroom buzzed. Each student hurried to finish their project, paint brushes dueled paper canvases.

Luke checked the clock. He added a few more finishing touches. A splash of color here, a brush stroke of a different color there. Sure that he'd finished, he gazed upon it and...

"Eeeewww! What's that?" a familiar voice said.

Luke found it difficult to breathe. Not again. Harriet ... and Taylor.

Harriet squinted at his picture, like her eyes hurt.

"Geez, can't you follow simple directions?" Taylor said, arms knotted across her chest.

Harriet and Taylor, best friends since the age of two. They thought themselves the best at everything. The b-e-s-t spellers. Numero Uno at arithmetic. The most creative artists. They also believed they brought the best lunches to school. Harriet and Taylor, exceptional at all these things, left no room for anyone else to be exceptional.

"I did follow instructions." Luke sank into his chair.

"You were supposed to paint a picture of a wrapped birthday gift, use squares and rectangles," Taylor said.

"Yeah, with patterned paper, bows and different colors." Harriet pointed to Luke's painting. "Yours looks like a wrapped egg."

"Who gives an egg for a present?" Harriet exhaled, her nostrils opened like parachutes, eyes looked towards the ceiling. She crossed her arms and began to tap her foot.

"And what's with that birthday cake? Who told you to draw a cake?" Both girls said and laughed loud enough to make the class look in his direction.

Harriet and Taylor waited for an answer.

Luke slouched in his seat, seemed like everyone's eyes drilled holes through his body. Difficult to breath, he stared at his picture, fought back tears. "What's a birthday without cake?" Luke said.

The girls marched away, their chins high in the air, together let out a "Hmmph."

"Class, time's up. Please hang your pictures to dry," Mrs. Flubdub said.

Luke crept from his chair, thought time had changed into the goopiness of maple syrup. He didn't want to hang his picture. Maybe he could hide his monsterpiece, like inside the big dumpster outside.

Luke hung his picture, clipped his painting backward, only his name showed.

Mrs. Flubdub took Luke's painting, turned it to face the class.

Luke wanted to disappear.

"Luke, you silly sot, be proud of your work," Mrs. Flubdub's warm smile did nothing to reassure him. "Art is a person's very own expression of what their mind sees." Her wink wasn't enough to melt his iceberg of embarrassment.

Luke wanted to believe his picture worthy, hung alongside all the other paintings. Most of all, he wished this school day to end.

Chapter Two – Point of View

Luke focused on his next lesson. A loud knock interrupted everyone's work. The Principal, Mr. McNoodle entered the classroom, followed by a girl. Curly black hair rested on her shoulders. She wore a long sleeved brown sweater, three small red hearts printed above the hem. A pink, red and white camouflage backpack slung over her shoulder. Large brown eyes scanned the room.

"Mrs. Flubdub, please accept my apologies for the interruption. I'd like to introduce Isabella, your new student. I'm sure all of you will make her feel welcome." Mr. McNoodle waved goodbye, left the room.

"Hello. I love your sweater," Mrs. Flubdub said. She placed a hand on Isabella's shoulder. "As a welcome gift, you may choose any of the new paintings we've finished today. I'll have the artist sign it, you can take it home in a frame. That's our tradition here. Go ahead, don't be shy."

Luke glanced at Harriet and Taylor. Each gave the other a knowing look, a nod, and a smirk. No doubt, one of their paintings would be chosen. They're the best at everything.

Isabella examined the artwork, gazed at each piece like a general in a military inspection. Luke went back to work on his lesson. She'd never give his painting a second thought.

"Have you made up your mind, sweetheart?" Mrs. Flubdub said.

Isabella nodded, reached for a picture.

"Wonderful choice, a beautiful piece of art. Bring it here, I'll prepare it for you, ready before school ends today." Mrs. Flubdub pulled a frame from her cupboard.

The room silent, Luke thought he had fallen asleep. Curious, he checked the room. Harriet and Taylor had their mouths wide open, eyes bugged out. Like the two of them sat on trays of mashed potatoes, green beans, and that meat mush covered in gravy from the cafeteria. The class stared at Isabella, smiles on most of their faces, others puzzled or lost.

Mrs. Flubdub said, "My dear, if I may ask, why did you choose this particular picture?" She held it up for everyone to see.

"My daddy says that in life, we sometimes need to look at the world in different ways." Isabella smiled. "Whoever painted that picture really sees the world in a different way."

Luke looked at Mrs. Flubdub, she gave him an I-told-you-so wink. Warmth spread from his nose to his toes.

Later that day, Luke signed his picture…

> *Thank you. You made me see, what I could not. Me.*
> *Your friend,*
> *Luke*

~~*

About the Author: Antony Villalobos has coached children and teens for over thirty-five years. His experiences as a high school teacher and athletics coach have weaved their way into his storytelling. In 2015, he placed second in the VCWC's Short Story Contest with *Paper Dragon*, published in the Ventura County Star. Antony is continually inspired by his son Corran. *The Picture* is based on an actual event and "Dreamtide" is the lullaby he wrote and sang to Corran for a decade.

I have a dog,

she's a collie mix.

She is four and

I am six.

We are different

in many ways,

different times

and different days.

Her name is Ruby

and she's my friend,

we'll be together

until the end.

~~*

About the Author: Juliet Ward lives in Ventura with her parents, her sister and their dog and two cats. She's eleven years old and looks forward to middle school next year. She enjoys reading and writing fiction and poetry. Her most recent published work is in the Art Tales 2015 compilation which has her first place short story from the 2015 Art Tales contest at E.P. Foster Library. Her present writing goals include completing a young adult fiction book within the next year.

"One lives in the hope of becoming a memory."
~ Antonio Porchia

While driving into Los Angeles from the suburbs, I wonder how long it's been since I've seen Rita, my former mother-in-law. Too long, but I couldn't miss her ninety-fifth birthday. I'm glad my son Steve told me about it. His dad is driving and Steve's wife and daughter sit with me in the back seat.

We enter the gloom of the Los Angeles retirement home where our granny has lived for several years. Fetid odors assail my senses and I hear Steve mutter to his wife, "I hate these places. Why do they always smell so bad?"

My three year old granddaughter, Samantha, dressed in a green and yellow striped pinafore, prances beside her Grandfather, my first husband. I hear him say, "Hey there, little pony, slow down."

At the end of a hallway, I recognize Granny Rita, a small, hunched figure in a wheelchair, swathed in a pink blanket—one of five or six other crumpled bodies also in wheelchairs. Near her is a plump woman secured with a belt from around the back of her chair. Head down, eyes closed, this woman is slumped over her left arm. Her lips protrude above her ample breast. Sleeping? Bored?

Samantha dances into the room and spins by the dozing figure. The woman, suddenly alert, opens her eyes and reaches out toward the sprite-like figure. Samantha turns around and, gently catching the outstretched hand, looks into the stranger's eyes and flashes a merry smile that seems to erase for a moment—the boredom I'd glimpsed a minute ago.

A third woman whose expressionless eyes had been raised toward the ceiling, leans forward, and I hear a barely audible, "Oh, isn't she darling?" I'm astonished when I see her spread her skinny arms over her head in an obvious expression of joy.

And then, Granny Rita sees her great granddaughter and smiles, revealing two ochre teeth that distract from her fluffed white hair and rouged cheeks. Slowly, she pulls her arms out from under the blanket and reaches forward. "Oh, my angel!"

The child eagerly leans in for a hug. White head nuzzles blond locks. Emotion tugs at my throat.

Samantha hands her a card. "Hi, Gate Gan'ma! We've come to celebrate your birthday!"

"You're kidding." Rita looks at her son, Ed, for confirmation.

He nods.

She chuckles. "My birthday? Really?"

"Yes," he says, "Your birthday. February seventh."

Puzzled, her face darkens, and then she nods, "Yes, February seventh. So, how old am I?"

Ed tells her she's thirty-nine.

She laughs.

I offer my former mother-in-law a little corsage of violets I've made. She stares at me, frowns and waves away my gift. I see that I scared her. She doesn't recognizing me. It has, indeed, been too long since I've seen her.

I am a stranger now.

My son's face clouds with concern. "Don't worry, Mom, she tends to be kind of abrupt with people she doesn't know." A little dart stabs my heart at the words "doesn't know."

Ed kindly makes introductions and Rita speaks to each of us like the gracious lady I'd known so well. When she hears my name, she stares for a moment and I see she still doesn't remember me. She says, "You certainly are pretty." We all laugh and I tell her I'll visit her every day if she'll continue to say such nice things.

Ed says, "Well, Mom, how 'bout some pancakes?" and we troop behind him as he rolls her through the lobby—to welcome fresh air—and to her favorite restaurant.

Throughout the time at the table, she holds her son's hand or he covers hers with his. She gazes at him with obvious love and adoration. "Are you my husband?"

"No, I'm Hughie, your son. Edward Houston, remember?"

She absorbs that bit of information for a minute and says, "Where's the boysenberry syrup?"

After a few bites, her eyes rest again on the white-haired gentleman sitting at her side. "You're very handsome."

"Thank you. I got my looks from my mother. And you're my mother."

She laughs—a funny story being fed to her.

Samantha pipes up, "I'm going to have a new baby sister!"

"Is that right?" Granny turns to focus on the child beside her. "A baby sister. My—goodness." I watch the very old and the very young converse with understanding and affection. As they talk, Granny's gnarled fingers rest on Samantha's plump pink hand. Her hand smooths the shiny flaxen hair, and plucks at the ruffles on the pinafore.

I am touched by the simple beauty of their interaction—the bonnie child, innocent and non-judgmental, so at ease and happy. Samantha never knew Rita as a mentally sound and vibrant individual. I envy her ability to accept the frail and elderly with uninhibited warmth. When I am ninety-five, I hope I'll get a hug from a dancing child.

About the Author. Barbara Fisher's interests include people's lives, and a love for animals and nature. Her published work includes interviews, personal experience and feature articles. While shepherding five kids, she worked as a technical writer and pursued the craft of writing with college classes at night. A second marriage expanded her flock to seven teenagers and an opportunity to delegate responsibilities. Thus freed, she completed her AA at Moorpark College, and took advanced writing classes at CLU. She's now focused on a memoir of her New England roots.

Post it – Courtesy of Wendell Ward

"We all have an inner voice, our personal whisper from the universe. All we have to do is listen—feel and sense it with an open heart. Sometimes it whispers of intuition or precognition. Other times, it whispers an awareness, a remembrance from another plane.
Dare to listen.
Dare to hear with your heart."
~ C.J. Heck, *Bits and Pieces: Short Stories from a Writer's Soul*

My husband, Mark, phoned from Chicago. "They've just closed O'Hare." His voice was husky from fatigue, frustration, apology. "I can't make it home in time for the thing in Malibu."

"I can't go alone," I replied.

"Bets, you could take on the world alone. Don't let an old boyfriend get under your skin. He probably won't even show."

It took a moment before I could say, "OK, OK, I'll go."

"Good for you. I love you. 'Bye."

If it had stopped snowing in Illinois that night and if it had warmed up the next day, my husband would have come home in time and we'd have walked into my college reunion together.

But it didn't stop snowing and they didn't open O'Hare and I drove through dark, winding Malibu Canyon to Pepperdine University with a big, empty pit where my stomach used to be.

I should have dredged up the yearbook or Googled the roster— anything to help me remember some of the faces I knew twenty-five years ago. Only two college friendships had survived the wear and tear of real life. One called, the other emailed to say they wouldn't attend tonight. I didn't blame them.

The only other person I remembered was Ralph, my college boyfriend. I prayed he wouldn't show and pleaded with the devil to bring him.

I planned to hurt Ralph—slide a dagger sideways between the fourth and fifth ribs on his left side stopping just as the tip grazed his quivering heart; watching his eyes as pain and realization filled them.

My weapon would be words. I had words. Steel only inflicts pain once, but what is spoken injures and when recalled, injures again, and again.

He'd used words and they had paralyzed me. I'd drowned in a sea of self-doubt.

We'd met in junior year. I was a very young twenty—small town girl in awe of this university, this location, these students and I was in awe of Ralph Masterson. He had a cynicism I mistook for wisdom. He was aware of culture and I thought it was knowledge. He disdained the ordinary and I fell in love.

We talked of marriage. I wanted it all—career, family, travel. He sniffed that having my babies would cost a ten year delay in getting to Europe. My babies.

I told him my desire to be a journalist—to expose the wrongs and help the vulnerable. He laughed at my idealism; said I'd never take the risks.

Ralph thought I hadn't the stomach, the words, nor the insight to reach that goal.

"Teach," he said. "Teach grade school. It's steady. You'll be around children. Very few people change the world. You're not going to make a difference." He left me for a silly blonde he deemed more worthy.

Twenty-five years have passed and I'm ready to face him. I beseech the gods to keep him away.

Signs directed cars to the parking lot in front of the event. An arch covered in balloons had been set up on the walkway. Cheerleaders—young boys and girls in blue and orange uniforms—posed with each couple as souvenir photographs were taken. There was laughter and music and lights. I drove past to another parking lot, another way in.

A light glowed over the back entrance. Someone was standing in the shadows. The red tip of his cigarette flared, then paled.

"Good evening, Betsy. You're looking lovely." He was still slender, mostly blonde, the same sneer, but older.

"Hello, Ralph." The night hid the flush washing over me.

"You've come alone." It was not a question.

"My husband couldn't make it."

"My wife couldn't make it, either." He snarled as he said it. I knew he meant something other than I had and I forced myself not to explain Mark's absence.

"So, tell me." He smirked. "Did you have all those kids you wanted?"

At their mention, the joy of my children and their births washed over me. Hannah arrived early with only a native midwife in attendance. Our adopted twins, Micah and Kai, were conceived in a rape. Their child-mother did not survive their birth. The village rejected them. We fought to keep them. Only Matthew arrived stateside in a sterile hospital with a doctor in attendance. Our babies, mine and Mark's.

"We have four."

"That's a lot. So you never got to travel."

I searched for the perfect retort that would wipe the sneer from his lips and the arrogance from his soul, but the smoldering rage began to flare and the words would not come. I fought to maintain my composure.

Ralph dropped the cigarette, ground it out with his foot and opened the door. "Shall we go in?" he asked.

A group standing just inside moved toward us. "Smile, Betsy." A flash went off in my face followed by more picture requests. When they subsided, I saw Ralph across the room talking to an attractive woman in a long black dress. He leaned with one hand on the hors d'oeuvres table, blocking the woman's escape. I chose not to approach. My anger had kept the scathing rebuke from forming, but it would come. I'd practiced many such over the years.

A glass of wine was offered. I clutched it and made my rounds of the tables of memorabilia brought by clubs and Greeks. A spread of yearbooks brought back memories. There were more pictures taken and, surprisingly, a few remembered faces—some dorm mates, a lab partner, the geology teaching assistant.

Our senior class president, Frank Jordan, gray but still youthful, stepped onto the stage and tapped the microphone for attention. "We have some awards!" he declared. "Where's Charles Monroe?" Frank shielded his eyes and scanned the room. "Charlie is with the US diplomatic service, currently serving in Kabul. He's come the farthest, more than seven thousand miles, to be with us here tonight. He wins dinner-for-two at Geoffrey's, here in Malibu!" The crowd cheered and cat-called. Charlie pushed through the throng, accepted the envelope and waved it high to more cheers.

Frank produced a poster of Barbara Harmon's painting, *California Oaks*, depicting the yellow rolling hills near Gilroy dotted with live oaks. It invited you to walk among them and it had been selected to hang in the California State Capitol building. More cheering and some, too, for Chamad Patel who was honored for having a textbook published.

I moved closer to the stage. Ralph sidled up beside me with a copy of *Jungle Confinement* which he held up for me to see.

"Our esteemed classmate, Stanton, is going to sign it," he said. There was derision as he pronounced *esteemed*. "Got your copy?" He pointed to the table on stage stacked with books.

There were no words. "Proceeds go to charity," I squeaked.

He shrugged. "I don't remember her, but a signed book will probably be worth something when she kicks it."

Frank tapped the microphone for the final award and held up his hands for silence.

"A journalist among us has risked her safety to visit enclaves of primitive existence encroached upon by our modern society. We are in danger of losing those cultures completely as they struggle to fit into our world. Elizabeth Stanton's insightful documentation along with her husband's photographs have made all the difference in preserving that heritage. They've gone a step further to help these vulnerable people by creating the Foundation for Endangered Human Cultures. Elizabeth will sign copies of their award winning series for you tonight. They have donated all proceeds to the Foundation." Cheers, applause, shouting. "I give you Elizabeth Stanton—our own Betsy Hill."

I turned to see Ralph's face startle with incredulity. "You're Elizabeth Stanton?"

Frank held out his hand as a welcome to the stage. I hesitated. He'd said—*risk, insight, making a difference*. Those were the words Ralph had used; the ones that had goaded me.

I accepted the crystal clock and held it up for all to see. Taking the microphone, I spoke to my classmates, "Thank you so much. Mark and I have been privileged to meet and share in the lives of these wonderful people. I hope you enjoy reading their stories and seeing Mark's exceptional photographs." More applause. As it died down, Frank placed a hand in the small of my back guiding me to the signing table. Before I sat and picked up the pen I searched the faces.

Ralph was at the back exit, one hand on the release bar, the other still holding my book. I waved and shouted across the chatter, "Ralph, Ralph Masterson, don't leave. I haven't signed your book yet."

As one, the crowd turned and looked in the direction I'd indicated. All eyes were on him. He didn't move.

"I wanted to thank you," I called out with sincerity.

"For what?" Bewilderment sounded in his voice.

"For all the things you said to me twenty-five years ago. I've kept those words close over the years. I don't know if I'd have persevered without them. *Making a difference* became my mantra. It kept me strong."

The crowd applauded. Not the thundering they'd given me, but an acknowledgement.

Even across the room I could see his eyes as pain and realization filled them. A blade had touched his quivering heart.

About the Author. Pat Caloia spent her career working with computer technology in the US and air traffic control software in the UK. When she retired, her creative side emerged. She joined the Ventura County Writers Club and a critique group where she has been working on a novel about four women friends of a certain age who suddenly find themselves alone. They think their long standing friendship will be the glue that helps them live together but friction occurs. It's not clear if they'll be able to resolve their issues before the schism is permanent. While her primary goal is the novel, she entered the 2013 short story contest with her story, "Revenge", which was inspired by a college classmate's experience. Pat lives in Ventura and enjoys working out, gardening and bicycling.

"We're going to crash," the woman had said in the seat next to Manny. The engines on their jet had fallen silent about ten minutes out from an early-morning landing in Denver. Through the window, Manny saw an electric blue glow on the front edge of the wing. Fine red dust rushed by the windows of the plane. He detected the impossible smell of burning

ozone. He knew that odor, like sparks made by old-time electric bumper cars in an amusement park. Nice image.

Oxygen masks dropped, startling the passengers including Manny's seat partner. He heard her say, "Holy Mary, Mother of God, pray for us sinners now, and at the hour of our death." In the back of the plane a baby began to cry. A man jumped from his seat in front of them and tried to open the cabin door. Two flight attendants grappled with him.

The plane jolted. Several passengers shrieked. The woman next to Manny screamed so loud it made him grip his leather case even tighter to his chest. His life's research.

He looked through the window again, stared at the red dust building up on the engines and wings. He saw the stricken engine sputter to life for a second then flame out again.

With each sputter another lurch, then another, first one side, then the other. A coughing backfire of red dust mixed with blue flame. The red powder flew everywhere.

Some passengers took out their cell phones. Manny heard a man across the aisle shout into his phone, "I love you. Tell the kids I love them."

A boy with a nose ring and dressed in black used his phone to shoot video, first out the window, and then back to the terrified passengers. "This is so cool." Manny heard him say. The girl next to him, also dressed in black, hit his arm each time he said it.

The woman next to Manny repeated her prayer only much faster now, as though she was chanting. Through his window Manny watched the shimmering blue glow disappear. He saw the fields outside the airport turn into runway.

Another lurch. This time accompanied by a whoosh and a roar. Manny turned to see the left engine catch and hold. The woman stopped chanting.

She opened her eyes then turned to Manny. He felt the hope he saw in her eyes.

The engine on the other side of the plane sputtered then roared back to life. Passengers cheered. The plane leveled out, tarmac rushed by a few hundred feet below. Big white stripes announced the beginning of the runway.

Too fast, it seemed to Manny. Too high. There's no way the captain would try to land now. Surely he'll go around and try again.

"Brace, brace," the captain said over the intercom.

Manny put his head down, grabbed his legs with his hands. His arthritic fingers burned with pain. Now he started to chant. "Please let me live to get my research to the conference."

Manny heard the voice of a man seated behind him increase in volume. "Though I walk through the valley of the shadow of death …" Too much talk about death.

Manny felt the wheels of the jet slam down on the tarmac, then bounce. Screams erupted. The boy in black said. "Not cool." He no longer shot video.

The plane came back down—hard. It seemed to Manny the wheels collapsed. The emergency lights flickered then failed. The sound of grinding steel drowned out the screams.

Manny clung to his legs, the pain in his hands close to unbearable. The plane skidded, slid for what seemed like an eternity, came to an abrupt stop. The dim lights sputtered back on. The smell of jet fuel filled the cabin.

Passengers stood up, heads turned first one way, then the other. He saw shock on some faces, happy surprise on others. Sounds of "thank god" floated in the stuffy air of the cabin.

The flight attendants jumped up, opened the doors. They shouted to the passengers in the emergency aisle to get the wing doors open. The woman next to Manny cried, this time happy tears. He helped her unbuckle her seat belt. They both got up, Manny behind her. They stumbled through the wing exit, covered with red powder. He tasted something like sulfur.

The woman grabbed Manny's arm and wouldn't let go. The flight attendant told them to jump on the yellow chute and slide to the ground. The woman screamed as Manny pried her fingers loose from his arm and pushed her onto the slide. Arms wrapped around his briefcase, Manny jumped, slid, got to his feet, paced away from the chute, stopped and looked around.

The jet sat in a ravine past the end of the runway, through the fence a few yards short of the main airport road. A red and yellow fireball rocked the landscape a short distance away. A private jet had also caught some of the red dust and crashed. No one jumped from that plane. He stared awestruck at the horrible scene, made surreal by the unnatural red haze.

An old pickup screeched to a halt along the top of the ravine. A young man in blue jeans and a sports coat climbed out. Manny clutched the worn leather briefcase to his chest, wheezed up the embankment. He felt his age manifest in his swollen joints. The dust floated everywhere, filled his lungs and made him cough.

"I need to get to the terminal," Manny said between coughs.

The young man who looked to be in his early thirties stopped at the sound of Manny's voice. He had his cell phone out, then put it into his pocket.

"I've got to catch the flight to Washington D.C. right away," Manny said. He noticed a CU logo in the back window of the man's truck. Was the man an educator? He seemed vaguely familiar, but Manny couldn't place him.

"Are you crazy? No planes can take off in this stuff." When he heard his voice, Manny felt certain he knew this man. "People are hurt down there. They need help."

Manny looked behind him then back at the man. "There's no fire. Nobody's seriously hurt. I have to catch my connecting flight."

The young man turned away, ran down the ravine toward the plane. Manny watched him head straight for the captain who directed the passengers away from the plane.

He walked to the man's truck. No keys. He looked up the road toward the terminal. There was no choice. He'd have to walk as quickly as his arthritic knees would let him. Manny turned and hurried up to the road, determined to get to the airport.

He couldn't understand why the young man wouldn't give him a ride. There wasn't anything he could do for the passengers of the plane. Where had he seen him before? He racked his brain as he walked.

This red dust came sooner than he calculated. He had to get to that science conference back East.

Then it dawned on him. The man's name was David Mitchell. He's that university professor from Boulder who got him thrown out of last year's conference. Arrogant educated fool. Thinks he knows everything.

A truck roared up, screeched to a halt in front of him. Again, arrogant David jumped out, but this time he grabbed Manny by the arm. "Where do you think you're going?"

Manny tried to shake him off. "I just got off a plane that damn near crashed because of your stupid comet, which, my dear professor is not a comet at all. But we don't have time to discuss this right now, do we?"

David dropped Manny's arm like it burned him, took a step back.

"You told people on TV yesterday we'd have some beautiful sunsets for the next few weeks." He waved his arm in the direction of the plane. "Is

83

this your idea of a beautiful sunset? You didn't consider what the tail would do this close to earth, did you, David?"

He recognized a look of panic in David's eyes. Manny nodded his head. "Maybe you believe me now? I tried to tell you about this last year."

The young man's mouth dropped open. He seemed to fight for control. "Get in the truck, old man. I promised the captain I'd get you back. Although why he should be worried about one crazy old goat is beyond me."

For a prize winning scientist, David didn't seem all that bright.

"Forget about the captain," Manny shouted. "This red dust is from your comet. You know it is. Why didn't you tell people the truth yesterday?" Manny watched David's expression morph from annoyance to shock.

David started back for the truck. "Do whatever the hell you want, old man. I need to get to the observatory."

Manny jumped in front of the truck, pounded the hood with his fist. "Didn't you hear me? It's too late for that. We need to get to that conference—NOW. They'll listen to you."

David ignored him, opened the door.

Manny ran to the door, grabbed him by the lapels. "If you don't come clean with what you know about that comet, a lot of people will die. They have a right to know."

David's eyes narrowed. He pushed Manny away. "It's too late. There's nothing we can do. Millions of people will die anyway. Now go away."

Manny didn't go away. He leaned closer. David backed against the doorframe of his truck. "What was your price?" Manny said. "A new observatory? A seat on the NSF board?"

David didn't move. Manny had him pinned with his summation of what might have happened.

"I have the evidence right here." He patted the worn leather briefcase clutched under his arm. "I'm taking it to that reporter you spoke with yesterday. She'll be interested."

For a moment neither spoke. David scowled at Manny. "Are you threatening me, old man?" He didn't get in the truck. He didn't push Manny away. Their eyes remained locked, neither moved. A fresh dusting of the red powder fell around them.

Manny held out his hand and caught some of the powder, then waved it at David. "You can help save lives. People will listen to you. Communications will be cut off in a few days. You know this. We've got to share this at the conference before it's too late."

David eyed Manny's briefcase. After a long pause he said, "Get in. I'll take you as far as the terminal." Manny smiled, got in the truck and slammed the door.

 *About the Author:* Recently re-introduced to creative writing as an adult by two veterans of the publishing word, Tim Malone has been practicing his craft over the past several years in hopes of producing a disaster thriller. Although his first novel is only halfway complete, numerous chapter reviews in writer's groups have convinced him there is something to the idea everyone has a story to share. Tim is a computer professional, employed as the IT Director for a private jet charter company at a major Southern California airport. He enjoys technology and science, especially astrophysics, combing elements of both in the story process. He is married to a published author, who inspires him to push ahead in the work of creating good fiction. They are parents of one adult son, also an IT genius.

Sailing on Ventura Harbor – Courtesy of Carol Malone

"I have to live if I want to be remembered."
~ Suzanne Young, *A Need So Beautiful*

3642 Maplewood Drive is a three-story flagstone house with a gabled roof and four-car garage, nestled deep within the protective arms of Red Fern Ranch, which is not a ranch at all but rather a gated community in a California suburb. In this neighborhood, the houses preen. Windows sparkle. The sidewalks are dutifully swept, the curbs are free of debris, parked cars do not clutter the streets. Gardeners come every Wednesday morning to trim the hedges, mow the lawn, rake the leaves. A family lives here. A mother, a father, and a son. I am born at 3642 Maplewood Drive at 8:53 pm on a Friday night. Not a soul in Red Fern Ranch knows about me. It is a dry, still night, static electricity palpable in the air. I am born in the attic.

On this Friday night, minutes after my birth, an argument simmers in the ornately-tiled kitchen. The son—Jason, a high school senior, admitted to Berkeley next fall—wants to go out with friends. But his mother is adamantly against him going anywhere.

"I just have a feeling," she says. "A bad feeling. I can't explain it."

Jason looks down at the granite countertop, silently runs his finger along the grout between the tiles.

"Please, honey. Stay here tonight, will you? Safe and sound."

"I'll be safe, Mom. I promise."

"Honey –"

"I won't even be out that late."

The father stamps into the kitchen and bangs cabinets, opening and closing them at random. He settles upon a bag of trail mix, which he pours into his palm. "Listen to your mother," he says, using his no-arguing voice.

"I promise I won't be out late."

"Jason, what have we talked about?"

The son sighs. "Fine. I'll be a loser with no social life."

The mother's face relaxes. She had felt tears welling up inside her, but she was able to tamp them down before an outburst overtook all thought. She smiles gratefully at George, reaches over and strokes Jason's hair. For a few moments, he stands there and lets her.

"Thank you," she says—to George, to Jason—to them both.

It is 9:02 p.m. We cannot choose the circumstances in which we are born. Once I am sparked to life, a single thought drives my existence: consume. *All I know is, I am ravenous. I cannot stop myself.* Jason ducks away from his mother and heads up to his bedroom.

"There's a movie on HBO tonight you might like," his father calls after him. "Some apocalypse action movie."

No response, other than the clomping of Jason's tennis shoes on the stairs.

George looks at Marie and shrugs. She shrugs in return, giving him a playful smile before turning away, her attention snagged by the sink full of dirty dishes.

She is wearing a long skirt that clings to her hips. Her hair—dyed a dark brown, gleams in the warm kitchen light. George is swept by the feeling of how it used to be—the two of them, together, apart from everyone else. It is this feeling that spurs him across the kitchen, wiping the peanut crumbs off his palms. Marie is bent over the big kitchen sink, arms in sudsy water, rinsing pasta sauce off dinner plates and dressing out of salad bowls.

George watches her shadowy reflection in the darkened kitchen window, her eyes cast downward, absorbed in her task. The steamy water fills the sink, a continuous rushing sound. He stands behind her, inching closer, closer, and then he's pressed to her, wrapping his arms around her waist, kissing her soft neck. She flinches, her body stiffening. George pulls away. She turns the water off and flicks her hands once, twice, three times. When she turns, finally, her expression reminds George of a frightened animal—of the squirrel they found one summer, trapped in the attic, desperate to find a way out.

"I'm sorry," she says. "It's just—I've told you—it's hard for me, right now. Being touched."

George takes another step away from her. He runs his hand over his thinning hair.

"It's not you," she says. "It's not anything to do with you."

"It feels that way, though."

"It's not, I swear. I love you. I'm just—I'm not there yet."

But will you ever get there? George wants to ask. *Will you ever be my wife again?* Eight months since they've made love. Two months since her last breakdown, when the doctor put her on that new medication.

"It's just that you've seemed better lately," he says. "I thought I could kiss you without—frightening you away."

"It's not you, George."

"I guess I was mistaken. Sorry." He raps his knuckles twice on the countertop. His smile is forced, worse than a frown.

"I'll be upstairs in my study," he says.

He works as a financial planner for small businesses.

"Got some emails to send."

Marie nods and turns back to the dishes. The water is scalding, but she doesn't turn it colder. She watches her hands, scrubbing the delicate china. She watches them as if they are someone else's hands. Her skin is a bright pink. Maybe, she thinks. Maybe tonight. Maybe I can try to stand it.

It is 9:14 p.m. Once you are alive, it is impossible to know what it was like before life. Yet I can taste memories all around me. This cluttered attic is drowning in memories. Christmas tinsel caught around a Popsicle-stick ornament. A Kodak Instamatic with half a roll of unused film inside. A child's rocking chair carved from redwood, a delicacy. I devour the memories, and then they disappear and I am left famished, raging for more. I am suffocating. I need oxygen. I need to breathe.

Jason flops backwards onto his bed, feeling suffocated in the emptiness of his bedroom, the vast hardwood floors stretching around him like a wasteland. His cell phone buzzes. Jason ignores it, knowing it's Danny or Steve or Brendan, one of the guys, wanting to know what time he'll be there tonight. If their parents give them a hard time about going out, they go anyway. Or they sneak out later, or they lie about where they're going.

Jason has never been able to lie. His face burns and his words run together. And it's gotten worse since his mother's last episode. She's always been an anxious person, fluttery and a hand-wringer, moved to tears by burnt breakfast toast. But Jason never thought he would see her like that: curled into a ball on the floor of her walk-in closet, her eyes huge and far away—rocking back and forth, back and forth, in a slow terrifying mechanical way. The doctors later referred to it as a panic attack, and she has been back to normal since then, her medication living calmly in the kitchen cupboard alongside the multivitamins and Tums. But Jason can't shake the image of her, wild-eyed and quivering, and he worries that any little thing could send her reeling back to that dark place. And what if the next time, she doesn't recover? What if her small yellow pills no longer work? What then?

His phone buzzes again. Jason pushes himself off his bed and reaches for it.

"So what time you want me to pick you up?" Brendan asks.

"I don't know," Jason says. "I don't know if I'm going."

"Dude, don't bail out now. You always bail."

"It's just … you know how strict my parents are."

"So sneak out. It's not a big deal. Listen, I'll pick you up at ten. Your parents will be asleep by then anyway. They'll never know the difference."

"Better make it 10:30," Jason says.

"Sure, 10:30. But seriously, don't bail on me, all right? I'm doing this for you."

"I know." Jason's social standing has nose-dived the past few months. He's declined so many invitations that he's fading into anonymity. Brendan, his best friend since sixth grade, confided that people think he's stuck up about getting into Berkeley. Brendan's a good friend. He wants to help.

"Thanks, man," Jason adds, feeling a surge of gratitude. "I'll be there." But Brendan's already hung up.

I am half an hour old, working my way through the boxes of old EPs,

Halloween costumes, baby clothes. The life-size paper-maché sculpture Jason made of Abraham Lincoln in sixth grade. The chest of wool sweaters no one has worn since the Reagan years, mothballed and delicious.

Before, when Marie heard the word "breakdown," she associated it with a sudden shift—something triggered. Like a twig stepped on by a heavy boot, snapped cleanly in two. Before: whole. After: broken. But Marie's breakdown was not like that. For her, the breakdown was something that built over a matter of days and weeks and months, a gradually increasing sense of claustrophobia—compounded by guilt that she was feeling anything but gratitude for her life. Because, Marie knew, she had much to be grateful for: a loving husband, a good son, a beautiful home in a safe neighborhood. Lunches with friends at the Country Club. Volunteer work at the library. She never worried about money. She had a life people yearned for and envied. An easy life.

As the weeks dragged on, the feeling within her expanded, and it was bigger than Jason, bigger than George, bigger than menopause or the onset of winter, the bare-limbed trees like ghosts in the yard. She went for long walks through the neighborhood, wanting to just keep walking, away, away, away from it all. Wanting to burn everything down and start again. Renewal in having nothing. Freedom in the ashes of what used to be.

Marie heard once that if you put a frog in a pot of water that is ever-so-slowly brought to a boil, the frog will not notice the increase in temperature, and will be boiled alive without even trying to leap from the pot. Her breakdown happened when she noticed. Her breakdown was an attempt at a leap.

I bide my time, keeping quiet, gaining ground without much notice.

It is 9:32 pm.

Marie lifts her knuckle to Jason's bedroom door and tentatively knocks.

"Come in."

The door whines as she opens it. Jason is flopped back on his bed, spiral notebook on his bent knees, the bedside lamp blazing a halo of light on his face.

"What are you working on?" she asks from the doorway.

"Homework. Thought I'd get something done since I'm not going anywhere."

Sometimes, when she looks at her son, Marie is amazed by how strange he seems to her. How unknowable. For nine long months, he grew inside her—she was his everything—and now. Now he humors her? Resents her?

"Thank you for staying in tonight," she says.

"It's no big deal."

"I just have a bad feeling. A mother's intuition. I know you think I'm crazy ...."

Marie trails off, but Jason doesn't respond. She waits a moment more, then says, "I'm going over to Safeway, to get groceries for the week."

"You're going now?" Jason sits up. "Is the store even open this late?"

"Till eleven. Anything you want me to get for you?"

Jason leans back against his pillow. "Mountain Dew."

"Okay," Marie says, not even putting up a fight about the amount of sugar or chemicals in that drink, his favorite since he was a boy. She understands Jason is bargaining with her. He is staying home tonight, and she is buying him Mountain Dew. She can do that.

"I love you," she says, and shuts the door before he can decline to say it back.

I am spurred onward by desire, not love. Need, not want. There is a difference. I do not love anything. I do not know what it means to be selfless. Yet there is honor in my pursuit: I am exactly where I am supposed to be, doing exactly what I am supposed to do. Consumption is my life's purpose. It must be. If not, why would it be such an irrepressible urge within me?

George is in his study, doing online Sudoku. Marie comes in without knocking.

"I'm going to the store," she says.

Ever since her last breakdown, she's been going to the store late at night, when no one else is there. George thought it would be good for them to shop together, or for her to go during the day or evening like everyone else, when she would have a chance to run into friends. He hates to see her withdrawing from the world like this—so scared, so on edge. But her doctor, a thick-haired pompous wearer of sweater-vests who George does not trust, sided with Marie, saying it would be best for her to avoid crowds and "anxiety inducing situations."

"Okay," George says now, not looking up from his computer screen. "Drive safe."

"I will. See you in a little while."

"I'll probably be asleep when you get back. I'm thinking of hitting the sack soon."

"Oh. Okay, then." The hurt on her face is what George wanted, yet it brings no satisfaction. Is this what they've come to—round after round of bruised feelings and subtle barbs? "It's been a long week," he adds.

Marie nods, then leaves, shutting the door behind her. It is 9:43 p.m.

I can detect life in the layers of house below me, creaking the floorboards, rattling the pipes. But they do not frighten me. They have no idea I am here. No idea how strong I am becoming with every passing second. Somewhere in this attic is a box that has not been opened in twenty-six years.

Inside rests a wedding dress, carefully folded and wrapped in tissue paper. It is the last thing I find before everything comes crashing down.

Jason stares at his bedroom ceiling, wondering what he'll tell his parents if he gets caught tonight. George stares at the Sudoku boxes, trying to fight away the image of his wife's timid, broken eyes. Marie climbs into her Lexus with her reusable grocery bags and backs down the driveway, thinking how monstrous the house looks at night, like a dark palace against the blue-black sky. Like something out of a grim fairy tale.

It is 9:53 p.m.

In the ensuing weeks, at George and Jason's funerals, people will try to console Marie with words, facts, scientific terms. It was an electrical fire. It started in the attic. There is no way anyone could have known. It was a slow-burning, smoldering nightmare. No warning. No smoke. The ceiling just collapsed, and by then it was too late. Nobody's fault. Just one of those bizarre freak accidents.

But Marie does not believe in accidents. Until the day she dies (June 16, four years later, her Lexus colliding head-on into a tree) she is convinced the fire is her fault. She is the reason it came into being. She is the one who left, who abandoned it all, everything, to burn.

It is 10:36 p.m. on Friday night. The back seat of Marie's Lexus bulges with groceries. She can see the smoke from all the way down Maplewood Drive. She presses her foot to the gas pedal, her heartbeat a blur of thumping. As if a part of her knows what she will find: fire trucks, an ambulance, neighbors crowding the street. The choking smell of soot and ashes. 3642 Maplewood Drive, engulfed in flames.

Our lives are short. That is the nature of any existence. I know I will die before I am ready—but, then again, won't we all? The men lift their hoses and gun me down.

About the Author. Ventura native Dallas Woodburn was a recent Steinbeck Fellow in Creative Writing at San Jose State University. She received her MFA in Fiction from Purdue University and studied Creative Writing as an undergraduate at the University of Southern California. A three-time Pushcart Prize nominee, she won first place in the international Glass Woman Prize. Her work appears in *American Fiction Volume 13: The Best Unpublished Short Stories* by American Writers (New Rivers Press). Woodburn's short story collection was a finalist for the Flannery O'Connor Award for Short Fiction and the Horatio Nelson Fiction Prize. She has published in *The Nashville Review, North Dakota Quarterly, Superstition Review, Monkeybicycle and The Los Angeles Times,* among many others. A passionate advocate for youth literacy, she teaches writing classes for kids and holds an annual Holiday Book Drive to benefit Ventura County libraries and children's programs.

Ladies, Ladies, let's have a party.
We'll wear gloves and pearls,
And our hats with wide brims.

Ladies, Ladies, we'll serve tea on fine china,
With cucumber sandwiches,
And savory sweets.

We'll talk of proper things,
Like gardens and flowers and recipes,
And maybe gallery exhibits and the latest books.

We'll share photographs,
Of our husbands, our children, and our homes,
And beam with pride at what we have.

Ladies, Ladies, we'll ooh and ah,
At diamonds on rings,
And talk of upcoming vacations and cruises.

But, Ladies,
Let's not invite you know who,
The one with the red hair,
Because she doesn't follow the rules.

She disrupts our conversation,
And talks of unpleasant things,
Such as
starving children,
homeless people, the declining environment, endangered species,
women's rights, and more!

Ladies, Ladies, is it not our right,
To wear gloves and pearls,
And hats with wide brims?

Mothering by Louisa Christina Angeli

Woman, rock your child as she suckles on stories of your youth

Let her taste the sweetness of your warm milk
Hum lullabies loudly and tap your foot
       to the beat and rhythm of semi-automatics

Press your child gently against your full breast
Let the softness of you shield her
       from the brightness of the blasts that spark the indigo sky

Smile lovingly as you bounce her on your lap
To disguise the rumbling and tremors of tanks passing by

Woman, let her taste the sweetness of your warm milk

Mothering – Courtesy of The Print Shop Deluxe

It doesn't make sense!

Why should we have to move?

I can't bear the thought of leaving my beautiful garden.

You knew the rules when you arrived.

How do you think I feel?

This has been my home since I was born.

You'd better hurry, Eve...

It's almost noon.

~~*

About the Author. Louisa Angeli was born in San Francisco, but grew up in Southern California. She has lived in Santa Barbara and Ventura Counties for most of her life. Louisa was an educator for over thirty years before retiring in 2013. During that time she also pursued a master's degree in clinical psychology and is a licensed therapist. After many years of focusing on her profession, pursuing further education and raising children and pets, Louisa has decided to enjoy lots of unstructured time in her garden, friends, traveling, seeking adventures, and  some volunteer service. She is a member of Women's Artistic Network and VCWC. Louisa has been writing for many years, but it has only been during the last decade that she has begun to explore poetry. Over the years Louisa has seen the spark of creativity change lives, and inspire infinite possibilities in children and adults. So she continues to seek adventure, the unusual, and loves living spontaneously.

A hard, late March rain beat against the panes of the hand-blown glass windows and whipped through the unchinked log walls like the breath of a vengeful witch. I was figurin' Sugar Creek Valley might as well be named Stormy Creek. My brother, Jared, and sister, Marie, and I were huddled against Ma for warmth.

"I'm so worried about your pa," my ma, Emily said, her voice rising over the screams of the wind. "He's been gone too long."

Jared, now tall at fifteen, leaned against my Ma's knee while she sat in the rocking chair Pa had made. Marie, cute as a button at seven, was curled up on her lap. And me, Charity, barely eighteen, sat cross legged on the sod floor leaning my head against Ma's other knee. The only warmth in our small cabin came from the dwindling fire in the large rock fireplace before us.

My pa, Harold Mitchell, left early for town to buy seed and supplies. He should'a been home by lunchtime. The clock on the mantel had just chimed seven o'clock. What could'a kept him? Visions of Pa lying dead along the trail made me heart sick. I shivered, but not from the cold.

"Jared, fetch more wood," Ma said to my brother. "Fire's dying."

"All right, Ma." Jared froze when we heard a noise out front. He jumped up, ran to the door, and yanked it open. Rain slanted in on the hard-packed sod floor, turning it to mud.

"Pa," Jared yelled and hurtled himself off the porch through the slicing rain.

Ma jumped out of her chair, rushed to the door, and closed it to protect the crude floor from more soaking. Marie and I scrambled to the windows. Through the rivulets racing down the wavy, bottle-like pane, I saw a stranger huddled on the wagon seat next to Pa.

Pa jumped down from the wagon seat and began to unhitch the horses. The stranger clambered down and followed Jared to the back of the wagon where they began to snatch up supplies from under the soggy canvas wagon-top. They headed for the cabin, heads bowed against the force of the wind.

Ma strode to the pot-bellied stove to stir the venison stew we'd eaten for supper. "Open the door, Charity. Let 'em in. Marie, set an extra place at the table."

I opened the door just as Jared reached it. He barreled through with his load. The stranger stomped in right behind him.

"Charity, fetch the lantern, and get towels," Ma said.

"Yes, ma'am." I grabbed the lantern from its place on the mantle, lit it, and brought it to the rough-hewn oak table along with towels I'd plucked from the kitchen shelf. I placed them on the table and watched the stranger who set a big box down by the door.

"Take off your coat, young man," Ma said. "You must be soaked clean through and frozen to the bone. Jared, get more firewood. Charity, hand the young man some towels."

"I'm right sorry for your floor, ma'am," the stranger said. "I seem to have made a mud puddle. I'll fix it up right as soon as the storm passes."

He had the voice of an angel, soft like, but strong and deep, like the thunder that rolls across the valley. Something strange happened inside 'a me. It felt like a lightning bolt swam under my skin clear from my head to my toes.

Ma smiled up at the stranger. "Never you mind. A little mud won't hurt us none. Charity-girl, stop gawking and do like I said."

I felt my face burn and not from the fire my brother had coaxed into a roaring blaze. I handed the stranger a towel after he removed his coat and hat. He rubbed the towel over his damp hair, turned, and grinned at me. I'd never seen such a fine-sculptured face on a man. He was younger than I thought, and more pretty than any man in six counties. I swallowed hard.

"Charity, girl. What's the matter with you?" Ma said. "Don't stand there like a statue. Take the young man's coat and hat and hang them by the back door. Quick now, so he can sit hisself by the fire afore he catches his death."

The young man smiled again, making my heart beat like the wings of a wild bird captured in a cage. "Yes, ma'am," I said and reached out to take his coat and hat.

"There now," he said. "You don't have to bother yourself with my wet things. Just show me where to hang them. I don't want to get you wet, too."

"I-I don't mind." I looked down at the floor so he couldn't see my cheeks flame. "It ain't no trouble, ah ..."

"Bill," he said. "Bill's my name. And you're Charity. That's a lovely name."

"Thank you." I looked up then, into the bluest eyes I'd ever seen– bluer than the sky right after a hard rain. There was mischief and something else in them that made me blush.

I nearly tripped over my feet when I turned to tromp to the back door. Bill followed. He smelled of rain, wet wool, and something heady like Pa's sandalwood soap. "You can hang them right here." He reached around my shoulder, hooked his hat on one peg and his dripping coat on another. There wasn't much heat in the back of the cabin, but I didn't need a fire.

I spun around and we were nearly nose to nose. My face must'a turned as red as Bill's cold cheeks. He shook rain water off his trouser legs then pulled his fingers through his thick hair. His hair was a deep, rich red-gold, like the color of the setting sun on clouds. Pa always said I'd stolen the sun's *goin'-down* glory and stuck it on my head. But Bill's looked more glorious. I fought like a wild cat against the urge to run my fingers through his damp curls.

Eyeing me closely, Bill grinned as he straightened. "You sure are pretty, Miss Charity."

My face flamed again and I turned away. "No. Just Charity."

"I got'a feelin' there's nothing 'just' about you, Charity."

Pa burst through the back door just then, trailing a freezing flood behind him. "Sure is a witch of a storm tonight, hey Bill?"

"Absolutely, Mr. Mitchell. We should have stayed in town like I suggested."

Pa chuckled, his eyes seeking my ma. "The missus would'a chewed my hide."

"Harold!" Ma called out in a heated voice.

Pa put up his hands as Ma rounded the wall separating the back of the house from the living area. "Please, sweetheart. Let me and Bill get dry afore you go carryin' on."

Ma placed her hands on her hips and glared at Pa. I knew that look– one part terrified exasperation, one part fierce loving. "All right, Harold Mitchell, for now. You scared the devil outta us tonight."

Pa walked to Ma, placed his hands on either side of her face and leaned down to kiss her. "I surely do love you, Mrs. Mitchell." He kissed her again. I turned away embarrassed, but Bill watched them with delight on his face. He turned and winked at me. My heart tried to thump its way out from under my rib bones.

After changing clothes and drying off, Bill and Pa sat close to the fire. I served them a bowl of warm venison stew. After they ate, Ma started in. "When did some shoppin' take all afternoon? You was gone far longer than needful and scared ten years off my life."

"Now, Emily, don't go on so. I ... we made it back in one piece. A little worse for wear, but safe." Pa clasped Ma's hand where it rested on his shoulder. "I'd like you to welcome Bill Hawks. He's going to be our guest for the summer, help work the farm."

Ma gasped. "But we can't afford—"

"Hold on, sweetheart," Pa said his eyes full of love. "Bill will work for us part time and in town the rest of the time. He studied writin' in a fancy college back east and learned to be a journalist. He's gonna open a newspaper office right here in Sugar Creek."

"Is that so, Bill?" Jared's eyes grew round. "There much money in newspapering?"

Bill laughed, that deep rich sound arrowing straight at my young untouched heart. "Not too much, but the ads will pay for the printing and my housing. Working for your Pa will help with the rest." He smiled at me. "It'll only be a monthly newspaper to start, then when the town grows, the paper will too. The press is a gift from my aunt and will arrive in May."

I'm right sure I stared at him with envy and admiration written all over my face. He winked at me. I giggled and blushed.

Already eighteen, I was considered an old maid in this valley of homesteaders and sodbusters. Many girls my age had already married and had a baby or two. I didn't want to get married yet and begged my parents not to offer me to any of the widowed farmers looking for a woman to raise their motherless children and breed more. I wanted to do important things with my life and dreamed of becoming a writer like Miss Jane Austen, whose stories I lost myself in during the hot summer months or the frost-riddled days of winter. I wanted a life of passion.

"What do you know 'bout that? Newspaper man. Right here in Sugar Creek." Ma sat next to Pa. Marie crawled onto Ma's lap, her eyes round.

"Our Charity's a bit of a writer herself," Ma said.

"Really?" Bill turned toward me, his face shone with admiration and curiosity. "I'd like to read something you've written sometime, if you'd let me."

I ducked my head. "Sure. I'd like that."

Jared laughed. "She's got so many stories, we're gonna need new pine shelves in her bedroom jest to hold 'em all."

I blushed and swatted Jared's arm. It was considerable warmer in the room since Jared kept adding logs and the room smelled like flour biscuits and the richness of the hearty stew. I considered Bill. He looked capable of helping Pa. He had the broad shoulders of a hard laboring man. His arms were thick and muscled and I wondered what it would feel like to be held in them. I bit my tongue when my eyes met his. Could he read my thoughts? Lurching around, I finished the chore of doing dishes to avoid the laughter in his sparkling eyes.

Later, after I retired to the small bedroom where I shared a pallet with Marie, I heard Jared and Bill settle down in front of the fire, and my parents' soft voices from their bedroom at the front of the cabin. Ma scolded Pa for scarin' her. Married women lived in constant fear of losing their husbands. What would a widow do on these harsh plains with three children and no man around? I shuddered to think of such a future for Ma or any woman.

The soft glow of morning sunlight drifting over my face like a downy feather woke me. I scrambled from bed to stand next to the blanket serving as our bedroom door. Warmth crept under it from the main cabin. I heard low voices coming from the living area as I pulled my cotton dress over my head and slipped my stocking feet into my ugly, mud-soaked work boots.

Ma stood by the stove frying bacon. The perfume of biscuits baking in the stove and the strong bold scent of fresh-brewed coffee made my mouth water. Soon Ma would need eggs from the hens. My chore. I grabbed my coat off the hook by the back door on my way outside then ran to the outhouse to perform my early morning toilette.

I scrubbed my face and hands with the icy cold water in the wash basin then brushed at my teeth as best as I could. Finally, I combed and braided my long hair.

Bill rounded the corner of the cabin just as I'd finished up and closed the door. He looked fresh, his hair combed neat and his face shaved. He smiled. "Mornin'."

My heart skipped a beat. I looked down at the wet earth. "Mornin'."

"What a glorious day. It's especially beautiful after the hard rain. Sorta washes away the gloom and dust, making everything new again. Don't you think so?"

Surprised, I raised my head. I'd always thought the same thing. His blue eyes were twinkling. I gulped, but smiled back. "Yes. It is beautiful." *Just like you*, I wanted to say.

"Can I walk with you?" he asked.

"I'm just goin' to the hen house to fetch eggs."

"Good. I need to stretch some after sleeping on a hard floor and sitting all day on the wagon seat. Not very comfortable."

I laughed. "It ain't made for comfort. That's why we rush to town and back. Someday maybe they'll make a wagon seat with our backsides in mind."

He chuckled. "I've always thought the same thing."

"Would you like to see the farm?"

"I'd like that very much."

I'd always been a shy girl–liking my books and writing over meeting boys and going to dances and such, but I didn't feel shy around Bill. He gazed at me and spoke to me like I was important.

We strolled past the hen house to the meadow where I loved to while away warm summer days and stopped at the place where Pa had started a crude fence.

"This will be the field of hay," I said then pointed across a muddy cow path as we continued our stroll. "And that field will be wheat. We hope to sell both in town and keep enough to feed our critters. Pa hopes to run a few head of cattle to sell to the Army. They always need beef for the troops and to feed the Indians."

"Sounds like an ambitious plan," Bill said, shortening his stride to keep pace with me.

I stopped ambling and turned to study his pleasing and manly face, his intelligent eyes. I nearly couldn't speak for the yearning that threatened to engulf me. "H-he's very excited to have you here. I hope you'll be able to help him with his dreams."

Bill took a step closer to me. I wanted to take a step back, but held my ground.

"Do you often ... go with the young men around here?"

I looked up at him like he'd grown a horn on top of his head. "Go?"

He smiled like Pa did when he was teasing. "Go. To dances. Picnics. Church socials. Go out with young men?"

I couldn't fight the bubble of laughter that forced its way out of my mouth. "For heaven's sake. Who'd ask me?"

Bill took another step closer, his blue eyes twinkling. I could feel his breath. "I'd ask."

My heart thundered in my chest. I couldn't breathe. Gulping in air, I said, "You would?"

"I would ... and I will."

He didn't say anything else just turned around and helped me collect eggs for breakfast. After that, he followed me back to the house.

Over the next four months, when Bill wasn't working with Pa or working his printing press, we often sat under the old oak by the stream. He would read me stories or walk with me to the meadow and beyond. He took me on those picnics and to church socials and danced with me like he said he would. I never felt more privileged or more cherished.

Finally the hot days of summer passed. Fall's chilly fingers would soon dust the harvested fields with frost's icy whiteness. I dreaded the day Bill would pack up and move into town. I knew one of those fancy town girls would catch his eye and he'd forget about the simple country girl. I prayed every night he'd ask me to be his assistant with the newspaper. I'd move to town, find a room in a boarding house, and become a famous writer like Miss Austen.

The day I watched him pack up his belongings into the second-hand wagon he purchased, my heart felt like it had been chopped in two and my belly felt like I'd swallowed a handful of tacks. I was in love with Bill.

I never wanted to love a man, but Bill had swept into our lives during a hard spring rain and stole my heart. It seemed fitting that he'd be leaving with an end-of-summer storm brewing.

I ran from the house, my long hair falling loose about my shoulders and flowing out behind me. I didn't care. My world had flipped upside down. I was losing Bill.

Tears dripping, I shook my head and continued to run. I shouldn't have fallen in love with him. He should have remained my friend, then his leaving wouldn't be breaking my heart.

"Charity." Bill called after me. "Wait up."

I could hear his heavy boots pounding on the sod behind me. I swiped at the tears in my eyes. He mustn't see how badly his departure had affected me. I'd let him go not knowing about my love. I stopped by a field of stubble, and clutched the rough fence post with my hands.

"What's the matter with you?" he said from behind me.

He then stepped in front of me and gripped my shoulders with his strong, calloused fingers. "Please look at me." He put a finger beneath my chin and raised my head so I had to look in his eyes. "You've been crying."

"So what?"

"Are you crying over me?"

"A'course not. Don't puff up your head."

"Charity." He chuckled, but it sounded exasperated. "Don't you know how I feel?"

My eyes must have widened as I gazed into his. "What are you saying, Bill?"

"This summer has been the best one of my life," he said. "I wouldn't trade working with your pa and coming to know your family for anything in the world. I adore your family."

"Is that all?" I frowned, curled my hands into fists at my side.

He laughed again. "No, that's not all, you silly goose." He took my curled hand, straightened it, and placed it over his heart. I thrilled at his rock-hard chest beneath my palm. The wild thumping of his heart matched mine. Did he? Could he?

"What do you feel, Charity?"

I looked into his eyes. I could drown in blue so deep. "Your heart's a' beatin'."

"Do you know who it beats for and always will?"

I shook my head.

"For someone so smart, you're pretty slow."

I unhinged my mouth to object, but he bent his head and pressed his lips to my open mouth. I never let anyone kiss me. But then, there was no one like Bill. I kissed him back, letting him feel my happiness through the touch of my lips to his.

He wound his arms around my waist, pulled me close. I threaded my fingers through his hair. We kept kissing. I never wanted to stop. I should have felt shame. But I didn't.

Then Bill knelt in the swirling dirt, gripped my hand in his, and tipped his head back so he could look me in the eye. "Charity, I love you. Will you marry me?"

I was too stunned to do anything but nod. Then I felt myself being swept back up into muscled arms. Above the whoosh of the wind, I sang out. "Yes, Bill. I love you, too."

And as we danced in each other's arms, the sky opened up and bathed us in a cool summer rain.

~~*

About the Author. Carol Malone writes romantic suspense to rocket readers back to an era of innocence for a fun *who-done-it* and to uncover a hard-fought happily-ever-after. Her first two published books, *Fight Card Romance: Ladies Night* and *Ladies Night Christmas* are romantic suspense set in 1950s L.A. and her third book, *Summer Holiday* is a historical romance set on a farm in 1905. Her works has been honored in a literary magazine, Amazon reviews, and in a VCWC short story contest. If not hammering out new tales, Carol is reading; watching sports, the Food Network, or HGTV; or hanging with her author husband in Camarillo. She has enjoyed the challenging process of combining contest winners and fellow member's submissions into this, the 2015 VCWC Anthology.

"Remembrance and reflection how allied.
What thin partitions divides sense from thought."
~ Alexander Pope

My grandfather slaps the damp paper bag onto the cutting board. He shimmies the contents, a blotched gray halibut, and sets aside the paper. His army green coat is streaked with brine, and as he removes his sealskin winter cap, I see the sheen of sweat that washes his bald head. With a slow dive, my grandfather lays the cap on the counter and whisks a bottle from the fridge.

Popping the metal top, he says, "Get going on the sauce, and tell your grandma the fish is ready."

"She's sleeping," I reply, lighting the stove.

My grandfather's brown neck loosens as he pours the alcohol down his throat. He runs his tongue over his thin lips, then calls, "Robeeerta!"

The glaze of his eyes is a net of crimson veins. He blinks several times, like after walking through a wind storm on Crescent Hill, and takes another drink. Grandma watches from the kitchen doorframe, pulling her limp hair into a low bun. "I'm here," she murmurs. Steadying herself, she rests her bony hand on my back. I lean into her, but my grandfather grunts and she slowly pulls away.

Grandma tightens her terrycloth robe before removing a steel knife from the drawer. Her skin has paled to an ashen straw color, and she's shaking more than the night of last week's chemo. When she takes a moment to breathe, my grandfather pushes her shoulder with his palm.

She hunches to the floor. "What?" he slurs. "I was just helpin' you 'long."

The knife scrapes the tile. I stay at the stove, stirring the rosemary marinade. My grandfather trudges into the living room with his beer, and I don't look as my grandmother rises.

"Are you all right?" I whisper, more to the molten sauce than to her.

"Fine, I'm fine," she answers. "Get me the paring gloves, will you?"

I grab the thick, latex gloves from the hook above the stove and hand them to her. She puts them on and focuses her strength into the halibut. I stop stirring and stare as she separates the head and tail, and slides the knife under the spotted sheath. She pushes the excess exterior into a lump at the end of the counter. Then, peeling away the skin, she dips the steel into the rose flesh and lifts a granular wire of vertebrae.

"Kitty," she says. "Throw these into the garbage bucket."

I try not to touch the dull, filmy eyes of the fish head as I take the bloody peels and bone and drop them into the can near the back door. The red fluid stems through my pajama shirt and stains the cotton. Even fish, the solitary schools buzzing beneath the icy lake, have veins. They have breath and bodies, the means to propel them through the world.

"Don't you feel sick?" I ask.

Grandma laughs, not a real laugh, but a low, startled cry. "I have breast cancer."

"No, I know. I mean from skinning. Does it make you sick?" I return to the stove and stir with the splintered wooden spoon.

"It's 'come a habit. Charles catches the fish, brings it home. I take care of it. The smell doesn't bother me anymore."

"But every Sunday, you skin. Then the rest of the week—sleep, go to appointments … you have your job at the library, too, and then you have to do what Grandpa tells you. Aren't you tired of it?"

"Life is about work and what comes from that work. If you're lucky, God rewards you, or you get paid," she says, putting the glistening cuts onto a plate. There's a strain in her movements as she lowers the halibut.

"Grandma, I know, but look at this fish. God gave it gills, a face, and a tail. But their minds, they're only so big, and they can't think the way that we do. If we were blessed with thought, then why don't we observe them, use it to live differently than them?" I ask. "Grandpa's always sayin' how we're the top. If we're the top, we don't act much like it."

"You know that's not true."

"I've tasted it," I say.

"In what?"

"The fish."

"It don't taste good?" she frowns, wiping her gloves on her robe.

"No, I mean when the fish comes home. When Grandpa beats you and you're coughing from the cancer. We're followin' the same paths and instead of drowning, we just keep breathing."

"We just keep breathing," she repeats. "Even though we're dyin', we're breathing. Think about what you're saying, Kitty. It don't make sense."

Flecks of gold sputter from the pot. I turn the heat down as the marinade comes to a boil. "Yeah," I reply.

"You prob'bly just have a fever. It's stuffy in here." She pulls me into a hug, her dry breath pounding my ear.

After Grandma unwraps her angular limbs, she tells me to steam the fish. Then, flaccidly, she reaches into the wood cabinet and bats her hand inside. She continues to do so until asking, "You know where I put my pills?"

I oil a pan and place the halibut on it. It begins to sizzle as I answer, "On the nightstand, next to your glasses."

About the Author. Erin Stoodley was born in Santa Cruz, California and is a rising senior who attends El Camino High School at Ventura College. She has been recognized by such organizations as the Johns Hopkins Center for Talented Youth, the Scholastic Art and Writing Awards, and the National Young Arts Foundation. Her poetry is published or is forthcoming in *The Adroit Journal*, *Belleville Park Pages* and *Euphony Journal*, among others. In addition to writing, Erin enjoys photography, morning hikes, walks with her dog, and Russian literature.

Magu Rock – Courtesy of Gregg Miller-VCWC Photography Chair

"They shall grow not old, as we that are left grow old:
Age shall not weary them, nor the years condemn.
At the going down of the sun and in the morning,
We will remember them."
~ Laurence Binyon

Warped – Chapter 11 – Brian's Bouncy Ride by Jodi Romano-Besket

I'm Joe, a junior in high school and self-appointed leader of a band of … not really misfits per se … maybe more like sort-of-fits. We fit together, but not really into any of the usual social cliques at our school.

My amazing group of friends had, just yesterday, experienced the best and worst luck of our lives. The best was we got to ride a rollercoaster that was not yet open to the public … the worst, something went terribly wrong. The rollercoaster went to warp speed with us aboard and we have been forever changed, given talents we never dreamed possible. All of our talents were revealed to us individually—but my favorite has to be my best friend Brian's because it's the best memory I have of our group's coming of power. I can bring that memory to mind in my head just like a video (if I had known what was going to happen I would have had my phone ready so I could have recorded it). That memory never fails to bring a smile to my face. At that point in time, I only knew that my younger sister, Mikayla, had discovered her ability—she can manipulate water—which is cool, but I don't really see the point of it other than some pretty epic water fight skills.

Anyway, our group had agreed to meet at the park that morning, mostly to make sure we were all okay after that crazy ride, but my ulterior motive was to find out if any of the others in our group had developed any powers without coming straight out with it and asking. Hey, I didn't want to come off as crazy.

The group rounds out like this: Cam, fellow football player and video game extraordinaire, is the shy, quiet troublemaker of the group. He has a knack for getting us into mischief before we even know what hit us.

Zack, the lanky, silent, brooding, but observant basketball star is our strategist. He's got a talent for seeing all the angles of any given situation. It's an important skill since Cam is so adept at getting us in trouble. Zack has gotten us out of a lot of situations that could have landed us in front of the school principal, our respective coaches, our parents, or all of the above.

Lexi, brainiac, cheerleader, and the worst driver I've ever had the misfortune to ride with, keeps everyone in line. She's our conscience—keeping a close eye on Cam and preventing us from getting into mischief whenever she can.

My sister Mikayla, in addition to her newly acquired mastery of water, has the gift of an empath–handed down through five generations of Native American ancestors. Since she has the ability to feel what another person is feeling, she keeps our group in balance. If any of us are upset or angry, she's the one who calms us down.

Brian, jokester, Eagle Scout, chow-hound, funky-toed best friend since kindergarten, is the group klutz unless he is goalkeeping for our school's soccer team–then he possesses the grace of a big cat pouncing on prey. Things just seem to happen to Brian—he has the worst luck and often gets us all into uncomfortable situations, but it's always entertaining. Every detail of the events leading up to Brian discovering his powers are etched in my mind.

When Mikayla and I arrived at the park, Zack was leaning against his car, talking on his cell phone. Brian drove up and parked next to my truck. Before Brian opened his truck door, he sniffed the air. "Joe. What's that smell? Something smells bomb."

"Mom sent breakfast burritos," I replied. "They're in the ice chest with

those warming things so they'll stay hot."

He lifted both arms in touchdown formation. "Yes. Is there salsa?"

"I don't know, dude," I said, handing him the ice chest. "I haven't even looked. Here, knock yourself out."

"Yes. There's salsa. The only thing that would make this better would be if Lexi brought Coffee Bean."

Zack pushed end on his cell phone. "That's who I was talking to, and yeah, she's bringing coffee. And Brian, she said not to eat all the burritos. She wants one."

Cam cruised into the parking lot, threw his car in park, and slid out of the driver's seat. He reached back in, grabbed his sweatshirt, slammed the door and walked over. "What's up?"

"Joe's mom sent breakfast burritos and Lexi's bringing coffee," Brian said through a mouthful of burrito.

"Really? Sweet," Cam said, reaching in the ice chest for a burrito.

I grabbed my sketchpad and a mechanical pencil out of the truck and sat down at the picnic table. I reached blindly into the ice chest for a burrito. Hot. I flipped it from hand to hand, then dropped it on the picnic table. Steam poured out of the wrapper, so I turned my attention back to my sketchpad. The lid on the ice chest snapped itself shut, but I didn't even notice because I was engrossed in my drawing.

I glanced up at Mikayla, who slid onto the bench across from me with a questioning look on her face. I could tell by her expression that she was wondering if we were going to tell everyone about her power.

Lexi screeched into the parking lot and bumped one tire over the island before settling back on four wheels. My heart lurched then settled. Whew. My truck was safely flanked by Cam's car and Brian's truck so it was relatively safe. But it would be a miracle if the coffees survived the ride.

"Hi, guys. What's up? Hey, Mikayla, will you help me with the coffees?"

Brian jumped up from the picnic table. "Here Lexi, I've got it." He grinned. "Hey, Joe, you should see this. They're in a box, with a towel covering them and the box is belted into the seatbelt." Lexi slugged him. "Ow. Why? Why do you have to hit me all the time?"

"Because you're so mean to me. I bring you a coffee and you still make fun of me. Did you guys save me a burrito? I only want half. Anyone can have the other half except Brian, cuz he's a meanie."

"C'mon, Lexi. I was just kidding. Sort of," Brian said under his breath.

"All right, fine. If no one else wants it, you can have it, Brian. But be nice to me for a change."

It was quiet as everyone munched and drank. I pondered again how we could broach the subject of Mikayla's water trick.

"Hey. Um. Did anything weird happen to any of you guys last night?" I tried to sound casual as I drew on the sketchpad in front of me. Zack pushed up off the tree he was leaning against.

"No, why?" His eyes locked on my face. Zack is six foot four, blond surfer hair, blue eyes. He's deceptively quick. The best way I can describe him is that he's always sort of coiled like a wary snake. I don't mean that in a bad way, it's just that he can be kicking back, looking relaxed, and then be up in your face in a flash if something ticks him off. Right now he was tense, and edgy, and a little more interested in what I had just asked than anyone else in the group.

I took note of that, but backed off. "I was just wondering if everybody felt okay after riding Warped, that's all," I hedged. "I was kind of sick to my stomach."

Mikayla and Lexi had moved to the soft grass. Dappled sunlight streamed through the trees, casting a kaleidoscope of color over their bare legs. They sat cross-legged, facing each other, strings pinned to each other's shorts, making those multicolored friendship bracelets. Mikayla had her hair covering one side of her face and kept her head down like she didn't want to attract any attention. Good thing. She was sort of an open book if you were looking.

"I was fine," Lexi answered. "Just a little queasy–but I feel good this morning. Why?"

"Oh, I was just wondering." I paused, looking at each of my friends in turn. My eyes landed on Zack. He wasn't buying it.

"Why, did something happen, Joe?" He sauntered over to the picnic table, swung his lanky legs over the bench, folded his arms and rested his chin on his fists. He was directly across from me, eyes probing.

"Uh … well it was probably nothing. Why? What happened to you?" I countered defensively.

"You asked the question. You must have a reason," Zack said.

Okay, this was weird. Why was he so up in my face about this? My gut instinct said to back down–to keep this to ourselves for the time being.

Trying to come up with something to diffuse this conversation, I focused on the drawing taking shape on my sketchpad. A grouping of crystals was emerging on my pad. I shifted it ninety degrees and added some shading. Thankfully, Zack let the subject drop.

I was so engrossed in my drawing, I missed the hot girl jogging along the dirt path, but, of course, Brian didn't. "Whoa."

I looked up. She was beautiful–but not really my type. She definitely had a nice rack, a long, blond ponytail swinging from side to side, blue eyes, white teeth, lips slightly parted to control her breathing.

She wasn't wearing much––tight, black shorts, one of those sports bra things, headphones and running shoes. Sweat darkened the sports bra at the cleavage and glistened on her tanned skin. Her breathing was rhythmic, her feet keeping a steady pace.

Lexi glanced up. "Geez, Brian. Put your eyes back in your head. That's so rude. She's just trying to get some exercise. You don't have to be such a pervert."

"Shut up, Lexi. I'm just being a guy, not a pervert."

Cam grinned. "Brian, man, you're gonna get a …."

"Cam!" Lexi cut him off.

"Eeeeeuuwwww. Guys are so gross," Mikayla added. Her face was beet red, an indication that her empath skills weren't limited to sorrow and anger.

Brian continued to watch the jogger's progress across the park, shaking his head. "Dude, she is hot." He cupped his hands at his chest, grinning. "Wouldn't you like to be her bra?"

I shook my head and grinned. Only Brian would come up with something like that. Still half concentrating on the shading in my sketch, I glanced up again, but Brian was gone. "What the hell? Where'd Brian go?" I looked around, bewildered.

Zack looked up, squinting and scanning the park. He had been texting since our conversation ended. "I don't know. Did he follow her?"

"Creeper," Lexi said. "That's just wrong. She was just jogging. Geez. You guys are so perverted. Oh, look, there he is. Oh, my gosh, he *did* follow her. He better hope she doesn't have pepper spray or anything."

"Nope. Definitely no pepper spray," Cam grinned.

Brian stood next to the tennis courts, nearly two football fields away. I couldn't believe my eyes. I cut a look at Mikayla and she stared back wide-eyed. "He disappeared," she mouthed. "I saw him." She looked more than a little scared.

Oh, man. Things were really getting weird. Now what?

"Joe, how the hell did Brian get all the way over there? He never moves that fast." Cam looked suspiciously into his coffee. "Lexi. What was in this coffee? Anything we should know about? Does it have an energy additive like Jamba?"

"Geez. It's just coffee, Cam," Lexi said. "Vanilla blended, no whipped cream, just like you like it."

We watched Brian walk back, his face beet red, repeatedly glancing over his shoulder at the jogger who was talking into her cell phone and glaring at him.

"Brian. What happened? Where'd you go?" I asked.

"You guys are not going to believe this." He sat on the bench and put his face in his hands. "I was sitting there watching her … and her boobs were so … bouncy. I thought, damn, wouldn't it be sweet to be her bra? To be cupping those … soft, round, firm … and the next thing I knew, I was. I was there. Acting as her friggin' *bra*. It was like my entire body was wrapped around her boobs and back and shoulders. But dude, it was gross. She was all sweaty and stinky. And the B.O. Ugh. She looked good, but dude, she seriously needed a shower. I mean what the hell?" He sniffed his shirt. "Ahhhh. Damn it. I need a shower."

"Well she was *jogging*, stupid. What do you expect?" Lexi, hands on hips, rolled her eyes. Amazing, she was focused on the sweat—as if that was the most unbelievable thing. I shook my head, stunned.

It was dead silent for maybe two seconds then we were all rolling around on the ground laughing. What a superpower. I can be a bra. It was so Brian. Dreaming of wrapping around some girl's boobs and then he actually gets his wish, then it's all stinky and wet. Priceless. I couldn't breathe. Oh, man.

I gathered myself up and looked around. Zack was staring at Brian intently. "Brian. How'd you do that? I mean you actually turned into a bra? Could you see? Smell? Hear? You friggin' shape shifted? Do you know what that means? Do it again. Turn yourself into something."

"I … I don't know. It just happened. Okay what should I be?" He cracked his knuckles.

"Not *my* bra. You stay out of my shirt," Lexi said, leveling a glare in Brian's direction.

"Okay. How 'bout I turn myself into pile of crap and you can eat it? Oh, wait. Crap. I don't want to be crap. Damn it, if I all the sudden turn into crap, I'm going to make you step on me. Wait. No. I don't want you to step on me. Crap. I better just shut up."

I was laughing so hard, I was crying again. Stinking Brian. That kid makes me laugh so hard.

Zack grabbed the ice chest. "How about this, Brian? Turn yourself into an ice chest."

"Yeah, okay, Zack," Brian answered sarcastically, giving him a thumbs down sign. "Pthththt, I'm an ice chest." He rolled his eyes.

"Seriously you guys. Has anything happened to anyone else?" I glanced nervously over at Mikayla. Everyone was silent. Huh. Only Mikayla and Brian? Interesting.

"Well," Mikayla said. "I made water shoot out of my glass last night." They all stared at her.

"What are you talking about?" Lexi asked.

"I took a really hot bite at dinner and before I knew what was happening, water shot out of my glass, and into my mouth." They were all still staring at her. "It did. Really. Joe, tell them. Tell them what you saw."

"After seeing Brian, I believe you. Geez, what'd your mom say?" Cam asked.

"Luckily she didn't see," I said. "I could barely gag dinner down. No way would I have been able to talk our way out of that one. She thought Mikayla just spilled it … which wouldn't be too unusual." Mikayla punched me. "Ow. Mikayla, I swear if you hit me again I will take you down." I said, glaring at her. "So, anyone else?" We all looked at each other. "Okay, well. If anything else weird happens to anyone else, send everybody a text message. We can meet back here and figure out what to do," I said.

Zack shifted nervously, staring at his shoes. I noticed, but he wasn't talking. "Zack?" I said. "Did something happen?"

"No, dude. I wish." But he couldn't meet my eyes.

I waited a beat. Okay, maybe he just needed some more time. "Let's get out of here. Does anyone want to come over to my house and play some Assassin's Creed?" I asked.

"I don't know, Joe. Can you walk through there? Last time I went in your room I thought I was going to get sucked under your bed by zombies or something," Zack said.

"Damn it. I have to clean my room. Anyone want to help?" I asked hopefully.

"Uh … I have to go shower," Brian said. He edged toward his truck, clearly afraid he was going to get recruited to clean my room against his will.

"Nah, dude. I need to help my mom do some stuff around the house," Cam said.

"No way, man. Your room is gross." Zack shook his head, pushed off from the tree he was leaning against, and headed for his truck.

"Last time I helped you clean your room I found an ancient, fuzzy, purple, hot pocket. I don't think you want breakfast burrito spewed all over your room. Besides, I have to go to work at noon. See ya, Mikayla," Lexi said. She hugged Mikayla goodbye, sprinted to her car, and started the engine.

I turned to Mikayla. "Why do girls always hug each other? It's just weird. I mean can you imagine me and Brian hugging every time we said hello or goodbye? I don't think so."

"You guys are just emotionally challenged. There's nothing wrong with hugging your friend. What if you never see her again?" Mikayla asked, eyes misting over.

I rolled my eyes. "Drama much? Brian. Come back here. I may never see you again and I need to give you a hug." I tried my last ace in the hole. I yelled to Cam, Brian, and Zack, "Mom's making lasagna. She said to invite whoever."

"I'll be over later," Brian replied.

"I'm in," Cam said. "Hit me up when you finish your room." He grinned, flipped his hair out of his eyes and slid into his truck.

Mikayla slid her arm around me, grabbed my sketchpad with her other hand and steered me toward my truck. "C'mon, Joe. We need to get our rooms done and then I want you to take me somewhere where there's lots of water. I know this stuff is happening because of that ride. I mean, what else could it be? We ride Warped and all of the sudden I can move water and Brian can turn himself into a bra? It must have affected all of us somehow. I wonder who's going to be next."

"I don't know, Mikayla." I slammed the door of my truck. Why did they get to have powers? I wanted powers. I clinched the steering wheel, frustrated.

"Hey, you left the ice chest," Mikayla said, pointing to the area where we had all gathered.

"Oh. *I left it*. Yeah thanks, Mikayla. You couldn't have picked it up?" I slammed the truck door again and headed for the picnic table. I scuffed my feet on the pavement, staring down. When I reached the picnic table, the ice chest wasn't there. I twirled around and stalked back to the truck, peering into the bed. The ice chest was there, up against the cab on the driver's side.

"Damn it, Mikayla. I didn't leave it. It's in the bed of the truck," I said.

"Joe, uh, I swear I saw it was on the table just a second ago. Are you sure you didn't … you know, move it somehow?"

"I'm pretty sure I'd remember if I was the one who moved it," I huffed out, annoyed.

"Maybe one of the guys put it there. Zack's still here. Maybe he put it there?" Mikayla said.

"Are you serious? Those guys just mobbed the burritos and left it there for me to clean up everything. I swear that's why my room gets so jacked up. Those guys come in my room and leave their trash and crap all over, and then I have to clean it up. You know what I found on my desk the other day? A petrified burrito and rancid ice cream."

She shuddered. "Well, let's get this over with. Argh. *I don't want to clean my room.* That would be a good power. Maybe you'll get the room cleaning power."

"Oh, that's great. The only one who'd like that power is Mom," I said.

I started the engine, waved to Zack, and headed home. I remember wondering whose powers would be revealed next. As irritated as I was, I couldn't keep the grin off my face, remembering Brian discovering his power for the first time. Even if I had known what powers would be revealed for each of us, I couldn't have anticipated how much our lives would change or that our town's safety would depend on our motley group using those powers.

~~*

About the Author. Jodi Romano-Besket is a native of Camarillo and has a deep love of family, humor, and reading. She loves kids—hers was the house where all the neighborhood kids congregated and she volunteered for many years as a team parent for the local sports organizations in which her kids participated. She has written promotional and sales materials professionally but this is her first endeavor into Sci-Fi/Fantasy tween novel genre. When she's not writing, she's consulting for a big data company or baking cookies for friends and family.

Camarillo Avenue at Ocean Drive Courtesy of Carol Malone

The sun sank behind the green hills, staining the distant mountains a rosy shade of pink. Erin sat on the edge of a large boulder, her hands clasped together in her lap. A twig snapped and she glanced nervously over her shoulder.

She was a pretty girl just entering the flower of adolescence. Soft, brown hair sprinkled with shades of chestnut framed her tanned face. Her smile could have charmed the heart right out of your chest.

"Erin."

The girl leaped to her feet, her hand flying to her mouth to stifle a gasp. Behind the rock, where moments before there had been nothing but darkness, stood a boy.

He was not tall, something that Erin had always regretted. But he had a nice smile, bright green eyes, and the sinewy body of a sprinter. He grinned wolfishly at her.

"Sorry, my bad. Didn't mean to scare you. What's up?"

Erin played with her hair, a dozen thoughts dashing frantically through her head. "Um, hey, Jake. Thanks for coming."

"Sure, no problem." He smiled again, but hesitantly.

Erin crumpled. "Jake, I'm really sorry. I know I've been a total jerk to you the past couple of weeks. It's just that I —" Her cheeks burning, Erin paused for a moment to calm herself. She spoke again in a more steady, controlled voice.

"Jake, I didn't call you back or anything because I thought you were still going out with Lisa. I thought you were trying to cheat on her. She's my friend and I —" She broke off again. "I couldn't let myself get involved with you, no matter how much I wanted to." Erin breathed deeply and looked him in the eyes. "I … I really like you, Jake."

She took a hesitant step forward, and Jake stood still, a smile spreading across his face. Erin took another step forward, and another, and another, until she was close enough to count his eyelashes. "I'm so sorry, Jake." She leaned towards him, her lips parted.

Jake leaned forward and their lips met in a kiss. Erin closed her eyes as her mind, which had frothed and boiled with confused emotions, straightened and faded out of focus. Everything seemed clear now—or was it hidden? It didn't matter.

She placed her hands on the back of his neck. Jake ran his fingers through her hair, stroking the line of her cheek, the curve of her spine.

After an unfathomable moment in time, they broke apart.

Jake wiped his mouth with the back of his hand. "Shouldn't have done that," he muttered angrily.

Erin, her eyes fixed on his beautiful face, barely heard him. "What?" she asked, her gaze tracing the strong line of his jaw.

"I shouldn't have done that!" Jake turned his back and began to walk away.

The beautiful placidity that had enveloped Erin's mind shattered. "What?" she cried. "What do you mean? I know you and Lisa broke up, Jake! We can be together now!"

Jake turned to look at her. "It's not that simple, Erin." He sighed. "But I wish it was."

"What do you mean?"

Jake looked up at the starry night sky. "Lisa and I broke up for a reason, Erin." He took a step forward. "I dumped her, Erin. Not because I didn't like her anymore, but because I had to protect her."

Erin looked at him, hurt, and full of tears. "Protect her from what, Jake?"

Jake paused a few feet away from her. The pale moon cast his face into shadowy relief.

"From me." His green eyes flickered yellow.

Erin took a step backwards. "Y-your eyes…"

Jake stepped forward. His eyes shifted between green and yellow. "I tried to hide it from you, Erin. I tried to hide it from all of you. But I can't. It's part of me now."

Erin tripped and fell on her back. Jake bent over her. His eyes were definitely yellow now, as yellow as dead grass before it is consumed by a crackling forest fire, as yellow as the dead eyes of a poisonous viper eyeing its helpless prey. As yellow as the innermost part of a hungry flame.

His hand seized her wrist. His skin burned like hot metal. "It's killing me, Erin. The hunger. Some nights, most nights, I just can't control it, no matter how much I try to think of something else, no matter how much I tell myself it isn't there. It's a horrible, empty feeling, Erin. It's eating me away from the inside. It won't be satisfied until I'm dead."

The sound of terrified shocked screams and claws ripping flesh cut into the chirping of the crickets. Thick blood splattered the boulder. Erin's screams faded into the night as a set of fearsome, powerful jaws crunched her skull.

Jake looked up at the full moon, the fur on his muzzle heavily matted with blood.

His yellow eyes looked down at the scattered remnants of a human being torn apart by insatiable hunger and unforgiving rage. A scream of bitter helplessness and grief built up in his chest. He threw back his head to beg for it all to end, to plead with God to end this living hell.

It came out as a long, mournful howl.

The wires fused into nerves, the brain coupled with a computer, steel and flesh became one.

The year was hard to discern. Humanity had spread far across the stars, throughout our galaxy and billions of others, breaking into cultures and sub-cultures and sometimes new species along the way. This brought about a tangled mess of different calendars, each based around a planet with an orbit of unique length. According to the calendar of the Revolutionary State, it was the four thousand six hundred thirty-second year since the settlement of the planet of Tercera. According to the old Gregorian calendar, which no one in that part of the universe used anymore, it was the thirty-five million five hundred seventy-two thousand nine hundred sixty-first year since the birth of Jesus Christ.

Vash rose to a sitting position on the operating table. Wires dangled out the back of his skull and his skin tingled as the new operating system came online. Data flooded his senses and he momentarily closed his eyes, scrolling through the data screens that appeared before his vision.

He turned to Jabu. "How did it go?"

"Not bad." Jabu stood from his chair. He was almost entirely human, with black skin and blue eyes that bore a distinct epicanthic fold. His only upgrade was a single metal hand he used to perform surgeries. Vash had always found the mechanic's refusal to upgrade himself further amusing because he was so good at upgrading others.

"You're one hundred percent operational."

Vash ripped the wires out the back of his skull and stood up. He was

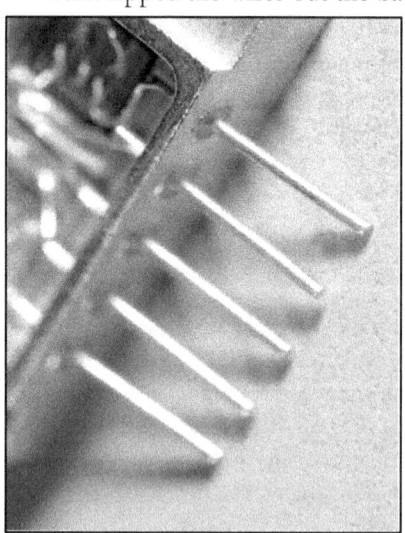

mostly machine, or at the very least artificial. A carbon fiber endoskeleton protected his organs, which had been built by humans and were designed for durability and resistance to disease. His torso was mainly metal, but his face remained organic, human tissue wired to the multiple processors that were his brain. Data screens flickered before green eyes that had been grown in a lab.

He ran a scan to make sure he had emerged unharmed from the surgery. A series of numbers and figures scrolled before his eyes:

system reports, weapons checks, program updates. Satisfied, he walked to Jabu's portal and retrieved the long jacket he wore to hide the illegal weapon upgrades that covered his body. "You know," he said as he programmed the coordinates into the portal. "Basinger still wants you."

Jabu bit his lip, which Vash's translator interpreted as a sign of anxiety. "I know, I know. It's just … I don't really want to … well, die."

Vash laughed. "What? You think the state will send an assassin after you or something? Come on! You're a mechanic. Those are a dime a dozen these days."

Jabu blushed. "I don't want to cause trouble," he mumbled.

"Look Jabu. You've been trapped on this miserable rock for your entire life. Do you really *want* to live in an oppressive dictatorship where the military is the state? You know what Basinger did to himself; he needs you to take care of him. He has more than enough power to keep you safe from the government."

"I'm not so sure," said Jabu, avoiding Vash's eyes. "Without me, the state would be short one mechanic, and, despite what you say, we're pretty valuable right now, especially with the war going on and all. I don't think anyone could keep me safe once the government knows I've deserted the revolutionary cause. They haven't caught any deserters in a while and I think they might want to make an example out of me."

"Jabu, you're making this much more difficult than it needs to be. Come with me right now to Feldon Station." He waved away Jabu's protestations. "Yes, yes, I know that's still within the state's borders. But it's easy to hack into the portals there and then we can be anywhere in this half of the galaxy within a few days. Even if they noticed or cared about your absence, the state wouldn't be able to find you. It'll be like you dropped down a hole with no bottom."

"Vash, I'm not leaving. I already risked enough upgrading you. That's practically treason in itself. Don't you know they declared you an enemy of the state? I wouldn't be surprised if they're already watching my house."

"Don't be an idiot, Jabu. You'll never get a chance like this again."

Jabu hesitated. "I-I … no, Vash, I won't." He met Vash's eyes and spoke clearly. "I've already taken enough risks because of you and Basinger. I'm not going. I'm done. I don't ever want to see you in this shop again."

Vash laughed. "If you say so, Jabu. Just remember what you said: I'm one of the state's most wanted criminals, and no one has ever been able to stop me from coming here." He grinned. "Maybe the state's not what you should be afraid of."

He winked at Jabu's frightened face and stepped through the portal into hyperspace.

His body smashed into a trillion atoms, then blasted through an antennae into millions of miles of empty blackness. Less than a second later, he reassembled at a similar portal on a space station in orbit above a moon of ice: Feldon Station.

Vash left the portal and began to stroll along the station's central boulevard. It did not seem possible that so much space could be enclosed by metal walls, on or above the surface of any planet. Vehicles sped around pedestrians in the road and fliers darted above their heads. Hundreds of people crammed the sidewalks, attempting to jam themselves into the gleaming buildings. Windows that stretched for dozens of meters revealed breathtaking views of the frozen world below—a world that seemed enormous, but in the great, infinite expanse of the universe, was so unbelievably small it was hardly even worth mentioning.

Vash turned off the main boulevard and onto a side alley. He took several more turns, his eyes constantly scanning the surroundings for any signs of hostility. He passed homeless people in the streets; people who were too poor to afford upgrades and so were almost certainly doomed to short, miserable lives of less than a century. He passed other sights too, the sort of things the governor wouldn't allow on the main boulevard: weapon upgrade dealers, smugglers, prostitutes—men and women who were desperate and would do anything to survive. Vash opened a door, nodded to a guard, and entered a small, windowless room.

"He said no." He sat down across from the most wanted criminal in the solar system. Basinger's eyes snapped up to meet his and Vash saw himself reflected in their glassy depths.

"He didn't believe you?" Basinger had long ago decided he felt nothing but contempt for weak flesh, and had upgraded himself to a degree few could or wanted to achieve. He was made entirely out of interlocking plates of Kevlar, which made him both flexible and incredibly durable. His eyes were black lenses, which whirred and focused on Vash's smiling face.

"No. He remains convinced the state will kill him to intimidate the other mechanics."

"He's probably right." Basinger's dexterous fingers fiddled with a spare weapons upgrade on the table between them. "The state needs them right now."

Vash kicked his feet up on the table and grinned. "Agreed." He retrieved a large parcel of freeze-dried flakes from his coat pocket and began to eat them nosily, relishing how they crunched between his metal teeth. "He also thinks they'll send an assassin after him if he runs. Can you believe that?"

"Don't get cocky, Vash," said Basinger sharply. "The state is desperate. If they lose any more mechanics, they might not be able to continue the war against the rebels, and then their precious ideals will be forgotten. I wouldn't put anything past them."

"Yeah," crunched Vash. "Definitely."

118

Basinger looked at him sharply, as if about to reprimand him, but then his eyes fixed themselves on the parcel of food. "Must you indulge in that disgusting habit?"

"What, eating? It's actually fairly healthy."

"And absolutely unnecessary. You should update yourself completely. Become a machine. Flesh inevitably decays and dies. Steel is forever."

"True. But pleasures of the flesh can only be enjoyed with flesh," laughed Vash, spraying the table with chunks of half-eaten food. "And I would rather not give those up."

"You're disgusting," said Basinger. "And you repulse me."

Vash laughed again, spraying even more food on the table. "All right, Basinger," he said, calming down. "Me and a few of the boys will go down to Tercera tonight. We'll hack into Jabu's portal. I'll talk to him, or kidnap him if he won't listen."

"Just kidnap him," said Basinger. "I've waited long enough. But be careful, Vash. Remember to watch out for —"

"Okay." Vash got up and crumpled his bag of seeds. He turned to go and tossed the bag carelessly over his shoulder. Basinger could not curl his lip in disdain, or even change his facial expression, but he did jerk back suddenly from the table as the crumpled bag bounced off its surface, his eyes focused on Vash and glaring with all the anger his black lenses could muster.

* * *

The shop was quiet when Vash stepped through the portal. He walked among the dark silhouettes framed against the triple light of the moons streaming in through the open window. The others stepped out of the portal behind him, tripped, and fell noisily.

Vash smirked as they scrambled to their feet and nervously looked around. His smirk deepened. Morons.

Two of the men quietly descended the stairs to guard the door. Vash and the other two searched the operating room, eventually finding Jabu asleep slumped over a desk covered in blueprints and charts of human anatomy. Vash took his hand out of his pocket and unscrewed one of his fingers, replacing it with a hypodermic syringe. He was about to jab the needle into the mechanic's neck when a loud crash reverberated from below.

Vash looked up, his face amused. "Which idiot was stupid enough to—"

One of his men fell into the room from the stairwell, his face sizzling and dripping. "It's the state!" he gasped before melting into a puddle on the floor.

"What the hell?" muttered Vash. He motioned to his remaining two men. "Go take care of it."

They dashed down the stairs, readying their weapon upgrades. An electric glow flashed into existence a few seconds later, momentarily blinding Vash before his eyes could adapt to the bright light. A crackle and the smell of burning flesh filled the air. The light and crackle abruptly vanished, but the smell of charred flesh remained. Vash glanced at the doorway again, then at the slumbering mechanic before him. He unscrewed another finger and jabbed a visual sensor into its place. He slowly approached the doorway and curled his finger around the frame.

Half-burned bodies with metal limbs lay horribly contorted upon the floor. A silent blue fire burned, painting twisted shadows upon the wall as it consumed the room.

The corpses slowly began to liquefy in the intense heat of the flames. A figure stood blocked out against the flickering blue light. It was metal, but humanoid, as if someone had sheathed a man in steel and breathed a mockery of life into him. Vash had never seen one before, but he knew exactly what it was: an assassin.

The assassin buzzed with upgrades. Blue arcs of light crackled and danced at the end of its left arm, which ended in not a hand but a series of bent wires. Its eyes burned a deep, electronic blue, the same color as the flames that blazed around it. It was the elite of-the state's military, a mindless machine that would pursue its targets to the end of the universe. It was utterly void of will and desire, and existed solely to destroy others.

Swearing viciously, Vash sprinted back through the room and to the portal. He frantically punched at the buttons, only to discover that it would not respond, and realized that the state must have hacked into it somehow and turned it off. He turned back to face the doorway to the room, knowing what he had to do.

"Vash? What are you doing in my house?" Jabu blocked his way, his eyes still crusted over with sleep. "And what in the galaxy is making that light downstairs?"

Vash shoved past him and ran to the racks of shelves that lined the walls around the operating table. "Arm me!" he hissed to Jabu, ripping off his coat.

"What?"

"Arm me, damn it! There's an assassin walking up your stairs!"

"*What?* How did it-"

"Shut up and arm me!"

Jabu hurried forward and undid the clasps that held Vash's forearms in place. They fell off his elbows and thudded to the floor. "I knew I should never have gotten mixed up with criminals like you!" whimpered Jabu as he ripped cylindrical containers out of a concealed compartment, tearing them open and jamming the illegal weapon upgrades within onto Vash's elbows.

120

He continued to whine as he clamped the arms into place and tightened them.

He shut up when the assassin entered the room. It saw them immediately and raised its arm to fire.

"Move!" Vash shoved Jabu out of the way and fired his left weapon. Flames so hot they were white blasted across the room, their heat so intense most of the metal shelves around them began to melt.

The assassin strode through the inferno, its eyes dimming as it turned off extraneous functions to cool itself. It raised its limb and weapon. A blue arc of light blazed through the air and connected with Vash's arm.

The limb was Kevlar, but because Vash still had so many organic components, his brain was programmed to feel even with the inorganic parts of his body. Pain like he had never experienced blotted all other sensations. The arm cracked and splintered, falling in a smoking pile to the floor.

The assassin was faster than any human, but Vash was no human, not completely anyway. He raised his other arm before it could strike again.

A projectile spat out of the upgrade and slammed into the assassin. The projectile exploded, the shockwave sending Vash and Jabu flying into the portal. The room flashed out of existence.

Vash got up off the floor of Feldon Station. He walked unsteadily towards Basinger and a few others standing at the computer that controlled the portal. Jabu groaned upon the floor.

"Close it," he said to Basinger, who nodded to one of the men. The portal sealed and Vash slumped against the wall in relief, grateful beyond measure that Basinger had somehow managed to bypass the state's security measures around the portal.

"What happened? Where are the others?" Basinger's ever-neutral face belied the anger that raged within him.

"Fried," said Vash. He turned to Jabu, who by now had managed to scramble to his feet and was looking about him in an extremely confused manner. "Welcome to Feldon Station, mechanic. I'd like to show you around, but I don't imagine we'll be able to stay here long, not with an assassin up our ass."

Basinger started violently, but Jabu spoke before he could say anything. "But we killed it! We shot it point blank with a rocket!"

"I doubt that did much damage," muttered Vash, examining the smoking wreck of his arm. "It takes more than that to kill an assassin."

"I told you to be careful," snapped Basinger, cutting off their conversation. "And instead you nearly get everyone killed. Did the assassin see your face?"

Vash nodded. He knew what that meant. The assassin, having presumably been programmed to kill anyone who aided Jabu in trying to escape, would now search until it found and killed him. He had always been a marked man, but never by a robot that existed only to destroy.

"But surely the assassin won't pursue us off the station!" protested Jabu. "I mean, what use am I to the state if I'm dead?"

"More than you are alive and aiding criminals. Besides, you're their example to the others now, remember? Defy the will of the state and be hunted by an assassin until death." Vash turned to the window. This one looked away from the ice-covered moon and towards the infinite, empty blackness of space. "The assassin will come for you. It will come for all of us."

"What are we going to do?"

"Run." The crowd surged by them in the streets of Feldon Station, and Vash could have sworn he saw a pair of burning blue eyes among the thousands of unsuspecting people.

~~*

★ 2012 Short Story Honorable Mention: The Last Look In Their Eyes by Max Morales

The call came while I was sitting in my unlit hotel bungalow on a warm summer night in the Bahamas. I was drinking a glass of my favorite merlot and had been enjoying the soothing tones of "Moonlight Sonata" when the phone buzzed and vibrated. I picked it up. Two words, one deep voice. "It's tonight." I disconnected, knowing that was all that would ever be said.

Sometimes I wonder what the guy on the other end looks like. Is he the stereotypical criminal, a tall man with a big black beard hiding his hideous scars? No, he's probably more like me: average looking, with the kind of face that wouldn't stand out in a crowd. The kind of person you wouldn't notice until they take the knife out of your back.

I didn't pack much. My Uzi. A few extra clips. A silenced handgun. A couple of knives. I like to travel light.

I walked out of my bungalow and onto the little boat tied to my private dock. The moon was a pale shadow of its usual self, and the resulting night was so black it beckoned murder with open arms.

The boat moved silently through the water at a few knots. I could have gotten there with my eyes closed and swimming backwards, but I kept the GPS on anyway. I don't like leaving things to chance. Chance is exactly the type of thing that gets people like me killed.

A few minutes passed in silence. I was perfectly relaxed, still humming "Moonlight" beneath my breath as death drew nearer to a fat old man with a lot of money. Nobody liked him, but he had money, and so everybody liked him. Or something like that. I didn't really pay attention to the details.

I'd memorized the bungalow's every detail and could easily pick the low building out of the gloom. I moored the boat, took the silenced handgun out of the bag, and walked up to the kitchen window. It swung open on its greased hinges without a sound.

I crawled in, careful not to knock the pots and pans around. I hate kitchens.

They're so crowded and noisy and filled with metal things that echo when they hit the floor. Bedrooms are better. Big, roomy, lots of windows. The perfect place for an uninvited guest to enter. But this wasn't a bedroom. Sometimes you just have to deal with these things.

I moved through the bungalow's rooms. I almost felt bad for the poor idiot that was going to die that night. He didn't know that he was staying in the same hotel as his murderer, didn't know that I knew him better than he knew himself. I'd been following him for weeks, and there wasn't a synapse that fired in his puny brain I didn't know about.

Snores emanated from the bedroom. I crept in and saw the still lump on the bed that was my target. I pointed my gun at him and poked the fat slob in the ribs. I like to see the terror on their faces before I pop them, the last look in their eyes before they die.

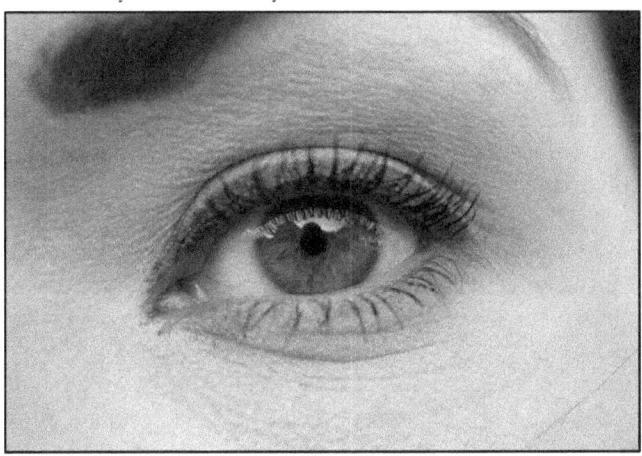

It's a weakness, I know. It will probably get me killed someday because it's the only flaw I allow myself to have. But even Achilles had his heel.

My target's eyes snapped open and for a moment we were linked more closely than husband and wife. I am the hunter. He is the hunted. I am going to kill him and he knows he is going to die. So much is said in those beautiful, wordless moments. It's a shame they have to end.

I pulled the trigger and the man's life ended in a silenced blast. There's a certain stillness that fills a room after someone has died, as if the walls could sense the departing soul. You would probably find that eerie. I find it invigorating.

I got into my boat and glided silently across the resort lagoon. Alone with my thoughts, and the moonlight. Back in my bungalow, I removed my blood-soaked clothes and folded them carefully, putting them in a plastic bag and then into my suitcase. I would burn them later when I had the time.

I changed into my finest, tailored Italian suit and finished my merlot. I checked my watch. I would only be a few minutes late to my date. I put on my evening jacket, excuses running through my head. But I didn't really pay attention to them. She would believe whatever I told her. People never want to hear the unpleasant truth.

I am the undertaker, the last person you will see in this world. I caught sight of my face in the mirror and grinned. My friends would call me by the name my darling, dead mother gave to me … or at least they would if I had any friends. And I don't.

* * *

Lisa looked great in the red dress I bought for her birthday. It brought out her blood-red hair, and made her white skin look even whiter, like the pallid hue of dead flesh or the color of dried bones.

When I apologized to her about being late, she was so gracious I almost laughed aloud. People are so cute when they try to be good. Because they're not good. Deep inside us all there is the capacity, the thirst, to do evil. You can spend your whole life trying to deny it, or you can give into the darkness. The first path leads to a life of constant, pointless struggle between your true self and the mysterious conscience "good" people use to justify their actions. The other leads to a life without fear. You don't have to be afraid anymore when you're the monster under the bed, the beast beneath the basement stairs. In the absence of fear comes hunger, and the freedom to satisfy it.

About halfway through dinner, Lisa wipes her dainty little mouth, looks down at her plate, and says in a quiet little voice, "I don't think this is working out, Jake."

A smile hiding a sneer. "What do you mean, sweetheart?"

"You know exactly what I mean, Jake," she says angrily, putting her fork down in her plate. "Our relationship. You have to respect me. You can't go off chasing skirts."

A moment of deadly silence in a restaurant filled with the chatter of happy people.

Lisa looks at me with a hurt puppy face. "You didn't think I'd find out, did you?"

The thick, red wine in my glass is reflected on the blade of my steak knife. I stare at it for a moment, transfixed by the serrated edge stained red.

"About what?"

"About Sierra."

Sierra's dead. I chopped her body into little pieces and fed it to her dogs.

"You can't go on seeing her."

Then I killed her family and buried them in their backyard. I still remember the black dirt slowly covering their white faces, pale as death itself. As pale as the pearl handle on my nine millimeter.

"I'm not seeing her."

"Jake, tell me the truth. Who do you love: me, or her?"

I still remember their screams, that high-pitched, halting music to my ears. They were all so shocked to die, so shocked to look upon their murderer that cold winter night.

I still felt the frigid knife handle clenched in my fist, still saw the blade squirm in delight as it tasted the flesh of their bodies, still hear my laugh as I watched the light fade from their eyes—

"Jake?"

The bright restaurant swirls back into existence before my eyes. I smile. "Baby?"

"You looked awful there for a moment. Are you all right?"

"Yes. Just ... remembering." I smile at her. "But rest assured, darling, they were memories of you. I think of no one else. I love you more than I can say."

She smiles. "Oh, Jake, that was beautiful. It's just that I saw that name on your contacts and I just had to wonder –"

"She was my old girlfriend. She's dead." Very flat, declarative, as if that was all there was to say.

"Oh, I-I'm sorry." She's silent for a moment, then takes my hand from across the table. "I love you, Jake."

"I love you." And that is why you must die.

We sit there for a moment, linked by the warmth in her heart and the murder in my brain. I don't like it when people try to find out who I am and what I like. Those things should not be brought to light. They're the dark secrets we all hide from prying eyes, the shadows we hold in the silence of our hearts. The darkness that creeps along the edge of our dreams.

Lisa smiles hesitantly at me, as if wanting to show she is sorry for bringing up words of grief. I smile back at her and she beams, confident all is well.

"Let's go to your hotel room," she says, grabbing the stupid little handbag all women seem to carry with them. "I want to make it up to you."

I act normal, tipping our waiter heavily, and even signing the bill with a flourish.

Lisa laughs, grabs my arm, and drags me outside.

The beach is deserted. Waves lap gently against the Caribbean shore as the moon creates a white path from the heavens down to the water below. It's all so dangerously romantic, as Lisa so flirtatiously whispers in my ear. "Yes it is," I agree. Very dangerous indeed.

I listen to her giggle as she hangs all over me. I laugh along with her, but my laughter is empty—a window to the black pit inside me. You could get lost in the emptiness there, in the dark, twisting labyrinth that is my shriveled remnant of a soul. I already have, and I never want to leave.

We enter my bungalow suite and Lisa falls into my arms. She's so warm and young and full of life. She loves the simple things: long walks on a misty beach, a good time over a good meal, a book in the warmth of her favorite chair.

Lisa steps back, shaking her long red hair out of her beautiful eyes. "Jakey," she says coyly. "Why don't you take off your shirt?"

I take off my evening jacket, and place it on the back of a nearby chair. I carefully unbutton the sleeves of my shirt and roll them up to my elbows in a businesslike fashion.

Lisa giggles as she kicks off her heels one at a time. I cross the room and lock the door.

That makes her giggle even harder.

She acts like she wants me to take her in my arms, but I brush past her. I look down at the contents of a black backpack strewn across the surface of the bed. My Uzi. A few extra clips. A silenced handgun. A couple of knives. I like to travel light.

"What's that?" asks Lisa, sensuously wrapping her arms around my waist and whispering into my ear. She's not even looking at the dark display before us.

I pick up the handgun and load it, saying, "Oh, it's nothing, Lisa. Why don't we just go back to what we were doing?"

Lisa backs away slowly.

"Jake …" she says softly, unbelievingly.

I pull back the safety. The bullets click into place. For a moment, I'm enchanted by the beauty of a .45 handgun, struck by the grace of a perfect killing machine.

Lisa stumbles backwards, tripping over her discarded heels. I tower over her, as I have over so many whining, pleading victims in the past … I too, am a perfect killing machine. As inescapable as death, as gripping as the cold fate that awaits us all.

Lisa looks up at me, tears filling her eyes. They all cry in the end, even the ones who think they're brave. They're all cowardly scum beneath the

126

tailored suits and the expensive dresses. Animals putting on a pathetic show.

I raise the gun wordlessly. "Jake … no …" She's too shocked to even scream.

I press the gun against the side of her head, searching for the one thing I crave: the last look in their eyes. The fear, the shock, and the hurt I live for are all laid bare for me in their blue depths. In that moment, I understand Lisa better than her own mother ever did. But what her mother gave, I will take…

Later, I finished listening to "Moonlight Sonata" and poured myself another glass of merlot. I took off my tie, undid the top few buttons of my shirt, and sat in the chair by the desk. My empty handgun lay on the desk in front of me and a silent corpse stained the carpet red on the suite's floor. I smiled and took a sip from my merlot.

I am the undertaker, the last person you will see in this world. I catch sight of my bloodstained face in the mirror and grin. My friends would call me by the name my darling dead mother gave to me, or at least they would if I had any friends. And I don't. Or: "call me by the name my darling dead mother gave me before she woke up one morning with her throat slit."

~~*

About the Author: Max Morales enjoys writing about the unusual and the grotesque—in this case, a werewolf, criminals living thirty-five million years in the future, and the twisted thoughts of a serial killer. Originally from Iowa, he has lived in Southern California for most of his life. He is currently a junior at Stanford University studying International Relations.

"Human beings do terrible things to each other
and the tragic thing about it all
is the way the remembrance of past hurt can rob us of our future and
become the narrative of our lives."
~ Richard Holloway,
On Forgiveness: How Can We Forgive the Unforgiveable?

California Winter by Marc Tapper

I sit with my coffee, as the temperature reads 30 degrees.

Clear, crisp, quiet, except for the sounds of far off traffic.

A kitty races across the yard following a squirrel, who beats him every time.

Sounds of morning.

Birds chirping and fluttering as they go to the feeder.

I listen … listen.

I was alone with my coffee, but not alone.

Nature shares with me,

And allows me this moment.

One time. One Life.

This moment.

I sit with my coffee.

A moment. This moment,

I am given.

East of here, a blizzard locks people in.

Ah California!

~~*

Sparrow Killer by Marc Tapper

The sparrow lay on its back. Fresh blood patterned as an arrowhead was still spreading on its throat. Nine year old Jimmy approached slowly and curiously stared at it. The elation he felt just seconds ago, when the bird was in his sights, was quickly ebbing. This same bird had been alive, hopping around, and picking at seeds. Now it was dead—the result of Jimmy's BB gun.

He picked it up by the tail and stared at it, then buried it in his backyard under the Chinese Elm Tree.

Not much sport, he thought.

Shooting from behind a crude hunting blind not ten feet away, and killing something hardly the size of his fist was no sport at all.

Jimmy carved his seventh notch in the stock of his Daisy Red Ryder Model BB rifle. That meant this brought the count to seven dead birds. "This is really stupid," he said aloud.

He had seen it lots of times on TV when cowboys cut a notch in their gun for every outlaw they killed. But that was TV. And that was 1955.

Days later, Jimmy stood poised in his backyard watching the Elm tree as a mockingbird landed on one of the higher branches. He took careful aim and he heard the distinctive "pop" that was made by the gun.

The mockingbird fluttered, began to fall, then flew away, apparently wounded. He watched it fly one-winged to a distant tree. Jimmy began for the first time in his nine years to question what he had done. The neighborhood boys had been doing this backyard bird shooting forever. He did it too, just because he had the gun and he had the skill and felt the power. But why? He wasn't really sure. His mind jumped back to the image of the dead sparrow. *No reason*, he thought. The sparrow was small and pretty and full of song before he, the great hunter, had killed it. Now the same picture jumped into his mind often. It was unsettling—nagging.

Spring came early to Jimmy's house. The cool morning air and California sun shone early each day. Jimmy slept with his bedroom window open all night. He felt the dawn and heard its sounds as they entered his room. The neighbor's puppy barking, a far off whistle of the freight train, and sounds of delivery trucks on the streets, all accompanied by chirps, warbles, and whistles of singing birds.

Just outside his bedroom window, a pyracantha bush had reached the height of the windowsill and blossomed. The bush had rich deep green leaves contrasted by round ruby red berries surrounded by long sharp thorns. A pyracantyha was one of nature's ironies. Pretty to look at and nourishing for the winged creatures who ate its berries, but painful for anyone unfortunate enough to stumble into its stickers. Jimmy awakened and lay silently listening and thinking about the day ahead. He heard a rustling sound. Not out of place, but curious just the same.

He moved on his side ever so slowly so he could view the pyracantha without disturbing whatever might be making the rustling. He heard the rustle again, it was rhythmic. Rustle. Pause. Rustle. Pause. Rustle, rustle, pause. Then he sighted the bird not more than five feet from his face, separated only by the window screen. He held perfectly still and watched with fascination as the bird pecked at a red berry, ate it, then jumped to the next one. So continued the quick methodical meal. Jimmy knew the bird saw him, but it did not take flight because Jimmy remained motionless.

As he watched, he noticed that as it hopped from berry to berry, the bird favored its left wing. It was a mockingbird. In fact, *the mockingbird* Jimmy had wounded last month. Jimmy became more certain as he observed a small dimple surrounded by a circle of missing down on its chest. Yes, this had to be the same one. For some reason he had chosen Jimmy's pyracantha for nourishment. The mockingbird kept eating for several minutes then, when done, it hopped to the lower twigs then to the ground. Jimmy realized that it could only move in short steps and could be easy prey for its enemies. After a few more hops it made a short fluttering journey to a nearby tree, then another short trip to the Chinese Elm, and up close to the top for its safety.

Early the next morning the same ritual repeated itself: the sound of hopping, the sight of the Mockingbird eating berries, and the departure up to the elm tree. Jimmy looked forward to this same little scenario each day. As he watched he found himself silently cheering for the bird, he admired its persistence and thought, *Com'on you can do it*. His feelings had completely turned around since that last day when he had pulled the trigger.

After several weeks Jimmy noticed something had changed. The bird still came and ate, but when he approached and left the pyracantha it no longer hopped and fluttered … it flew. The wing had healed itself over time and the Mockingbird appeared strong and healthy. Jimmy knew that healing had taken place, and not just to the mockingbird, but to himself.

He understood he had no need to kill animals. After all, he lived in the suburbs where food was found in the grocery store. His mother provided him with ample food. There was no need for him to hunt. There never had been. Watching that bird fly had changed something inside Jimmy. Maybe it wasn't love, just respect for life.

From that time forward when he was asked by his friends to bring his BB gun to go shooting birds, he always had the same answer. "I lost my gun," he said. "I lost it and doubt I will find it."

~~*

About the Author. S. Marc Tapper writes short stories and poems to educate, entertain, and amaze his readers; the thoughts and events expressed therein are born purely from a fertile imagination. In the nonfiction genre, Mr. Tapper has created hundreds of ads along with movie scripts and sales training materials. His company, S. Marc Tapper & Associates, located in Encino, California, is a consulting firm which specializes in marketing and sales strategies.

It's been held long enough to be called a tradition. This year, however, it's going to be different.

Every January of every New Year, Sara, Blanche, Grace, and I meet at my house to give each other a little boost to our New Year's resolution. And every year it is the same resolution. We are all determined to lose weight this year.

"I only have sugar-free sugar," I said, while I poured each of my friends some coffee.

"Don't worry," Sara said, "I always carry the real stuff in my purse."

When the other girls reached for their purses, I knew we wouldn't need my sugar substitute.

"Did you know there's a new gym in the old bank building? Why don't we meet there once or twice a week?" Grace suggested.

Sara looked over the top of her coffee cup. "I hear the gym's upstairs and there's no elevator. Isn't there another gym somewhere that's on the first floor?"

Blanche made what seemed like a sensible suggestion. "I see people walking in the mall. Why don't we meet there once a week? We can meet at that new plus size dress shop."

Grace raised her hand. "Or at McDonald's," she replied. "I know exactly where that is."

"I don't think so," Sara protested. "I hardly ever go to the mall because I always have to park so far away."

Grace chuckled.

"Did I miss something?" Blanche asked. "Why are you laughing?"

"I just remembered what my friend, Helen wrote on her blog. She suggested that instead of worrying about losing weight, we hang out with people who are bigger than you. You'll look and feel thinner."

I was hoping Sara wouldn't notice everyone staring at her.

"I'll bet she's the same lady who puts a cherry tomato on a sundae so she can call it a salad." Blanche laughed.

"Has everyone started their diets?" I asked.

Sara broke the silence. "I'm going to wait a couple of more weeks. There are some things I want to eat first. I mean there are lots of leftovers from the holidays. We should never waste food."

"Well, I'm going to start mine today," I announced. "But I can't have any of those donuts left here. I'll just scarf them down after you leave. You gals have to help me out."

They were all very gracious to make sure I didn't have that problem.

~~*

About the Author. Theresa Schultz's winning essays and short stories have won the hearts of many throughout the years. Her column "This I've Learned" in RAW (Real Authentic Women) magazine inspired her to write a collection of self-help books. Her books include: *Dear God, I'm Divorced;* delivers comfort and lessons for anyone experiencing being once again single. *It's Like … Getting 25 Years of Experience as a Real Estate Agent,* offers lessons drawn from her own experiences as an agent. And *It's a Happy Face Day – Simple Rhymes for Happy Times,* is a delightful book designed for a grandparent to promote fun conversation when read to a child.

Beach in Ventura – Courtesy of Dallas Clemmons

I was staring at Mark Robinson's red brick home with the rose bushes in the front yard from my car. My fingers were still tapping lightly on the steering wheel as they had been for the past ten minutes. At least they weren't gripping the wheel so tightly that my knuckles turned an abnormal pale color.

Today was Mark's thirtieth birthday. If he was serious about what he said when we were twelve then he would not be surprised to see me. But if he was just joking around and didn't even remember what he said, then I was certainly about to make a complete fool out of myself. Especially, since I was dressed in a ridiculously sexy red dress—Mark's favorite color, and black stilettos—Mark's favorite shoe to see on a woman. I leaned back once again in the driver's seat and continued to stare at his house.

My mind wandered back to my twelfth birthday party that I had at my father's beach house. It wasn't quite a party, just a few friends over: Maggie, Reggie, and Mark.

We were sitting around a bonfire with our bare toes sinking in the sand, roasting marshmallows, and talking. Suddenly, Maggie's eyes widened when she came up with the brilliant idea to play truth or dare. Finally, it was Mark's turn. "Cheyenne," he said to me, "truth or dare?"

"Dare…" I said with a giggle.

Mark shoved his gigantic, black rimmed glasses up higher onto his nose and grinned, exposing his braces. He cleared his throat then challenged, "I dare you to marry me on my thirtieth birthday."

There was shocked silence around the bonfire. Reggie was the first to snap out of the silence by nudging Mark then said, "You're such a dork. We're playing today, not for when we are old. What kind of …"

Mark regained his balance on the rock that he had been sitting on and held up his hands. "Okay, okay, wait … hold on … let me finish what I have to say. I know we are all kids, but Cheyenne is my best friend. We've known each other forever, and we have fun, and she's starting to look hot. I'm thinking after she does her whole college thing, traveling thing, get all the guys she'll be dating out of her system, eventually she will want to settle down. Who better to settle down with than your best friend, right? So all you have to do, Cheyenne Gauthier, is show up on my doorstep on my thirtieth birthday, and we can get married."

He sputtered his speech out quickly and was out of breath. He looked as if he had more to say, but both Maggie and Reggie seemed to have had enough.

They both started throwing marshmallow's at Mark. I never had the chance to answer him.

Still sitting in the car, my stomach churned, and goose bumps appeared across my skin. Mark was right. I did all he had predicted I would do. Now, I wanted my best friend. We have been going out to the movies and dinner for the past few months, almost every weekend since neither of us was dating anyone. What if the chemistry I thought we developed was all in my mind? What if he was just joking that night? What if he forgot about it?

I squirmed in my seat. It was getting cold, and the windows were fogging up from my nervous breathing. I took one last breath and finally got out of the car. I was sure the whole neighborhood could hear the obnoxious click, click of my stilettos on the concrete.

I tapped lightly on the door rather than ringing the bell. A moment later, Mark answered the door. He grinned, and I immediately felt tingly inside. "Cheyenne," he said almost breathlessly. He cleared his throat and blinked his eyes.

"Hi," I said with a smile.

"I didn't think you were coming today."

"It's your thirtieth birthday. Why wouldn't I come?"

His dark brown eyes searched mine as if waiting for something. His hand was still gripped tightly around his door knob, and I was still outside in the cold. Maybe this was a mistake. What had I been thinking? Maybe he was hoping someone else was knocking on his door. What if he had a real date tonight? I bit my lower lip then said in a low raspy, almost desperate voice, "Mark, truth or dare?"

He reached for me and wrapped one arm around my waist, the other behind my neck and kissed me the way he should have kissed me a long time ago. I felt giddy and excited and … just … alive. I felt at home. Finally, he pulled me inside and said, "So, you'll marry me?"

"Absolutely," I said.

~~*

About the Author. Giselle Lumas mostly writes romance novels, but she also writes children's, teen and sci-fi. She currently has eight novels available in paperback and e-book via Amazon, BN.com, Nook, Kobo and Smashwords. Some are also available in audio on Audible.com and *i*Tunes. When she is not writing, or working her day job, she is at the baseball field at one of her son's baseball games, or hanging out with her daughter, dogs and crazy bird.

I've Lost My Chicken by A. Bernie Barnes

I've lost my chicken.
Though I have looked everywhere—
And began past steps retrace.
I'm resigned its loss to bear
And I must bleak future face.

I've lost my chicken.
Of course, heard no squawk or noise,
Nor have friends seen it go by;
Cannot go far, I suppose,
My rubber chicken can't fly!

Mysterious Sorghum by A. Bernie Barnes

The year was 1937, the time of the Great Depression, in Nebraska.
This place was part of what came to be known as the Dustbowl of the United States. My father was a dry land farmer in the sand hills of Nebraska. Some of his crops were white corn, sweet potatoes, and melons.

As a boy of eleven years, I was impressed by the sorghum cane with its small corn-like leaves and seed carrying spires on top. The cut stalks about four to five feet in length, were squeezed of juices which were then cooked into a thick syrup called sorghum. I remember eating pancakes covered lavishly with the sorghum molasses I helped to make—how good it tasted.

One day, a giant mill was carried to our farm in a large wagon pulled by a team of four horses. I hadn't seen anything like it before. At its center core were two iron rollers about sixteen inches in diameter, each mounted vertically side by side. Sprocket teeth mounted on the bottom engaged a cogwheel drive ring. A long beam attached to the gears reached out about twenty feet just outside the round catch basin located under the rollers.

A small, gaunt brown horse was fastened to the beam with a single-tree for a one horsepower machine. While the horse walked around and around, we followed and pushed the cane stalks, butt end first, between the rollers.

Greenish juices flowed down from the mill into the catch basin, then into buckets below. This operation lasted all day long. As the morning wore on, clouds began to darken the sky and winds soon whipped up the sand,

135

spitting it almost horizontally. I still remember how the sand stung my face and got in my eyes.

The buckets of raw juice were poured into a huge shallow pan about ten feet long by four feet wide and about five inches deep, protected by a lean-to shed.

Underneath were the grates loaded with wood and cobs for fuel. My job was to help skim off the foamy scum that formed on the surface of the simmering liquid. Normally, the juices boil down into syrup in about three hours, however, a problem arose.

A mysterious thing happened during the next stage of the delicate production of the sweet sorghum. The winds blew so hard it became difficult to keep the fire burning hot enough. Although the big pan was in a roofed shelter, the fire was at a lower temperature than planned. Therefore, the cooking process went on and on. Four hours went by and it still hadn't finished. I was getting very tired and bored, skimming and stoking.

In the very early morning hours, I was sent to bed. My parents, bundled up against the cold wind, worked on through the night.

The all night cooking produced what I now call the miracle molasses.

In the year 1995, my mother got out several small jars of that sorghum she had kept stored at room temperature all those years. Still as fresh and unspoiled as when they were made that summer of 1937.

It always amazed me that the batch had been preserved for that long period of time as a result of the unseen force—the wind.

The scientific explanation would probably be that the unusually slow heating caused by the wind had changed the chemical makeup of enzymes that normally would deteriorate the liquid.

But, my explanation is that some mysterious forces were at work on that day, long ago making the delicious sorghum last for years.

~~*

About the Author. A. Bernie Barnes has written and published books of poetry and will be publishing his first novel soon. He is a graduate of the University of Nebraska and a U.S. Navy World War II Veteran. An engineer, inventor, and scientist, he served several years in industrial and consumer marketing and corporate management before retiring. His other activities include family relationships, cooking, church, community service, gardening, and membership in several writers clubs. Father of four, he has six grandchildren, and two great grandchildren.

A high-pitched train whistle echoed through the grand atrium. The
sound reverberated off the curved ceiling of skylights and glass walls of the
soaring space. Nick and I stood on the mezzanine balcony under a gold and
black clock, the hour hand as tall as a man. We watched the locomotive roll
toward us through the open end of the station. Accompanied by screeching
brakes and one last gasp of steam, the train eased to a stop at its platform.

An emaciated man in a light blue three-piece suit stood at the door
between the first and second cars. Thick swirls of steam shrouded him like
a cloak, but they could not hide his fiery orange beard and matching hair.
Nor did they conceal the anguish in his eyes. The man stepped down onto
the railway platform, a leather-bound portfolio under one arm, and a small
framed mirror under the other. He scurried along the platform and climbed
a spiral staircase, passed through one of the enormous archways along the
sides of the building and disappeared behind a set of double doors exiting
from the grand hall.

More passengers spilled from the train. A serious old woman wearing
a long black dress and a white bonnet held the handrail as she stepped onto
the platform. With a white handkerchief produced from her pocket, she
dabbed her forehead and upper lip. Turning toward the front of the station,
she gathered her skirts and picked up a black satchel with her free hand. She
ascended the stairs with careful attention to each step. Like the emaciated
man, she passed under the chosen arch and through the double doors.

I looked down at the train once more. A few passengers trickled from
the caboose. Two sensuous brown-skinned women wearing summer
dresses, one with a flower tucked behind her ear, smiled as they emerged.
They sauntered the length of the platform, as if they were walking along a
breezy shore with not a care in the world. Like their predecessors, they
climbed the stairs, passed under the arch and through the doors.

Nick and I glanced at each other, then nodded in silent agreement. We
followed the travelers' route to the double doors. Nick pushed and shook
them, then knocked loud and long. The man with orange hair, the wise old
matriarch and the two contented women were locked-in with whatever
secrets they held.

I looked back at the clock.

* * *

My dream changed to reality. The massive hands had shrunk to fit my
travel alarm. I awoke with a start.

"Nick, it's time to get up."

A familiar arm slid around my waist, slipping into a spoon-style hug.
"What's the hurry, Michelle? It's the last day of our vacation."

137

"We can relax when we get home. Today is Monet Day! There are museums to visit, and lunch at the Eiffel, then…"

"Okay, I know—you're right."

I jumped in the shower while Nick shaved. In typical charming old-hotel fashion, steam fogged up the mirror.

"I can't see what I'm doing," Nick said, cracking open the door.

"Be careful, Nick. I don't want to set off the alarms."

The fresh air entering the bathroom swirled the steam, briefly reminding me of the night's dream. *Who were those people on the train?* The ring of the room phone interrupted my memories. Nick answered and reported we'd gotten lucky. On Thursday night, the Musée d'Orsay stayed open late and their historic restaurant served an after-hours dinner to a select few. By a stroke of luck, the concierge had procured tickets for us when another couple cancelled. My dream and the fascinating people behind the doors were temporarily forgotten.

* * *

During the morning hours, we admired the works of Monet at the Musée Marmottan, including *Impression, Sunrise* from which the impressionist movement took its name. The excitement of lunch at Restaurant 58 in the Eiffel was followed by the peace of Monet's *Water Lilies* in the oval hall of L'Orangerie.

Early evening, we strolled across the Seine footbridge, Passerelle, toward our last event of the day. Thousands of padlocks, referred to as love-locks by the vendor, hung on the side of the bridge. Nick and I couldn't resist. We scratched our names on the surface of a much-too-expensive lock, attached it to the bridge, and threw the key into the Seine. Following a romantic whirlwind five days, it felt right to proclaim our love, publicly and privately, on our last evening in the City of Love.

We walked toward the Musée d'Orsay, hand in hand, happy to be alive. Once inside the grand hall, we picked up a guide map and hurried to the fifth floor to complete our Monet quest before dinner. I was mesmerized by the artist's impression of an ethereal woman holding her parasol, her scarf waving in the breeze. Monet's renderings of boats and bridges, haystacks and train stations took me to another time and place.

The rest of the museum would have to wait until after our meal. We rode the elevator down to the third floor and entered the restaurant promptly at seven. The brilliant chandeliers and gilded ceilings transported me to 1900 when the restaurant opened as part of the original hotel and train station. I imagined we were aristocrats in a forgotten old world, having dinner on the banks of the Seine.

Diners trickled in fashionably late until patrons filled every seat in the large restaurant. The interesting first course, a foie gras terrine, arrived at eight. The second course, baked cod flavored with cocoa, arrived forty-five minutes later. The French natives didn't seem concerned about the time, although the few tourists in the restaurant were surreptitiously looking around, as were we. It's not that Nick and I didn't have much to talk about—we simply weren't accustomed to relaxing into the slow pace of a quintessential French restaurant.

The waiter passed us time and again with trays of banana crème brulee. Studying the layout of the room, we realized our table may be served dessert last. Many diners finished eating and headed off into the night. Only several large groups, perhaps forty people total, stayed for after-dinner drinks.

"I'm worried we're not going to see the Van Gogh," I said.

"Which of his works did you want to see?"

"A self-portrait, one of forty-three he produced by studying himself in a mirror."

"What makes this particular one special?"

"His eyes. When I drew *your* portrait for my art class, I found the eyes most difficult. An artist needs to portray more than physical appearance. Van Gogh revealed his tormented soul through his eyes."

While waiting for our last course, we planned our route to the self-portrait, plus several other famous works. Once served, we inhaled the dessert, but skipped the cognac. A few minutes before ten, we exited the glittery dining room to reenter the museum, intent on finding Van Gogh.

We walked in the only direction possible, following a short hall enclosed by glass protective railings which looked out into the atrium. Both above and below us, the five levels of the great hall stood completely in the dark. Following the path of floor lights, we descended the circular marble staircase to the landing one level down. All of the hallways on floor two were closed and secured.

I grabbed Nick's hand. "Is this the right way?"

"We couldn't go any other way. C'mon, I'm sure we can get out on the entry level."

The further we descended, the darker it became. The side galleries were pitch black. The minimal floor lights on the circular staircase and random dimly lit areas cast everything in dark eerie shadows. Nick and I felt the need to move quickly.

"I'm scared," I whispered to Nick.

"This *is* rather strange." When we reached the first floor, a small rectangular area enclosed by walls of translucent frosted glass surrounded us on three sides. Residual light from the stairs behind us revealed a pair of closed double doors flanking us on each wall of the room. Like the walls, the doors were also made of frosted glass. Each featured a small square clear glass block, reminding me of a larger version of a peephole. A four inch thick metal bar barricaded each door.

A slow controlled feeling of panic began to take over my body. As my anxiety grew, my shoulders slumped, head lowered and hands started to sweat. We were locked in a glass room of a dark museum, after-hours, in a foreign country.

"We're not supposed to be here," I whispered.

Nick began to push, shake, and bang on each set of doors. "One of these doors must open. If not, we'll make our way back upstairs to try and find help."

"Be careful, Nick. I don't want to set off the alarms."

Uttering those words transported me into an impressionist painting of steam and dreams. Staying close to Nick, I pressed my face against one window. I could see nothing recognizable, but I thought I heard a noise.

"Did you hear that?" I said to Nick.

"Hear what?"

"A high pitched sound, like the wind rushing through a tunnel," I said.

"I didn't hear anything. Your imagination is playing tricks on you, Michelle."

"Stop banging on the doors for a minute."

I reached out for Nick's hand. In the City of Light, we stood still in the dark.

"I hear it now, like a whistle," Nick said.

We looked into the room, completely distorted by the glass block, but saw nothing that explained the sound. Beyond the shadows on the far wall, in the dimmest light imaginable, my eyes were drawn to a fiery orange shade. The color matched the man's beard from my dream. Gradually, all of his facial features came into focus. I had found the self-portrait of Van Gogh. His eyes stared at me with understanding, revealing that his soul knew how it felt to be locked in.

I looked to his right. I saw the old woman in a white bonnet, sitting in a rocker, grasping a handkerchief in her lap. I looked toward his left. The two exotic women sat on the beach, whiling away time as if it held no meaning.

The muted sound again diverted my attention. *The train? The screeching brakes?*

Nick quickly pulled his hand away from mine, and frantically began banging on the set of double doors. "I saw someone," he said.

I spotted her, too. A museum worker, a docent it seemed, reached into her shoulder bag and pulled out a fashionable scarf. She began wrapping the length of color around her neck as if she were preparing to leave.

We banged and yelled. She jerked her head in our direction, then squinted at us through the glass block. Our faces were squeezed together looking at her. She appeared to speak, but her voice did not penetrate the armored glass.

As if exasperated, she pulled the scarf off her neck and stuffed it into her bag. She glanced at us, shook her head, and disappeared out of sight. A few long minutes passed. I spent the time staring at Van Gogh's *Self-Portrait*, *Whistler's Mother*, and Gauguin's *Tahitian Women on the Beach*. They were forever frozen in time, but I remembered each of the subjects arriving in the Musée d'Orsay railway station and climbing the staircase. The people in the paintings felt alive to me.

The docent reappeared with three male security guards in tow and pointed to us peering through the door. With perturbed voices, the men chattered on walkie-talkies. The annoyed woman wrapped her scarf round her neck and left without waiting for our release.

The guards turned off the alarms, raised the metal heavy bar, and retracted the electric pegs on the top and bottom of the door. They spoke to us in French. We understood only the stray word "restaurant" and shrugged our shoulders in response. The men finally led us out a special narrow hallway and through a maze of security doors to a small staff exit. Without any good wishes or even *au revoir*, they opened the door to the night.

Disoriented from the adventure, and seeing tall buildings where I thought the Seine should be, I could not find my bearings. We'd been let out of the back of the museum. Nick's good sense of direction took over. He led me around the building, eventually pointing towards the Seine river bridge leading to the metro line and our hotel. We seemed to catch our breath. Walking on the path toward the bridge, we both began talking at once, then burst out in laughter.

"Can you believe what just happened?" Nick asked.

"Not really. Did you see that docent's face when she saw us through the door?"

"First shock. Then disgust," Nick said.

"I wasn't sure if she went to get help, or if she'd left us stranded."

"And those guards ... they weren't happy either."

"They seemed to blame the restaurant," I said.

"I'm glad they didn't blame us. They probably wondered if we were innocent looking thieves. We don't even have official identification. Our hotel has our passports."

"Picture the headlines. *Ventura Couple Accused of Attempted Art Heist*," I joked.

Numerous groups of people sat on the bridge enjoying the balmy night. Revelers passed underneath on festive boats strung with strands of bright bulbs. Spotlights beamed from passing barges, illuminating famous buildings along the shore. We stopped midway on the bridge, looking back at the Musée d'Orsay shining brightly in the night.

The lights of the city and stars in the sky reflected on the river below. In addition to seeing the self-portrait, I'd hoped to see Van Gogh's *Starry Nights* in the museum. Although I'd missed the painting, the real scene spread out before me. I felt free—invigorated and uplifted.

Our adrenalin kicked in and we joked our way to the nearest metro stop. The station doors were closed and locked for the night, which made us giddy with laughter. While searching for an open station, we admired the city, alive with street music and artists.

Hand in hand, we rambled through groups of picnickers and lovers drinking wine in the Tuileries garden and the Louvre Museum plaza. Couples in street cafes sat sipping steaming cups of after dinner espresso, watching us meander past. We'd set out that morning to find the great art in the lovely city of Paris.

At the end of the day, we became part of the enchanting canvas.

~~*

About the Author. Constance Mukherjee is grateful to have found her true passion, writing, after an enjoyable thirty-five year career as a Speech-Language Pathologist. "Connie" enjoys writing a variety of genres including novels, short stories, and poetry. In addition, she is exploring the world of screenplays. The anthology short story, "Tourist Trap", is derived from the vacation adventures of a good friend. Connie is also the author of a work of fiction, *Nanibala's Belief*, which was published in May of 2015 to a flurry of high praise. Connie is also the mother of an adult son, Misha, and resides in Ventura County with her husband, Ajit, and family dog, Madison.

A distant rumbling
reveals
the cerulean separated
cut through by
the tiny silver shape
slipping through clouds above.

Its voice at odds with
the weightless flight
that seems
more float than engine
more flower flowing
down a silent blue current
than propellers and oil and gleaming steel.

Alone among the wisps of white above
its flight now free
from the noise
that falls
landward.

~~*

About the Author: Diana Caskey believes that the act of creating is vital to her sanity and wellbeing. She has written and painted since childhood. Poetry has always been a way to process what was going on in her life. She majored in Art in college, but went on to a career in social work for the County of Ventura. She is retired and, in addition to writing and painting, enjoys gardening and volunteer work. She is married, with two children and five grandchildren.

The Magic Act by Antonia Burgato

Entertainment was scarce in Marano Lagunare, but there was plenty of imagination for creating one's own. The evening passeggiata, walking arm in arm with your special one, up and down the cobblestone main street, was a revered pastime. The weekly visits from market merchants, with their display of goods, provided diversion from an otherwise soporific town. Boys honed their sling shot skills shooting at feral cats and played soccer in the muddy poppy field on the far side of the canal. Girls re-enacted stories from fairy tales narrated to them by their mothers or pretended to be the love-sick heroine of the screen. Yes, there was a screen in this fishing town.

Every Sunday evening an open lot was converted into an outdoor movie theatre where theatre goers sat on a chair in the sultry lagoon air not far from Venice. Children were not allowed if there was any kissing, but *Dracula* was admissible to everyone and *The Bicycle Thief* was a repeated favorite. Movies became a spirited activity for days to come. The Maranesi talked of the story for days, tearing it apart or praising it as if it were a live drama unfolding before their eyes. So widespread was the prattle that it replaced the local gossip for a week.

It was no surprise that the visit from a magician at the school during my second grade, left me spellbound for the rest of the year. A rope cut in to many pieces in the magician's hand became whole again; a scarf changed colors in front of my eyes, and six white doves flew out of a hat. It was a performance which defied everything I knew about nature and it made me question: How can broken things be made whole again? How can ribbons change colors? How can six doves fit in a hat? What other secrets loom outside this medieval burg?

My mother, who had never seen a magic show, had no answer.

She asked around town about the magician's performance. "It's all tricks. The devil has a hand in it."

The magician was invited to perform again the following year. There was not a chance of my dawdling home for lunch the afternoon on the day of his visit.

This year the school charged five lire for the performance. I rushed home to get the money—the price of a licorice stick, which I liked but seldom had. My father would have given me the coin without a thought, but I rushed home knowing well that my mother, frugal as she was, wouldn't deny me this thrill.

"I don't have five lire," she said.

"I want to see the magician," I pleaded.

"Go back to school."

"He was here last year, and I never saw anything like that before. I must see his magic."

"Tricks. That's what he does. Go back to school."

"I'll be the only one without the five lire. I can't go back." Rivers of tears gushed down my cheeks. I thought of the humiliation that awaited me as the only student denied admission to the show because my mother wouldn't part with five lire. "If you won't give me the money, then I'm staying home."

"You're going back to school."

"What am I going to tell my friends and the teacher? That you're too mean to give me five lire?"

"I don't care what you tell them."

"I can't go back to school." I washed away with my tongue the snots that joined the salty tears above my lip.

"You will go back to school if I have to drag you there."

The words stabbed me at the heart. I straightened my back and puffed my chest, ready to do battle. I looked her straight in the eyes and said, "No."

"What did I do to deserve a daughter like you?"

I heard her vent this question to the air many times before, and each time I heard it, my inner core became a little harder, a little colder. "You can do anything you want to me. I'm not going back."

She took the little bristle broom she gave me as a present on my seventh birthday and began to hit me with it, sweeping me out of the house.

More than kill me, she can't hurt me, I said as a mantra to give me strength to stand up to her. I repeated this in my head over and over again to block out her fury, until she successfully managed to sweep me out into the street in full view of onlookers.

"I can't go back. I'll be the only one left out of the show."

The whisk of the broom swept me forward; the onlookers on the street asked, "Natalia, what has she done?"

"Stubborn. Disobedient. She has to have her way." I heard her public tirade of my short fallings and felt the eyes of the townsfolk on me. "Pigheaded. Disobedient. Selfish. Gotta have her way. I'll teach you," she continued and whisked me at my feet.

I couldn't hold back tears and snots. My cries were loud. People on the street stopped their activities to look at me. I could feel their stares, judging me, pitying me for receiving my just punishment, pitying my mother for having such a recalcitrant child. She swept me all the way back to school with the broom at my heels, as though she were chasing a rat from the house.

I wished that I could have disappeared with the wave of a magic wand or metamorphosed into a malaria-bearing mosquito and bite her. Life was peachy when she came down with malaria last summer. Instead I found myself in front of the school, where my mother gave me a final whisk of the broom and ordered me not to come home until school was over. I used my sleeve to dry my face, but the tears kept coming. The teacher took pity on me and gave me the five lire.

I stopped crying then.

I entered listless into the classroom where the magician did his act. When the show ended, I felt nothing—nothing captivating and nothing disappointing. I walked home from school with a hollow feeling, drained of emotions. I was broken.

I faced my mother that evening with a heavy silence.

My father asked me, "What's wrong?"

I didn't reply. I was busy building an emotional wall through which neither pain nor humiliation could penetrate ever again. By evening's end, I had built such a wall that no bombardment of words or beatings could break me again. That day was the last time I, the child, cried.

Alas, barriers cannot discriminate what to let in and what to block out. I was successful in keeping out pain, but as an unintended consequence, no joy entered my life. My inability to cry stifled my ability to laugh. I could neither laugh nor cry, neither love nor hate. Beauty, too, had its limit. The beaches of nearby Lignano Sabbiadoro, with their white stretches of sand, shaded by pine woods at one end and disappearing into an emerald sea at the other, made little difference to me, who could swim in the muddy lagoon of Marano Lagunare with almost equal apathy as in the crystalline waters of Lignano.

I was a good wall builder. Reprimands and compliments bounced off my fortress like ricocheting bullets. A rejection from the high school cheer leaders because I wouldn't smile? Big deal. A praise for a pretty dress made with my own hands? Big deal. There was nary a tear nor a smile on my face, and I had become an unlovable child at a time when I most wanted to be loved. Until I began dating on my eighteenth birthday.

I was excited about my first boyfriend. And my second. And my third. There were so many one-night boyfriends, and so few that stayed a little longer. I could feel them trying to get through to me, trying to open me up, but the little person I had trapped inside was petrified and offered no help. I wanted to cry, but tears wouldn't come. I realized then that the wall inside me didn't separate me just from other people but also from myself. I had to work on getting that little person out of her jail.

My mother came to visit me years later. I was well into my third marriage; this time to a man who's been constructive in helping me tear down my wall. I told her about this childhood incident. It was the first time that I had ever spoken of it. She said, "Oh, you remember it. You were such a stubborn child."

~~*

 *About the Author.* Antoinette Zanon, a.k.a. Antonia Burgato said: Think being a teenager is tough? Try being a first generation immigrant who becomes a teenager in America and your parents are old country and old school. Think about the generation gap, cultural gap, and inadequate language proficiency to express yourself. Antoinette had to learn English fast, and when she did, she couldn't put that language down. She went for a bachelor degree in English, some graduate work in Comparative Literature, then a teaching credential so she could teach English language arts, and finally get her Masters. She loves the old classics and never tires of rereading them. Right now, she's on a mission to discover the new classics. She places Susan Minot on that pedestal. Love of writing followed her love of reading. She's written many biographical sketches for artists, feature stories, essays, short stories and even received a coveted award for a poem. Currently, she's writing a biographical novel. As varied as this may sound, all her writings originate from a moment in her life—a person that moved her, a site that awed her, a feeling that rocked her. We all have these moments; they are the fabric of our creativity.

"Do you remember those days?
Back porch, sunshine, mason jars" – she paused at
remembered sweetness –
"we were so foolish then...thinking there was a big ol' world out
there to conquer."
~ Melissa Marr, *Graveminder*

I'm in this murky pool hall in Kailua, Kona, sweating like the main course at a luau. I'm sweating because I'm in the middle of a best-out-of-seven match for the Kincaid Pool Cup and losing big-time—three games to none. My opponent is my older brother, Jack, who turned fifty years old today. I flew over from the mainland yesterday to help him celebrate.

We have this pool tournament every time he and I get together. I won the last time we hooked up, which was in Ventura about five years ago. Whoever holds the cup always brings it along whenever we plan to meet, and right now it's sitting over there on a ledge next to the pool cues. The trophy looks like gold, but it's really only a cheap plastic thing. It has a brass

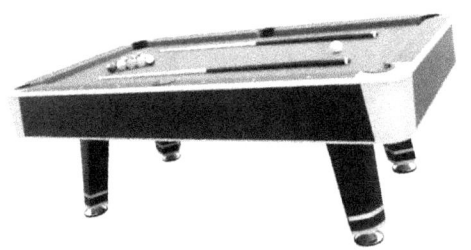

plaque on it though that reads "THE KINCAID POOL CUP." And underneath that, in smaller letters, it says: "Current Champion." It ain't much, but we both covet it just the same.

Coming into the pool hall this afternoon, I figured he'd be a

pushover, because Jack's been drinking beer all day. But his hands are steady and his eyes are icy with concentration. My heart's pounding and I'm feeling a little weak in the knees because I'm in real danger of being swept here.

Even though I'm half in shock, I have enough sense left to realize I've got to stop giving him such a tight rack. So this time I rack 'em real loose so the balls won't go anywhere when he breaks. That's what you do when someone's shooting like he is. I'm determined not to let this guy sweep me, even if he is my brother and just turned fifty. I didn't come all the way over here to give him the Cup as a birthday present. And besides, if he sweeps me I'll never hear the end of it.

I haven't given up hope because the one thing I've got going for me, the thing I've always had going for me, is luck. Even when life knocked me down I'd look up and there'd be Lady Luck standing there with her hand out to help me up. But you could never say the same thing for my brother Jack. If it weren't for bad luck, he'd have no luck at all.

So I stand back and watch him sock the cue ball into the rack and only three or four balls skitter out and roll weakly towards the railings. The rest of the balls just sit there clustered loosely in the middle.

"Nice rack," says Jack, sarcastically.

"Sorry," I say, innocently.

Now we both know we'll have to select our shots carefully. We'll have to hunt and peck and look for openings and play defensively. No more of this slamming balls into the pockets left and right like he's been doing. Now it's a tactical game, a game that will be decided by strategy, and of course, luck.

My brother lives over here on the Big Island. He came here about ten years ago, and it was the best thing he ever did. He must have left most of his bad luck behind, because ever since he came here things have been going well for him. Back on the mainland he was about to go under.

All my brother's bad luck began when we were teenagers back in Ventura. He got his first car when he was sixteen. It was an old beat up '48 Dodge coup. He spent a long time tinkering with the engine, transmission and brakes; then he slapped on some new retreads and a $50 Earl Scheib paint-job. It turned out primo. That winter he decided to show off his new machine and take a few of his buddies (and me) up into the mountains above Ojai to goof around in the snow. This turned out to be a very bad idea.

Once we got up there, we stopped by the roadside and filled up a cardboard box with a bunch of snowballs and went barreling up the mountainside pelting road signs as we went. Pretty soon we started bombarding families building snowmen alongside the road, and then we started in on passing cars. We blasted one old guy's windshield, but then watched in alarm as he slammed on the brakes, turned his car around and started chasing after us. So Jack zoomed up the mountainside bent on escape. He rounded a hairpin turn, spun out on a patch of ice, and slid sideways into a berm alongside the road. The car rolled over, like in slow motion, balancing momentarily on two wheels. I looked out the side window and saw we were hanging over a five hundred foot precipice. Oh, no!

The guy sitting shotgun opened the door as we went over and my brother and his two buddies fell out into the snow as the car rolled over them. But since they were in the doorway they didn't get crushed. The car started rolling down the slope sideways with me and another guy in the back seat. The car went airborne a couple of times, spinning like a high-speed lathe. One of those times it landed on the roof and the windows popped out. My seat-mate was catapulted out of the back window and into a tree where he got hung up in the branches. Unable to get out, I rode the tumbling car all the way to the bottom where it came to rest upside down. The roof was flattened down level with the body, both doors ripped off; the hood was gone, as was the trunk door and the front seat.

Everyone was all beat up, but no one was killed or seriously injured, and no one even got any stitches. The one who got hurt the most was my brother, of course. He broke his collar bone when the front seat of the car came flying out of the air and landed on his shoulder. So, my brother lost his car, not to mention nearly killed us all. Bad luck, you might say. I figure the only reason we lived through it was because I brought along my good luck.

Meanwhile, back in Kona, I hunt and peck and scratch and claw, and somehow luck my way to a win at that loose-racked game. My brother is stunned. He was on the verge of a great victory. Inconsolable, he turns and reaches instinctively for his beer. But there is no beer. Why? Because this place doesn't serve beer. It's a family billiards joint. It was the only place we could find to play. What a break for me. Now the game score is 3-1. Having escaped a sweep, I'm feeling more confident now. Jack racks 'em up and I blast off into game five.

My brother's bad luck continued. He knocked up his girlfriend when he was nineteen years old. She was seventeen. Being a sincere, thoughtful boy (and not wanting to go to jail), he did what he thought was right. He married her. This was another idea that didn't work out like he planned.

To support his wife and child Jack got a job working for the state of California on a highway survey crew. He also started attending classes at Ventura College three nights a week so as to better himself. On the nights he wasn't at school he washed dishes in a local restaurant to help make ends meet. Not surprisingly, his young wife got bored sitting around the house all the time, and took to cruising Main Street in his '56 Chevy. She met some cute guy and started playing around.

One night, the owner of the restaurant where Jack worked had a heart attack and was taken to the hospital. The restaurant closed and Jack got home early that night. He walked in and found some stranger sitting on his couch with his feet on Jack's coffee table, a can of Jack's beer in his hand, and an arm around Jack's wife. My brother went ballistic, dragged the guy outside and began beating on him. Jack's wife called the cops and when they pulled up to the rented house, there's my brother with the guy in a headlock, running him into a telephone pole. The cops arrested my brother for assault and handcuffed him. As they drove him off to the station, Jack looked out the rear window and saw his wife with her arm around the guy, helping him back into the house.

Several months later he found out his wife was pregnant again. When the kid was born it looked like the guy with the big bump on top of his head. My brother got divorced and ended up paying alimony and child support for two kids.

Because I'm feeling confident now, kind of hitting my stride, I win game five going away. Game score is now 3-2. My concentration is getting sharper by the minute, while Jack's seems to be slipping. Grumbling, he racks 'em up for game six.

So my brother got a Harley Davidson and joined a motorcycle club called Los Borrachos (The Drunkards). He figured he'd start having all the wild fun he'd missed when he was married. About this time he met a foxy Oriental lady in a bar and asked her out. Before long she was pregnant. So my brother wound up marrying her and they lived together until she got sick and tired of him being drunk all the time and riding his motorcycle all over the county bar-hopping with his buddies. She divorced him, and so then he was paying alimony to two wives and child support for three kids.

I win game six easily. I'm sharp. I can't miss. Game score tied at three all. One game to go to decide the championship. One game to decide who goes home with the vaunted Kincaid Pool Cup. My brother is the one sweating now, and after each missed shot he turns around looking for his beer. "Damn this place," he hisses. "What kind of pool hall is this anyway?"

So my brother was going downhill fast on the mainland. He quit school and his dishwashing job. He wrecked his bike on a weekend ride and got arrested for drunk driving. He lost his job with the state. When he got out of jail he met an ugly bar troll. But looking through a haze of alcohol and cheap pot he was convinced she looked like Cleopatra. He asked her to marry him, and she, seeing nothing but dollar signs, agreed. But it didn't take her long to realize that her meal ticket was all punched out because of Jack having to pay so much alimony and child support. So she asked for an annulment. She was willing to settle for a one-time pay-off of a thousand bucks. It was all he could scrounge up, but it was worth it. He was now broke and unemployed.

He eventually found a job humping lumber for some house-framing contractors. After he proved himself to be a hard worker they began teaching him some carpentry. After a year or so he thought he was getting pretty damn good at it. That is, until the day he inadvertently cut off the ends of three of his fingers with a circular saw. Oh, brother. So then he was maimed, unemployed, and on the dole until his hand healed.

While he waited he spent most of his time in bars. He got into fights—one-handed, one-sided fights. One sadistic bully took particular delight in beating him up every time they met. My brother finally got fed up and bought a handgun. One night the bully ran into him in the parking lot of some honky-tonk, but before he could beat my brother up again, Jack ducked into his car and pulled out the gun. He didn't shoot the guy, but started firing angry shots into the ground and into the air while yelling at the guy how he was sick of all this s#*@. The cops came, of course, and arrested brother Jack, again.

This was when his luck began to turn. After he got out of jail and his hand had healed, he joined the carpenters' union and started finding work.

151

By some miracle, he met a fine, decent woman who saw something in him that nobody else did. They got married. One Christmas they came out here to Hawaii to visit her parents who were retired on the Big Island. The island life and its distance from the source of all his trouble appealed to Jack, and they decided to move out here. In the meantime, his first two wives remarried, and so he was off the hook for alimony and child support.

It took him awhile, but he eventually got a full-time job (with benefits) with the Big Island County Parks Department doing construction and repair work in beach parks around the island. Before long he was able to buy a house way out on the rugged Puna Coast, far from all the bad memories and the people who had tortured his soul for all those years. And he was truly happy for the first time in his adult life.

Blam! I sink the eight ball and win game seven, thereby accomplishing one of the greatest comebacks of all time!

Maybe I should have let Jack win, seeing how it's his fiftieth birthday and all. If this had been the game of life I would have. But it ain't. This is pool, man.

~~*

 *About the Author:* Terry Tallent grew up in Ojai and Ventura. He took up surfing when he was fourteen and later wrote numerous stories about surfing during the early sixties. After graduating from Ventura High School and Ventura Junior College, Terry transferred to Chico State where he earned both a Bachelor and Master's degree in English. He joined the Peace Corps after college and went to Western Samoa in the South Pacific. Teaching experience, adventure and romance blossomed there, including the meeting of his future wife. After returning to California, Terry taught at Hartnell College in Salinas offering courses in literature, composition, and a seminar on John Steinbeck. This seminar led to him becoming a Steinbeck scholar and being selected as a featured speaker during the statewide Steinbeck Centennial in 2002. After Terry left teaching, he worked at various thought-provoking jobs around the country. He published his first book, *Making The Reata* in 2012. A second book, a collection of short stories, is due out in 2015. Extensive travel and living in various parts of the country, twice overseas, has provided Terry with many tales to draw on in his writing. Currently, Terry lives in his old home town of Ojai where he is a semi-retired part-time librarian, owns a small business with his wife, and plays senior league softball for the Ventura Classics.

In the 1960's, I lived in San Francisco. In those days, some of us were looking for cool transportation—a brightly colored motorcycle with a slick-chick on the back seat. Before I dropped out of college at the end of the second year, I was dating a girl with beautiful brown eyes and black hair who wore it in a long ponytail. When guys saw her, they took a second look. Beth didn't like bikes. She was altogether against them. "Too dangerous," she said.

I bought a red and yellow motorcycle. She looked great riding on the seat behind me with her black helmet and long black ponytail all fizzed up in the breeze as we tooled down the pike. I decided to join a bike club, The Counterculture that met at the Red Pagoda Restaurant which was owned by Ping Wong and located on the south side of Chinatown. Beth was against my joining it at first, but after I joined the club, she joined too and was always beside me at the meetings. Most of the meetings were rather dull, discussions of motorcycle safety. The talk about the then existing "credibility gap" between the President and his crappy Establishment and the honest citizens was a good subject for discussion.

Beth made a few friends at the club. Judy and Dapper Dan were the two she liked best. Judy was a middle-aged woman, about forty-five, and sported a bouquet of roses tattooed on her upper left arm. She was always seen with windblown hair. I don't think she ever combed it, and always had a sad countenance on her chubby face, except when she was close to Dapper Dan. Then she beamed.

Dapper, in his twenties, had long brown hair slicked down with fragrant oil so that it reflected light, a pencil-thin mustache and neatly pressed pants, a charcoal gray shirt with a hot pink tie, he looked like he had just stepped out of a men's fashion magazine. Judy frequently held Dapper's hand at their table to give people the impression they were lovers. He didn't seem to notice her. He spent much of the time rubbernecking around the room.

I wore a short crew cut which seemed out of place at the time and I questioned the meaning of life and was open to a lively discussion of it. Beth told me the other members of the club were just not her type, whatever that meant. But she said I was her type. However, I didn't see her as my type. No matter. I still dated her and she never dated another man that I know of. She was a faithful companion and fun to be with.

As much as I was angry with the Establishment, Beth was enthusiastic about her religion. Sometimes she talked to me about Jesus stuff. Like, I didn't have to be good to be saved and go to heaven. I just had to believe that Jesus had already done everything necessary at the cross and I would just have to trust Him for it and have eternal life. So if I murdered someone, I could still be saved and go to heaven. That didn't make much sense to me at the time. Beth meant well with all her religious talk. I just patiently listened.

Like I said, most bike club meetings were pretty dull, but this night was different. First old piano, then a gunshot. They changed my life.

In the back of the room was an old piano. I heard someone plink a few keys as they walked by. Then I saw Beanpole Ben, head ducked under his table, and took a few puffs on a joint. After hearing the piano, he pinched out the glowing end and put it in his pocket. He had a tall, skinny frame and when he got up, he stumbled toward the piano, ensuring his balance with the aid of chairs in route. When he got to the piano he turned and faced the snickering crowd and slurred, "The Twelfth Street ... Twelfth ... Street ... Rag." He turned and flopped down on the stool and put his fingers to the keys. His hands chased each other up and down the keyboard at warp speed. The music ended with a resounding crash. Pounding out the ragtime tune mesmerized those present.

When Beanpole Ben stood to leave, some shouted, "More." "Play Sweet Georgia Brown." "How 'bout, Tiger Rag."

Beanpole turned and sat down again, stared at the wall for a moment, and glanced at the ceiling. His fingers gently rested on the keys. Strains of Beethoven came forth. While he played, the chatter of the audience competed with the music. Someone yelled, "Enough of the junky stuff. Boo! Boo! Boo! We want ragtime." Others echoed the sentiment. Beanpole continued to play until he had finished the piece. He stood up and faced the jeering crowd and said with an ugly face, "You all go to hell."

As he was finding his way back to his seat, Beth beckoned him to come over. "That was a magnificent rendition of Beethoven's Sonata No. 8, Ben. Beethoven himself couldn't have played it better." Beanpole stared at Beth, smiled, gently touched her shoulder, walked back to his table and sank down into his chair.

I glanced at my watch. It was 11:30. People were starting to leave. They looked like they'd had plenty to drink. The sound of motorcycles leaving The Red Pagoda faded into the night. Suddenly, the restaurant door banged open. There stood Dragon, the guy with a tattoo of a dragon encircling his neck. He glanced around the room.

"I'm looking for a guy named Phil Powell. I'm going to see his blood before I leave this place," he shouted.

Beth looked up from her glass of wine and said, "Get out of here, Phil, as fast as you can. I've heard about Dragon. He's crazy and he carries a gun." Before I could move, Dragon spotted me.

"You stole my girl, Beth," Dragon yelled, "and you're going to pay for it with your life. You're going to die, and die tonight." He came toward me, knocking over chairs as he came.

154

"What the hell are you talking about, Dragon?" I said, "I'm not afraid of you. Beth is my girl and you can't have her."

Dragon stood before me and slowly removed a Colt .45 from his waistband. Someone shouted, "Douse the lights! Duck, Phil!"

The lights went out immediately. I heard, "Bang!" Something flicked the top of my right ear. I touched it. It felt wet and sticky. I heard chairs bumping around in the darkness and excited voices. Then came a gargling sound and coughing.

The lights came back on. Dragon lay flat on his back in front of me, both his hands clutching his throat. Frothy blood came from his mouth. It spurted between his fingers. His throat had been cut. He twisted. He turned. He kicked. His gun lay beside him. With one final cough, blood shot upward and then back onto his face. Then he lay motionless in a pool of his blood.

By this time, most people in the room came to see what had happened. Someone whispered, "That guy is really dead, his throat cut from ear to ear. Who did it?"

Ping Wong scanned the room with his eyes and a twelve gauge shotgun to discourage any additional violence. Everyone froze in place. Ping yelled, "I'm calling the cops. Stay right where you are. No one leaves or touches anything." Soon sirens could be heard in the distance and coming closer. The sirens cut off as cars screeched to a stop.

The door swung open. Two cops stood there. One ran to the back door to prevent anyone from escaping. Then two detectives showed up. "All right, who got shot?" barked one of the detectives.

"I did," I said. "Look, right here on the top of my ear. See? Dragon shot me." The blood had dried. The detective was not impressed.

"The body is over here," Dapper Dan said to the detectives. They examined Dragon's body.

"Wow!" exclaimed one *dick tectivo*, "deader than a doornail, throat cut from ear to ear."

Using his ballpoint pen, one detective picked up the Colt .45 and slipped it into a plastic bag while the other dick examined the bullet hole in the wall. "I'll get our forensic man to dig out the bullet for ballistics," he said.

The front door opened again. A man walked in wearing wrinkled pants, a pajama top and bedroom slippers. "The dead man is over here,

Coroner," said one of the detectives, "It looks like the handiwork of Cutthroat Charley."

"I think you're right, done by a razor sharp blade about eight inches long, neck cut clean to the backbone. Nice guy. It's definitely Cutthroat Charley's handiwork."

One detective shouted, "The knife has to be in this room. Everyone empty his and her pockets and put the stuff on the table."

"Women, empty your purses on the table," demanded another. "The murderer's knife is here in this room and we'll find it."

After a while, the chief detective shouted, "We haven't found the murder weapon yet. It has to be here somewhere. We're not through. Now, there will be a strip search. Men, line up in front of the men's room. Two cops strip down each man. Make a thorough search of the clothes."

After about a half hour, the chief detective yelled, "We haven't found the murder weapon. It has to be here somewhere. Search this room and don't stop until you find the knife."

At 2:30 AM, after a thorough search, the chief detective shouted, "We haven't found the weapon. You may all go home now."

About three weeks later, Cutthroat Charley was captured. This psychopath boasted of his murders, except for the one at the Red Pagoda. He claimed to know nothing about it. I thought that was strange. But on the other hand, there was no real evidence he had even been there. Someone killed Dragon, but who could it have been? Someone saved my life. I couldn't get that out of my mind.

Two months later, Beth, Dapper Dan, Judy, who was holding Dapper's hand as usual, and I were sitting at our regular table at The Red Pagoda for another club meeting. We were talking about the capture of Cutthroat Charley and how he customarily murdered his victims with a razor sharp knife. Then, Judy interrupted us. "Beth, do you have a fingernail file in your purse I could borrow?"

"Sure, Judy, I'll get it for you." Beth reached deep into the pocket of her Levis. Her hand stretched down to her thigh.

"Beth, you have a hole in your pocket."

"Yes, I know. This is where I keep my fingernail file." She slowly pulled up an eight-inch long fingernail file with a few layers of duct tape for a handle.

"Be careful with it, Judy. I made it razor-sharp so I can use it in an emergency."

I heard the phase, "razor-sharp." That caused me to think—no it couldn't be her. "Come with me, Beth. Did you do it?" I asked.

She turned her head away. "Do what?"

"You know what I'm talking about. Did you kill Dragon with your fingernail file?"

156

Beth lowered her head and hesitated. In a moment she raised her head. With a smile and sparkling eyes, she said, "Yes, Phil, I did it. That's because I love you. So, that makes it all right."

~~*

About the Author. Phil Powell enjoys writing Christian stories and poems. He places much of his work in the Christian blog entitled, Potpourri Place. Before retiring he was an aerospace electrical engineer. He never had formal training in writing and is a native Californian with three daughters which are his pride and joy.

*Stairs - Ventura - * Courtesy of Wendell Ward

News of the Japanese attack on Pearl Harbor at about noon on Sunday, December 7, 1941 shocked me. I was working at my part-time job tending the YMCA locker room in Fort Worth. As a twenty-one year-old college sophomore, the attack fired up my determination to strike back and opened a new page in my geography. Hawaii, then a U.S. territory, would not become a state for another nine years.

Adolf Hitler's trampling our European friends concerned us seriously, but not enough for us to reach for our guns yet. We let Great Britain and their European allies deal with him. Suddenly the fight crashed in our back door. Our Pacific Naval fleet and our country suffered enormously in lives, ships and aircraft.

I wanted to fight for our country as a pilot, but got shot down before I sat in a cockpit. I failed the eye exam required by the Army Air Corps. When the U.S. Navy offered male college students an officer-training plan, I signed up for its V-12 program and passed the physical exam. It offered male students the opportunity to finish college as Navy cadets.

Upon graduation and completion of ninety days training at the U.S. Naval Academy, cadets would be commissioned as Ensigns. Several months later, orders came for me to report for duty on July 1, 1943, at Texas Christian University. *What a break.* I'd continue as a student right there at home, at the same university I had been attending, on the same campus I had roller skated across many times on my way to elementary school.

Classes went well through the first semester, but about two weeks into the second semester, commandant, Lt. Decker, called me into his office. He said, "Gill, I hate to tell you this, the Eighth Naval District Headquarters ordered us to dismiss two cadets to bring our unit within quota. In reviewing your file we found that you don't meet physical requirements to become a line officer. You are one-half inch too short and your eyesight is below the requirement." I thought, *here we go again with the matter of my short stature.* Lt. Decker added, "We'll give you two weeks to stretch half-an-inch and eat carrots by the bunch to improve your vision."

I failed to measure up and, deeply dismayed, I bid goodbye to my college buddies and boarded a train to boot camp at Great Lakes Naval Training Station on Lake Michigan as a second-class seaman.

Disappointment and bitterness hung over me during the several weeks of training. Eventually, making good friends and enjoying fellowship with crewmembers helped torpedo those negative feelings. The end of my story would have been quite different if I had completed the V-12 program. Little did I imagine the Lord had more extraordinary plans for me before the war ended, despite my shortness and imperfect vision.

Boot camp resembled my experience as an ROTC cadet in high school. Marching, close-order drill, military discipline, sighting-and-aiming exercises were all very familiar to me. When time came to select the type of duty I wanted to perform, I chose to be a radio operator.

The Navy sent me to radio school at Miami University in Oxford, Ohio, and taught me to receive and transmit messages in Morse code. I had learned touch-typing in high school so typing the characters I heard in the headphones came easily and developed an automatic response. What I heard transferred to my fingers on the typewriter keys.

Once trained as a radio operator, the Navy assigned me to a seaplane tender, the USS Suisun. At Houghton Shipyard on Lake Washington near Seattle, workers finished outfitting the Suisun as its crew assembled. Clad in our dress blue uniforms on the day we commissioned our ship, we became Plank Owners and I celebrated my twenty-third birthday.

In effect, the Suisun and I shared the same birth date.

We embarked, cruised out of Lake Washington through the Chittenden Canal into Puget Sound and the Pacific Ocean. We cruised down the coast to San Diego to conduct the ship's shakedown cruise. The crew tried out all the ship's systems and equipment much as you would do with your new car.

On December 7, 1944, exactly three years after the Pearl Harbor attack, we departed from San Diego to help win the war in the Pacific. After less than a week at sea we encountered a storm that tested our sea legs, and the stomach of a signalman named Burnam who bunked across the aisle from me. That poor guy suffered every time we hoisted anchor no matter how calm the sea.

Fortunately for us, reclaiming of most of the Pacific had been accomplished by a lot of brave guys who gave their utmost. A few of my shipmates who fought the Battle of Midway and earlier engagements could attest to that. Most of the destroyed Japanese Navy housed sea-life on the Pacific Ocean floor by the time the Navy deployed the Suisun.

The Japanese, in a desperate attempt to thwart our gaining complete control of the Pacific, began hitting our Navy with Kamikaze aircraft and mini-submarine attacks. Earlier in the war, the Ulithi group of islands served as a major Japanese naval base. After the U.S. Navy routed the Japanese from the area, Ulithi became our Navy's Third Fleet Anchorage, and its islands provided rest and refreshment for sailors who had come from further west in the Pacific.

Fleet Commander, Admiral Chester Nimitz created there what he called his "secret weapon". He arranged to install floating repair facilities in those protected waters approximately 6,500 miles closer to the Pacific war action. It enabled repair crews to return our damaged naval vessels to action in less time compared to repairing them on the U.S. Pacific Coast. The islands also provided rest and refreshment for sailors who had come from action further west in the Pacific.

At dusk on March 11, 1945, feeling safe from attack, crews of ships in the anchorage, including the Suisun, were permitted to sit topside to watch movies. About ten minutes after our movie began, a violent explosion shocked us. Less than a mile from our ship, one of two Japanese Frances aircrafts had crashed into the starboard side below the flight deck of the aircraft carrier USS Randolph. The Kamikaze killed twenty-five sailors and wounded one hundred and five more.

Years later, I learned that the second pilot mistook a lighted baseball diamond on a nearby island for an aircraft carrier and dived harmlessly into it. The pilots had dropped chad—particles of aluminum foil—to obscure their appearing on radar and sneaked into the area undetected.

The two Japanese planes were all that remained of a much larger attack force. This squadron of twenty-four bombers had begun training a year earlier to attack all of the aircraft carriers in the Ulithi anchorage. Weather, accidents, navigation errors and engine failures over the several months of training severely weakened the attack force according to a Japanese report.

The Suisun was designed to serve as a floating gasoline station to refuel Navy seaplanes used to bomb Japanese maritime shipping and photograph results of bombing missions of other U.S. aircraft. Our ship established a seaplane base in the calm waters of a Palau lagoon formed by an atoll near Babeldaob Island. From there our squadron supported the Lingayan Gulf landing of U.S. troops to reclaim the Philippine Islands. Because enemy troops left behind in the Japanese retreat prevented safe access to the nearest island for recreation, our captain ordered the ship's carpenter to build a raft to be floated on empty oil drums.

When it was completed, boatswains anchored the raft about a mile from our ship. Groups of four off-duty crewmembers were taxied in a whaleboat to the raft for a swim. As my group pulled up to the raft the coxswain said, "Strip off your shoes, dungarees and skivvies and leave them in the whaleboat." Along with a case of beer, he gave us a mop to remove seagull droppings from the canvas covered deck and said as he left, "I'll return in a couple of hours to pick you up."

After my first beer, I suggested, "Hey guys, let's have a clay pigeon shoot. Save your first empty bottle and when you finish the second one, toss one in the air and throw the other one at it." We gave no thought to the danger of being showered with shattered glass. Fortunately, by the time we emptied a few bottles and began "shooting", the only thing that might have been shattered was the ego of any aspiring baseball pitcher among us.

A few weeks later, our mission in Palau completed, we cruised northward to Kerama Retto, in the Ryukyu Islands, to set up a seaplane base several miles off the southwest coast of Okinawa. One day I volunteered to serve on the garbage detail. I don't know how ship's garbage is disposed of in these days of more serious environmental concerns. We dumped garbage from our ship in the ocean outside the anchorage.

The Ensign, perhaps a former Navy V-12 cadet, who skippered the small landing craft used as a garbage scow, brought a surfboard to tow behind his boat. Those who chose to took turns at surf boarding behind the boat after we were out of sight of the other ships in the anchorage. At top speed, probably about fifteen knots, the boat managed to lift the surfboard to support the rider in its wake for a few extraordinary moments of recreation before shoveling the garbage into the ocean from the craft's lowered tailgate.

Off duty late one afternoon, I relaxed at the starboard rail to view a peaceful scene of the sunset behind the island west of us. Suddenly, a Kamikaze, undetected by radar, flew low over the island west of us. He used the sun's glare behind him to elude detection. Pilots from the "Land of the Rising Sun" used the setting sun to their advantage. I spotted that one just before it slammed into the large red cross painted on the hospital ship USS Pinkney near us. *So much for the Geneva Convention.*

Another attack occurred in Kerama Retto at about 0945 hours one morning. A bogie—enemy aircraft—apparently escaped the anti-aircraft fire of our Navy's picket ships outside the anchorage. Our general quarters alarm clanged and the boatswain ordered, "All hands, man your battle stations." I climbed to my position as communications man at a 20mm gun tub on the flying bridge, the uppermost deck of the ship. In a few moments, I spotted a Japanese Tony. At a low altitude he flew directly toward us from the east. This pilot also used the sun's glare behind him to his advantage.

I yelled, "He's coming right at us! He's coming right at us!" As the plane bore down on us, I prayed, "Please save us, Lord!"

Our gunnery officer stood a few feet from me, looking the other direction. He heard my alert, turned to see the attacker and gave orders to open fire. Our five-inch gun crew fired one shell. A puff of black smoke appeared near the plane's left wing. The shell's proximity fuse exploded the shell close to the plane and probably peppered it with shrapnel. The pilot immediately banked leftward and crashed into the USS St. George, a larger seaplane tender anchored close to us.

As it says in Psalms 34:4, *"I sought the Lord and he answered me; he delivered me from all my fears."* Thank God, the 500-pound bomb aboard his plane

161

failed to detonate. Three heroes on the St. George gave their lives for our country. The crash destroyed a crane that the St. George used to hoist seaplanes aboard for service and repairs, and disabled its ability to perform its job.

God saved us. Had that Kamikaze crashed into our ship, the explosion and fire would have surely ignited the 80,000 gallons of aviation gasoline stored in our ship's hull. How ironic. The less-than-perfect eyes of the guy who was too short to become a line officer, were good enough to help save about three hundred of us aboard the Suisun from mass cremation.

After our troops secured Okinawa, our ship relocated to refuel seaplanes in Buckner Bay, Okinawa. There, on August 15, 1945, we learned that after the second atomic bomb leveled Nagasaki, Japanese, Emperor Hirohito, "got the message" and agreed to surrender.

A few days later in the Suisun's radio shack, Radio Operator Wayne Sholly copying encrypted fox messages—weather and other information for all ships at sea—motioned to Chief Radio Operator Sobke who stood nearby. In the message heading, Sholly recognized the call letters of our ship. The Chief stood close enough to hear the Morse code message beeping over the headphones. He listened intently and watched to correct any error Sholly might have made. Sholly confidently continued to type what he heard and tilted his chair on its back legs as the Chief moved closer. When Sholly leaned forward, the chair's front leg pinned the toe of the Chief's shoe against the deck. Rather than risk causing Sholly to type an error, the Chief didn't move. Two others of us in the radio shack watched the Chief's dilemma and bit our lips to keep from laughing. Sobke, usually a man of few words, said nothing even after the end of the message.

The message, when deciphered, ordered the Suisun to join nine other ships in Sagami Wan on the south coast of Japan's Kyushu Island and proceed into Tokyo Bay. Only a week had passed since the second B-29 atomic bomber released its bomb on Nagasaki as if to say, "We really mean it, SURRENDER!"

The next morning at 0400 hours the first light of day spanned the horizon. Our general alarm clanged and the boatswain's mate piped, "All hands, man your battle stations."

Shortly afterwards, Captain Vaughn announced, "This is the captain speaking. In compliance with orders of U.S Armed Forces, the white lattice markers along the banks of the channel will show locations of heavy-gun emplacements."

Seven other ships followed us. Each one had been selected for special material or services it would provide. The task unit formed a complete infrastructure to support the surrender event. From my battle station on the flying bridge, I had almost 360 degrees of unobstructed view of our surroundings.

The Japanese heavy-gun markers appeared to be no more than a hundred yards apart among the dense underbrush and trees we saw on the way up the channel. It gave me an uneasy feeling. We had no assurance the Japanese would honor the ceasefire. At about 1800, hours we welcomed the recall from general quarters. After the stressful fourteen-hour cruise into Tokyo Bay, I began to relax.

So after that our crew refueled the seaplanes that taxied VIPs to and from the battleship USS Missouri. The Missouri, on which the peace document would be signed, was anchored about a mile from the Suisun. We were blessed with ringside side seats at this most extraordinary event.

At about 0900 hours, September 2 1945, Captain Vaughn announced the beginning of the surrender ceremony. We listened to the proceedings over our ship's sound system. Upon the conclusion of the ceremony the din of ships' bells, horns, whistles and thousands of cheering seamen filled the air, and the most glorious air show ever began, a fabulous fly-over. Squadron after squadron of military aircraft of the allied nations droned above us for perhaps fifteen minutes and thrilled several thousand sailors aboard the vessels assembled in Tokyo Bay.

I praise God for the extraordinary privilege of attending the peace signing. Looking back at my dismissal from the Navy V-12 officer-training program, He had blessed me mightily.

Gratefully, I tell my grandchildren, with due respect and appreciation for the Kerama Retto Ensign, I celebrated the end of my Navy career, as a Radioman 2nd Class in Tokyo Bay, rather than perhaps as the skipper of a garbage scow towing a surfboard on the waters of Kerama Retto.

~~*

About the Author. Alastair Gill writes feature articles about personal experiences. Born of Scottish parents, he grew up in Great Neck, NY and Fort Worth, TX. After earning a BA degree in psychology and sociology from Texas Christian University and serving the U.S. Navy in WW II, he began a thirty-year public relations career. As a prospective employee-relations executive, he gained oil field experience and was asked to found and edit an employee safety magazine. Gill later became a writer/photographer for the company's shareholder magazine and retired as executive producer of public relations films. His photography, a hobby and friend since teen years, has won cover positions on several publications. Alastair and his wife raised a family of five children. A widower, he visits and encourages his children and their families who live in five western states, serves on his church senior-care team and lap swims to stay healthy.

Be careful what you wish for. His long dead mother's voice whispered to him, or was it the rustling of the autumn leaves overhead? Some days he wasn't certain whether he heard the present, or his memories. He talked to his mom, too, in his head. At least, he hoped it was in his head—that he didn't say anything out loud. If he did, no one seemed to notice.

No one heard him; no one saw him. He had become invisible. Other pedestrians' eyes never met his with any spark of acknowledgement. On the contrary, they averted their eyes and walked right at him, like they could walk straight through him and feel no resistance. He shuffled along the crowded pathways, yielding the way to everyone.

From his park bench, he strained to look up at the trees overhead, no easy feat for his uncooperative neck. Golden years, indeed. Whoever labeled them that had not themselves endured the indignities of old age. First his body, that he had cared for over the years, abandoned him to near immobility and persistent pain. What good had it done to feed it low fat foods, to deny himself favorite sweets? Ungrateful, that's what his body was. Next, he expected his mind to leave him. As it was, it took frequent vacations, sending him postcards. Wish you were here.

What was the point? Why had no one warned him about the unending nothingness he faced? Yet, even at 82— or was it 83?—he remained his mother's son. Hers was the voice that reprimanded him. Shame on you, Charles! Be grateful that you've been given another day!

He looked around the near empty park. Another day for what, Mom? Even the pigeons lost interest in him after he threw the last bread crumbs on the ground. They flew off to more promising territory. A young woman walked toward him pushing a baby stroller, large enough to hold half a dozen kids. He leaned forward to take a look, see how many she had in there, but she whisked the carriage past him and was gone.

Some excitement. That's what I wish for, Mom.

His head dropped to his chest, and his eyes fluttered shut. Loud voices from the far corner of the lawn drifted to him on the late afternoon breeze. How long did I sleep? He raised his head, and saw the sun had dipped behind the trees. Young boys swaggered toward him on the path, jostling and pushing at each other.

"Can't stay on the path, fool?" the tallest said, as he shoved at a companion. By size and attitude, he led the way. The others bobbed and weaved in his wake. As they got closer, Charles could make out their saggy-baggy pants and their sideways baseball caps. What gangster yapper-rapper had inspired that look? Three young kids trying to look menacing.

Huh, they don't scare me, Mom.

Charles used his cane for balance, and pulled himself to his feet. He moved until he stood in the middle of the walkway, facing them, and directly in their way.

Excitement is about to be created, Mom.

"What you lookin' at, old man?" the smallest one said.

Always the smallest one has the biggest mouth, right Mom?

"Looking at you lemmings in all your finery," Charles replied. He planted his cane in front of him, and leaned on it.

"Who you callin' lemons?" a squeaky adolescent voice said.

"Why he callin' us lemons?" another said.

"Easy guys. He's not right in the head," the tall leader said.

"I called you lemmings, not lemons. Lemmings are rodents noted for…" Charles began.

"Rodents. 'nother name for rats. He callin' us rats." The diminutive boy moved closer, and bounced in a tight circle around Charles like a miniature prize fighter, fists raised.

Charles turned in dizzy confusion, and stumbled.

Charles, Charles, now see what you've gotten yourself into. His mother's voice sounded sad and disappointed.

He lost his balance, his hat … and some measure of his dignity. As he flailed with his cane in a desperate attempt to stay on his feet, his knees buckled and he braced for the inevitable crash to the ground. Instead, hands caught him in his arm pits and pulled him upright toward the bench.

"Easy there. Sit down," the lanky boy said. The boy's hat had fallen off, too.

Charles's eyes burned, and he blinked. He'd be darned if he'd allow himself to cry. His body trembled, and he crossed his arms over his chest to camouflage his distress.

"Nobody callin' me no rat," said boxer boy.

"Back off so he can breathe."

"Okay, okay. Not worth bothering about the old—"

"Shut up and get out of here. Go on," lanky boy said.

"You comin'?"

"Later."

The two boys strutted away. Charles willed himself to stop gulping for air, to breathe in and out, settle into a regular rhythm.

"Hey, you all right?" The boy scooped up Charles' hat, brought it to him, and folded his body onto the wooden seat next to Charles.

"Never better." Charles plunked his felt hat down on his head, hard, and yanked it back up off his ears.

"Don't look like it to me." He eased his baseball hat into place, twirling its bill to the left.

Charles shook his head. "Why do you wear your hat like that? Looks stupid."

"Not good to mouth off to strangers." The boy wagged his long index finger close to Charles' face.

"Not mouthing off. Just stating a fact." Charles sat up straighter. "Like, for instance, there are facts I know about lemmings."

The boy gave Charles a long look. "And you gotta tell me."

"Lemmings migrate," Charles continued. He saw the boy wrinkle his brow. "Stick together, follow each other, even if it means jumping off a cliff into the ocean."

"They swim?"

"They do, but they misjudge the distance to the next land. Most don't make it."

"Why they jump then?"

Ah, this boy has a good mind, Mom.

"Biological urges … how they're made … forces them to follow the crowd, wherever it leads. No choice."

"Still don't get it. We walkin' along, mindin' our own business, and you go callin' us lemmins."

"Lemmings." Charles drew out the syllables. "Think about it. Ask yourself, how are my friends and I like lemmings?" Charles looked up into the sky. "Okay, Mom, I will," he said.

"Hey, who you talkin' to?"

"My mom. She's always after me."

The boy's eyes swept the sky above the tree tops. "What she say?"

"Told me to be nice to you."

The boy hooted. "You somethin' else, old man."

"My name is Mr. Charles Crenshaw, not old man." He stamped his cane for emphasis.

"Right, Mr. Crenshaw. Call me Mr. Uptown."

"You're Master Uptown—too young to be a Mister. Don't you know anything?"

"Be nice, Mr. Crenshaw, or your mom will send you to your room." He pointed up.

Charles bowed his head. "Right. She gets mad when I'm rude. Sorry."

"No problem. Gotta be on my way." The young man stood.

Charles slid forward to the edge of the bench. "I have an encyclopedia volume that tells all about lemmings—shows a photo of them, too. I'll bring it to the park tomorrow."

"A picture of lemmings, huh? Wow, that's temptin'," the boy replied.

With effort, Charles stood. "Mom likes everyone to be nice to each other," Charles said.

The boy looked into the tree top above them. "Sorry," he said.

"See you tomorrow?" Charles leaned forward and looked up into the boy's eyes.

As they stood face to face, like mute statues in the fading day, the park lights switched on. Golden pools of illumination dotted the pathway at regular intervals into the distance.

"Name's Victor," the boy said. He winked up at the sky, pivoted, and jogged away.

~~*

About the Author. Carol Fogel's short stories have won prizes in the 2010, 2011, and 2014 Ventura County Writers Club short story contests. Her prior publications also include articles in academic and women's periodicals. She is currently writing a novel based on her short story, "Rosie Sees the Light." Avid international travelers, she and her husband Ronald have traveled to sixty-six countries. The couple resides at Lake Sherwood, California.

I remember the day I first met her.

I was slinking through the park scanning the ground anxiously. As dusk fell, fireflies lit the cobblestone path and flitted through the darkening trees. My heart beat quickly, and my eyes searched even more so. Catching sight of a well-dressed couple climbing out of a carriage, I darted into the bushes. *He has to be around here somewhere,* I thought.

That's when I heard it, a laugh, not the loud, threatening, booming noise my father made when he had had too much liquor, but a sweet, gentle laugh like the stars had found their voices. Venturing farther into the trees, I came upon a small clearing, and sitting in the center of it with a kitten in her arms and a parasol next to her was a young girl. She looked about my age at the time, maybe eleven or twelve.

"Hello," she said, "Look at this kitten I found! Isn't he cute?" I was filled with relief at the sight.

"Th-that's my kitten," I said. "I've been looking everywhere for him."

"Can I play with him? I just love kittens! He is so adorable! What's his name? Do you want to play with me, too?" The words kept spilling out of her mouth and a smile played on her lips.

"Um … yes." I complied. She squealed in delight. My fingers tugged at my ratty shirt, but she didn't seem to care that my clothes were old or that my face was smudged with dirt. I told her, "He doesn't have a name yet. I just found him yesterday. Do you want to name him?"

"Really? You'd let me name him? You're a great friend." Her sudden use of that word startled me, but she had already moved on to the naming. "I think I'll call him … Ocean. See, his eyes are pretty and blue like the ocean. I love going to the beach. I'm going there tomorrow with my papa. Will you come too?" Ocean started squirming in her arms.

"Cora! It's time to go home," a distant voice called.

"Oh, that's my papa. I have to go. I'll see you at the beach tomorrow." She plopped the kitten into my arms and started to rush off.

"Wait, you never told me your name," she said, stopping short.

"I'm Will."

"My name is Cora. See you later!" A gust of wind whipped the soft good-bye out of my mouth as I watched her walk off with a tall gentleman and get into a carriage. Just like that, in the park at dusk I had found my kitten and something else, something new … a friend.

What if she doesn't come? A thousand thoughts ran through my head, each one more anxious than the last. *Even worse, what if she doesn't remember me?* Ocean struggled in vain to escape my grip. I knew that cats don't like water, but I figured that Ocean should at least see his namesake. Besides, if Cora didn't remember me, she might remember my kitten.

"Will, you came!" a familiar voice said. I turned to see Cora running across the sand toward me with a bucket in her hand and a smile on her face.

"Hi, Cora," I said shyly.

"You brought Ocean too! He can help us collect seashells."

"Seashells?" I asked.

"Yes, it's what I always do at the beach. I have a huge collection at home. My papa is resting in the carriage, so as long as we don't wake him, we can play for as long as we want." She took my hand and led me down to the waves, and I finally had to let Ocean run off to safety.

"Where is your papa?" Cora asked. "Does he mind that you are at the beach with me?"

"He doesn't know or mind. My father isn't home very much," I responded.

"Oh. Where is he? Won't he worry if you are not at home?" she asked.

"I don't think he'll notice. My father always spends his time at the tavern," I told her. She looked very confused at my explanation.

"My papa goes to the tavern sometimes, but he still worries when I don't tell him where I am going," she insisted.

I smiled sadly.

"Look, there's a seashell. Is this the kind you like?" I asked.

Her face brightened. "Yes, that's perfect!" As she reached down to pick it up, I splashed her arm.

"Hey!" she squealed. She looked surprised, but then her expression melted into a smile, and she splashed me back. The day slipped away into a flurry of water fights and seashells.

We agreed to meet again to play the next day, and the next, and the next. Sometimes her father would walk on the beach with her, and I would have to hide, but he was usually tired from his job and slept in the carriage. Each morning, the one thing that filled my mind was when I would get to see Cora. I had never had a reason like this to be happy about the day. Once as we were saying good-bye at the beach, she leaned forward and whispered in my ear, "Will, you are my best friend."

Several years passed in this way, before life decided that it was time for us to grow up.

One day, she was late coming to the beach; she was never late. When she finally arrived, the look on her face told me that something was very wrong.

"Cora, are you all right?" I asked. She avoided my gaze.

"Papa said that I need to start acting like a young lady now, so he is sending me to a boarding school in London. He doesn't want me spending time with … people like you. I'm sorry!" Tears spilled from her eyes as she ran to the tall silhouette standing beside their horse-drawn prison, standing between me and the one person I could ever call my friend.

I remember the day she left.

The train station was crowded with people, young and old, leaving our sleepy coastal town for the excitement of the big city. I watched her board the train, but I didn't let her see me. As the train carried her away, I bid farewell to joy and hello to my former best friend, solitude.

Nearly five years passed before I saw her again. I had grown so much; it was amazing that she even recognized me.

I found her strolling the beach, without the childlike freedom of before, but with a new elegance and grace. How could a street urchin like me talk to an angel like her? *We were friends once. That has to count for something,* I thought.

"Cora." I could barely keep my voice from shaking. She looked around in surprise until her eyes fell on me.

"Will?" She remembered me.

"How are you, Cora? It's been a long time."

"Yes, it has. I finished my schooling, so I am home to stay."

"That's good news," I said.

"I'm sorry. I have to go. Good day," she said. She walked quickly off toward a waiting carriage. *Perhaps past friendships don't count for anything after all.*

That night I slunk through the back streets of town that I knew so well, taking the shortest route to her house. I had followed her home once, but she had warned me never to visit her. Tonight I had come prepared with pebbles in my pocket even though I knew that a visitor at her window would not be welcomed. I was about to turn away when a voice whispered, "Will? Is that you?" To my surprise, there she was at her window looking down at me.

"Cora, I know you told me once not to come here, but I had to see you. Why are you avoiding me? Why can't we just be friends? You know I would never hurt you."

"Will … hold on. I'm coming down." A few minutes later, she appeared in the front garden.

"Does your father mind that you are out here?" I asked.

"Papa is a heavy sleeper, and he goes to bed early. And our maid just left a few minutes ago." Silence fell.

"How was London?" I asked eventually.

"London was wonderful, but it didn't have a beach," she replied. "Whatever happened to your cat, Occan?"

"He died a few years ago, happy and fat from all of the mice I caught for him." I chuckled. Silence again. "It's been lonely here without you around," I said.

She looked away. "I'm sorry!" she cried suddenly.

"You keep saying that."

"It's not that I don't want to spend time with you; I do. It's just, Papa doesn't approve…"

"He doesn't know that we are meeting now, does he?" I said.

She looked at me strangely. "What are you saying?" she asked.

"We could meet every night, and your father would never know about it. It's perfect! What do you say?"

Her emerald eyes lit up. "Okay, but what if he finds out? It would really hurt him," she said softly. I didn't understand the concern she had for her father, but I reassured her anyway.

"That's why we have to make sure he doesn't find out," I replied.

She smiled; it was the first time I had seen her smile since she had left. I finally felt like things were going to work out.

Of course, fate had other plans. Everything seemed to be working at first: her father would go to bed, she would signal me from her window, and then we could spend time together. We would talk and laugh and forget that the rest of the world existed until the bell tolled midnight, and then we would part. Why did it have to end?

"What?" her eyes widened in disbelief.

"I said that I have been drafted to serve in the British army. I have to leave for my post in a week." The words were like poison in my mouth.

"But, why? Why would they do this?" She wrapped her arms around me.

"I am going to serve our country and protect you. It is an honor," I said more to convince myself than to convince her.

"Promise you will come back," Cora whispered.

"I promise," I replied, holding her close.

"You have to come back because … because I love you." My heart skipped a beat.

"I love you, too." There. I had said it. Now I could die without any regret.

On the night before I had to set out for the battlefield, as I began to leave for the last time, I started to say those fateful words, "Good—"

"No," Cora cut me off. "Will, don't say goodbye. That makes it sound like you are never coming back."

"What would you like me to say?" I asked.

"Just say … I'll see you when the morning comes. It will be a dark, lonely night without you."

I smiled. "All right then, Cora, I'll see you when the morning comes." We kissed and parted.

The night seemed to last forever on the battlefield. One fight after another drained my strength, and the blood was never-ending. More than once I thought I was dead, but somehow the memory of Cora waiting for me pulled me through. At long last, we were packing up and heading home to England. It was a miracle.

When I reached my hometown, I went first to see Cora, and I didn't care if her father saw me or not. We had not been able to write to each other during the war, and she did not know that I was still alive. I pounded swiftly on her door, but there was no reply. I knocked again. Again nothing.

"Are you looking for Cora?" A man's voice startled me. Turning I saw her father standing at the end of the garden. He looked much older than when I had last seen him; his dark hair was now streaked with gray.

"Yes, where is she?" I asked. He pointed behind the grand house.

"Thank you," I said and rushed to see her.

But she wasn't there. The garden was empty. It was just the same as it had always been except for one thing at the very center: a dark gravestone with seashells scattered all around it.

"She became sick while you were gone." Her father stood behind me. "The physicians tried everything, but there was nothing they could do. In the end, all she did was ask for you." He slowly walked back to the house and left me alone with Cora.

As if in a trance, I walked up and put a hand on the gravestone.

"I'll see you when the morning comes."

I remember the day I first met her.

I never even had the chance to say goodbye.

~~*

About the Author: From a young age, Carolyn Richards has loved everything magical, and she has discovered the perfect way to express herself and her imagination— writing. She is currently working on several short stories and a fantasy novel. She attended Villanova Preparatory School in Ojai where she was encouraged in her writing by teachers and friends. As she moves on into college, she plans to continue writing and learning about the world. Her winning short story, "When the Morning Comes" was inspired by a collage of pictures provided by her creative writing teacher, including images of a fashionable girl and a boy alone on the beach.

They come in dozens and packs.
They spill out of my mailbox like pills out of a bottle.
They dance before my eyes with colorful new things,
to buy or try and view and while the cost makes you stew,
And all you can say is **whew.**

> Then throw them out or put them in the bathroom
> reading pile.
> Then every few weeks you sort, clean them out,
> but new ones arrive—all shapes,
> sizes and names.

You stack them in piles,
drawers and baskets.
They ply you with new fads,
trends and numbers
you can call or go online.

> Shipping is free if you buy many
> And they never ever stop or
> Hear your plea
> Please take me off your list,
> I am so pissed.

~~*

About the Author. Maxine Landis earned her BA from Antioch University where she worked as a volunteer for Project InterAct at Morningside High School with the Inglewood School District. She compiled an anthology of the students' poems and served as their adopted "Poet in Residence." She has published nine chapbooks. Her work has also been published in scores of prestigious literary journals and anthologies. While in the graduate program at CSULB, she was chosen for the Santa Monica Writers' Program and the previous year was accepted at UC Davis, "Art of the Wild, Writers' Program at Squaw Valley. Her many memberships included the Society of Children's Book Writers and Illustrators, Poetry Society of America, California State Poetry Society, Women Writers' West, California Poets-in-the-Schools, Academy of American Poets, L.A. Collective, and a long-time member of VCWC. She is married and has four grandchildren. She published a book called *Wildflowers and Weeds*, as well as many anthologies and has a Children's Book, titled *Argonauts Adventures.*

Jolie woke to the sound of plates clattering far off down the hall in the kitchen. Today was the day. Adrenaline pulsed through her. She lay in bed and looked around her room, wanting to remember everything. The ceiling sparkled with shiny flecks. Her papier-mâché Jimi Hendrix head sculpture that sat on the dresser. The psychedelic Janis Joplin concert poster that was taped to the pink wall above her record player.

She took her time getting ready. She stepped into the blue plaid skirt, the hemline exactly three inches above the bend in her knee. She buttoned the white blouse over a white bra. All undergarments were required to be white. She pulled on navy-blue knee socks and slipped into the clunky white-and-black Oxfords.

After dressing, Jolie paused in the doorway to the dining room. Her brothers were eating breakfast while her mom stood talking with them, her purse and car keys in hand. Her dad was already at work. The conversation halted. They gaped at her.

"Whoa," James exclaimed. "I never thought I'd see the day."

"At least you won't have to think about what to wear," Jon said.

Her mother shot them a look and smiled at Jolie. "I'm going to be late for my Women's League meeting." She gave Jolie a hug. "It's going to be fine, sweetheart. You'll see. Don't miss your bus. I want to hear all about it tonight." And she was gone, out the door.

Her brothers left shortly after. Jon off to college in his VW Bug, and James to high school in her father's old, green Ford pickup. The house was still.

Jolie walked back into her bedroom and changed into a skirt, tie-dyed T-shirt, and butter soft knee high moccasins. She opened her closet and picked up her pack. From her top desk drawer she plucked out an envelope and walked back through the house.

On the kitchen counter was a note from her mom. The note pad was printed with *Have a Nice Day* next to a yellow smiley face.

> Jolie,
> Saint Mary's Girls School is not as bad as you think. You'll meet new friends. Focus and I know you'll graduate early.
> Love, Mom XOXOXO.

She tore off the note, folded it, and put it in her wallet. Her stomach was in knots. Breakfast was out of the question. Out on the deck, she gazed over the red tile roofs and canopy of green trees. Boats in the harbor looked miniature, bobbing in the blue water. After seven months, the oil slick had dissipated into small seeps. It was a beautiful morning, and she drank it in.

A muscle car groaned up the street and turned up the driveway. They were on time. She walked back through the kitchen, picked up her pack, and placed the envelope on the counter next to the notepad. She paused, lifted the letter and brushed it to her lips. "I love you, Mom and Dad," she whispered. "Please understand, I have to do this."

She set it back down and walked out of the house, not daring to glance back. A newer blue Camaro idled in the driveway. Will sat in the passenger seat. A young woman stood by the open driver's door. She was dressed in pale yellow poplin shorts, a matching top, and a wide, white plastic belt.

"I'm Pattie. I guess I'm your ride."

"Nice to meet you, Pattie. I'm Jolie."

Jolie pulled the seat forward and slipped into the backseat. Pattie got in, and the car purred down the driveway. Will looked back at her and smiled his wide, disarming smile.

"Emancipation day!" he said.

"Isn't she a little young for you?" Pattie said, scowling at Will. "Where exactly are we going?"

"Seven hundred miles north of here. It's on your way. It's just a short detour outside of Dunsmuir. You can drop us off at the Ranch and be on your way."

"What's at the Ranch?" Pattie said.

"Friends."

Pattie studied her in the rear view mirror. "So this is Jolie? How old are you, Jolie?"

Jolie glanced at Will. Hadn't this all been prearranged? He had told her Pattie was going back to college in Portland and would give them a ride. She looked into the rearview mirror. Jolie could hardly speak. Her heart was in her throat. "Eighteen."

So this was how it was going to be. She was already lying about her age. She put her head back and closed her eyes. The engine's steady hum and vibration cradled her as Pattie drove north on the 101 freeway. Will periodically reached back and squeezed her hand. They stopped only for gas and food. All Jolie knew of their destination was it was a ranch where Will's friends lived in the mountains of Siskiyou County, somewhere in Northern California.

More than once, Jolie caught Pattie's concerned gaze in the rearview mirror. If Pattie suspected she wasn't eighteen, would everyone else?

Pattie and Will talked up front. "I want to become a journalist," Pattie said.

"You don't need a degree for that. Write for an underground news press," Will said.

"No, I want to have the skills and credentials to work for a big news agency. I want to work overseas, on assignment."

"Trust me, you're wasting four years of your life. Plus, they don't send women overseas. That a man's job," Will said.

Jolie cocked her head toward Will. What did he just say? A man's job? That didn't sound like the Will she knew. Wasn't he all about equality?

Pattie shot him a glance. "We'll see about that."

Jolie gazed out the window. The knot tightened in her stomach. She was with Will, and they'd be together now. They'd been drawn to each other from the moment they'd met. He had persuaded her they could make it together, out there, wherever that was. She had put her trust in him.

Pattie drove north into the darkening light. Will changed the radio station every time they lost the signal. Jolie inhaled deeply and closed her eyes. This was really happening. She sank back into the seat.

By now her parents would have read her good-bye letter and would be mad. Mad she hadn't followed through with the first day at Saint Mary's Catholic Girls School. Mad she wouldn't conform and obey. But their mold for her couldn't contain her free spirit.

Hours later they neared Lake Shasta. "I can't drive anymore," Pattie said.

"Let's find a rest stop and crash for the night. We'll start fresh in the morning," Will said.

Pattie cruised into a rest stop. Jolie curled into a ball in the cramped back set. Her world would never be the same. What were her parents doing right then? Had they called the police? She lay awake a long time before falling into a fitful sleep.

In the early morning darkness, a rumble woke them as truckers idled their diesel engines. At dawn they piled out of the car and stretched. They drove on and stopped at a roadside café in Dunsmuir and ordered the Logger's Special: pancakes, eggs, and hash browns. Will made notes in a well-worn leather notebook.

Pattie fidgeted with her spoon and coffee cup, glancing repeatedly at Jolie. "Let's hit the road. I want to be in Portland tonight, and we have no idea where this so-called Ranch is."

Will turned to a page in his notebook. Cryptic directions were scrawled on the back of a song he was writing. "X marks the spot." Will pointed to a small *x* drawn at the end of a squiggly line.

From Dunsmuir they drove toward Sawyers Bar through Fort Jones and Etna. The pavement ended abruptly, and a cloud of dust enveloped the car. They had gone too far. Pattie did a U-turn and slowed when they came upon a store, a phone booth, a ranger station, a few houses, and a small post office.

"This is the middle of nowhere," Pattie said. "I thought you said it was a short detour?"

Jolie peered out the back window. "Do people really live here?" Where was the Ranch? She'd imagined a horse ranch off the side of the highway with a white fence that ran for miles and horses galloping wild and free.

Will looked at the map and guided them on. They turned off the main dirt road onto a rutted one lane track. "The Ranch is eight miles ahead."

"This is so primitive. I'm not sure my car will make it," Pattie said.

"I'll drive," Will said.

After switching drivers, Will drove, up and up, mile after mile, until they reached a crest. "Look at this." Will stopped the car. When the dust settled, they got out and looked over the valley. Folds upon folds of blue green mountains were stacked against each other as far as they could see. Small cloud wisps wrapped the far off peaks. The evergreen forest was lush with fir and pine. A deep green river snaked through the trees far below.

Jolie took a deep breath and exhaled. The tightness in her stomach loosened. Two brown and gold mosaic-patterned hawks rode air currents, floating effortlessly in large meandering circles over the forest valley. They were free, and she was free. Free from her parents. Free from Saint Mary's.

"Are you sure about the directions?" Pattie turned the ring on her finger over and over. "I mean, there is nothing out there."

Will nodded. "I trust my friends."

They drove on, bumping down the twisted mountain, granite cliffs on one side and the green winding river far below on the other. A rusted brown station wagon lay overturned partway down the mountain. Jolie closed her eyes to calm her stomach. The drop-off was dizzying. If the wheel got too close to the loose edge it would be all over. Will inched down the rutted road, navigating hairpin turns for three more miles. At the bottom, the forest opened up and the road ended in a meadow.

Will parked in the grass. "We have arrived."

Jolie took a deep breath and exhaled, relieved to be off the harrowing road. An old homestead with a hulking brown farmhouse sat on one side of the meadow. Opposite the farmhouse was a teetering barn. Both were in need of repair.

Will got out of the car. Pattie and Jolie paused and then eased out and stationed themselves by the Camaro, the car almost unrecognizable under layers of dust. Will strode toward the farmhouse.

Jolie glanced around furtively. A dozen or more goats nibbled tall meadow grass on the knoll and bleated incessantly. This was nothing like the ranches she'd been to. Where were the horses and riding corrals?

The screen door creaked open. Out stepped a young woman with waist-length brown hair wearing a long skirt and halter top. A bearded man with a blond ponytail, jeans, and no shirt appeared behind her. A bowie knife poked out of a sheath strapped to his belt. They stood rigid on the porch.

Jolie clasped her hands together. Who were these people? Why was the man wearing a bowie knife?

Will stopped twenty yards from them and addressed the man. "Peace, brother. We're here to visit Allen and Haley."

"They're away," he said.

Jolie stood straighter. They weren't there? Now what would they do?

Will paused. "I'm Will. They invited us to visit."

"They're in San Francisco," the man said, studying Will. "How do you know them?"

Jolie clasped her hands tighter; a sinking feeling ran from her head to her stomach. The man looked her way. His gaze was too intense to hold, and she dipped her head.

"Allen and I were roommates at Berkeley."

Jolie hadn't thought about his life in Berkeley. There was a lot she didn't know about him. The man stood silent on the porch.

"And after college we shared a house. Haley, too."

The man studied them and then conferred with the woman in a low voice. Jolie wiped the sweat off her brow with her hand. It was unbearably hot in the sun.

The couple descended the porch steps and walked over to Will. "I'm Mark and this is Jasmine." He held out his hand to shake Will's. "Friends of Allen's are friends of ours."

Jolie smiled and murmured, "Hi." Jolie followed Mark's gaze to Pattie. The girl looked wildly out of place in her matching yellow outfit, standing rigid with her arms crossed.

"If I'm going to make it to Portland tonight, I'd better head out now," Pattie said.

"We're getting ready for lunch. Don't you want to stay and join us?" Jasmine asked.

"No thanks, I need to be off."

"Don't you want to see the Ranch?" Mark asked.

"No, no thanks." Pattie looked at Will. "Do you want to get your packs from the car?" Jolie gave Pattie a hug. The steep winding road they had traversed loomed behind them. Pattie could not be looking forward to the drive out by herself.

"Thanks for the ride and everything," Jolie said.

Pattie hugged her back. "Are you sure about this? This Ranch? And Will?"

Jolie nodded. Was she sure about this? She hid her fear and put on a smile, but she did wonder. The Ranch wasn't what she had expected. She watched Will get their things out of Patti's car. Everything would work out. He had told her that. She just wasn't used to it yet. This was her new life, a new adventure.

Will stacked his guitar, their packs, and bedroll in the grass and hugged Pattie. "Thanks for the ride."

Jolie stood rooted in place, her eyes riveted on the trail of dust as Pattie's car disappeared from view on the spiral assent up the crude road. Jasmine's voice startled her, and she turned back to them.

"Let's put your packs in the house. We're getting ready to join the others for lunch, down the way, in the summer kitchen."

Jolie followed Jasmine's gaze. The others? Who were the others? She looked at Will and forced a smile. Her journey had just begun.

~~*

About the Author: Joye Emmens enjoyed a successful career in environmental health and biotechnology before to pursuing her dream to write fiction. Her first novel, *She's Gone*, was published in January 2015. *Readers Favorite 5* Star Review of *She's Gone:* "Joye Emmens deftly explores the political landscape of 1960s America ... Emmens' descriptions of the historical topography ... greatly elevates the story's engaging veracity. *She's Gone*, besides being an entertaining exposition into the counterculture that reigned in America's mid-twentieth century, is a captivating tale of a girl's adventuresome transition into womanhood." *San Francisco Book Review:* "*She's Gone* is an excellent story of a young woman who struggles to find her identity in the midst of chaotic times. Joye lives in Ventura, California with her husband. She volunteers as a Big Sister and mentor with the Big Brothers Big Sisters of America.

I never wanted to be Jeff Gordon. I don't know NASCAR from a three-legged race. I don't even have a car. Who can afford one? You have to be a cop to own a good car. Hey, no offense.

I stumbled into the Jeff Gordon thing. It wasn't my idea, it just happened. It found me, or it grew around me, or whatever. Yeah, sure, you could say I started it. I go into the Burger King this one time....

I'm dining in. When you're dining in, they always ask you your name. I always say "Orlando". What do you say? You tell 'em your name, right? They're onto something at Burger King. Like, who we are is how we get fed, as much as the money. Like your ma hollering outside, "Orlando, time to eat!" Your friend can't run in and take your place, right? It has to be you.

Only, this time, I don't tell 'em "Orlando." I say, "Jeff." I don't know why, I swear. I'm just trying it out, see how it goes. I say "Jeff."

When she says, "Jeff, your order's ready," I get a little buzz. I kinda like it. She smiles at me. I feel like a Jeff guy, not the usual Orlando. I'm getting away with something. No big deal. No one's getting hurt. There's no "Jeff" dude missing dinner.

That night, that same night, Jeff Gordon wins some big race, somewhere, I don't know where, some big race. He wins. There's champagne, somebody is kissing him, he's all stoked. Yeah, I notice—he looks a little like me. Not that much, really. I never look that happy.

If I'm really Jeff Gordon, I can buy Burger King. I can name everybody who works there "Jeff", the girls, too. I can call all the customers "Jeff." "Jeff, your order's ready!" All day long, if I'm Jeff Gordon.

Okay. Then it gets a little creepy. Not like bogus creepy. Just like, who's-in-charge creepy, know what I mean? Sometime, I don't know, maybe a week or two later, in the mail, in my box, with the Orlando stuff, there's an envelope addressed to Jeff Gordon. No, really. It's a water bill. I don't pay water where I am. The house numbers are just like mine, but the street is maybe four blocks over. Any other day, I'm walking the letter over, or, I'm leaving it in the box, flag up, "NOT HERE", right?

This time, I'm like "Hey! I got mail!" Like, champagne kisses, happiness, the whole bit. So, I take it to the library, to get me a card, a Jeff Gordon card. You guys wanna pin me for fraud, you got me. Wanna look for a stash of books, missing books, somewhere? Be my guest.

I read the papers, magazines, sometimes. I've read a few books, but I don't need to have them. See what I mean? I was after the card. Be Jeff Gordon a little, no big deal. "Okay, Mr. Gordon, these will be due October 19th." No big deal. Nobody gets hurt. I drop the bill back in the box, "NOT HERE", that's that.

So. It's not about fraud. Or identity theft. It's not about that. That's why I'm talking to you guys. You know more about it than I do.

The girl was in the bathroom, at the library. I never saw her before. I don't know nothin' about her. I push the door open, she's standing by the toilet, I start to leave, she says, "Lock the door. Shave or something. I need a few minutes."

I say, "You didn't lock the door."

She says, "I forgot."

So, okay detectives, so, check it out. This girl has something on her mind. She forgets to lock the door at the public restroom? She's tearing little strips of paper, and folding them smaller, and dropping them into the bowl. I stay by the sink.

I push the hand dryer button.

"What are you doing?" I ask her.

She says, "I'm making poetry."

"Fine," I say. "More poetry, less poverty."

No, no, once in a while I can say things like that, certain occasions. When I'm around women. I over-reach, sometimes. Hey, you guys, ever happen?

"What's your name?" she asks me.

I kind of panic. It's like BK truth-telling time in there, and I say, "Orlando."

And, she goes, "Okay. I'll be Dawn."

That's all I know. She never tells me another name. She's Dawn, the whole time I know her, okay?

She says, "Your name's not Orlando." She's telling me my name's not Orlando, in the bathroom, at the library?

So, I go, "No, it's Jeff, Jeff Gordon."

She goes, "Sweet Jesus under a microscope!" She stops tearing the paper, and she says, "Can you drive?"

I say, "A little." Because I can drive, I just can't afford to.

Then she says, "Do you trust me?"

Look, you guys get around. Who says, "Do you trust me?" In the bathroom, first meeting?

So, I say, "Okay Dawn, but you leave first, and meet me by the bike rack, if this is for real," I say.

There she is, at the bike rack, when I come out.

"We need to be in Boca Raton by 6:15 tomorrow," she says.

You guys, I don't know about cars, I'm not a car buff, but you saw the car on the news, right? She gives me the keys.

So I say, "Why aren't you driving?"

And, she hitches up her pants, her pant legs a little, and I see this metal stuff, where like her ankles would be, and she says, "It hurts too much." Then she says. "A.M. 6:15 A.M. Can you do it?"

I do it. I did it. 5:25 in the morning, we pull in there. I don't see her after that. I don't know nothin' about her. The keys are in the ignition. She hands me this little package, that one right there, she says, "Thanks, Jeff." I didn't ask for it. I don't know where it came from. You guys counted the money. I saw it in there. I never touched it.

I read the note. I don't want the money. Sure, sure, I thought, "I'll get me a latte, now! I'll get everybody in line a latte." I never had a latte. But I don't wanna do no crime. Money finds a way home, it always does. Let 'em have it, those guys at the track, fix the bathroom. I don't need it.

I never saw any gun. I don't do guns.

Once, when I was ten, my uncle and my dad thought they'd teach my brother and me how to shoot a rifle, and it was my turn, and I had my finger on the trigger, and they were saying "Go ahead!" and, my little sister, Aggie, runs out across the road, right in front of where the rifle is pointing. No, no. She's okay. I didn't even pull the trigger. That was enough for me. I don't do guns.

So.

This Dawn, she shoots up this men's room, all the urinals and the mirrors, and the sinks, and the toilets, and does a full lap around the fairway, walks away from the car, on those metal leg-thingys, and you guys can't find her?

I have no idea. She slept a lot. No, not the whole way. We talked. She talked about poetry. She could say poetry, lots of it. Not out of a book, she wasn't reading– stuff she knew. Like Shakespeare, you know, and somebody named Dickens, she said, or Dickenson maybe. Some girl poet.

Kinda deep stuff. But I could understand that Dickens girl. She could probably make some good songs if she set her mind to it.

She said her own stuff, too, mixed in there, Dawn did—or whatever her name is. She did go on this one rant.

We stopped to take a leak. Just pulled over, you know, and she's on her side, and she calls out, "You dudes can just use a bottle. You don't even have to stop. That's the difference. Not that you're stronger, or braver, or smarter."

When she got back in, she kept going. "The pit stop is a girl thing. You dudes don't need it," she says. "You can drive 'till you croak. World peace is indoor plumbing, with a mirror. It's a girl thing, too. You don't need it."

I never thought about it. It's sort of true. I don't have to tell you guys this. I wanted to put my hand on her, just on her leg, while she was sleeping. I didn't.

She said, "Do you trust me?" For openers, you know? There's a poem. Right there. To me.

Yeah, I trust her, I got her there. You could say she used me. I don't mind, didn't hurt me none. I was dang near bona fide Jeff Gordon there, somehow, I have no idea how, what it means, or what she's up to. The note's no help—one of them little Dickens poems.

Maybe you never do find her. Or, maybe she tries it again. I give up. Orlando will do from here on. That's who it was I was the whole time, anyway. I never wanted to be Jeff Gordon. There's enough Jeff Gordons already. There's one about four blocks from me, I guess.

I'm back to Orlando.

I didn't even get the card.

~~*

About the Author. Joe Vandenberg is a real character, so they say. "Had to be You" is his first short story. In the screenplay ending, Joe sees Darlene (her real name) taking a job at BK. She's disguised, a little. She surprises "Jeff" into love with her. Re-born identity.

My Bridge by Peter Pohl

One day, while at my drafting table a dream walked by.
My heart stood still; oh my!
Tall and of regal bearing, her walk hit a cadence on the wood floor.
Who are you? I need not know more.
It was an electrifying moment in my life.
I knew then – I wanted her to be my wife.

It's been sixty – four years since we wed.
I carried you to our bed.
Through the years your contagious laughter,
I remember every day thereafter.
The way you grinned, like a pixie,
When you rode your horse named Dixie.

Twenty-two years ago you left me for the heaven above.
But I still treasure you; talk to you. My bridge to you is Love.

~~*

Death Drives a Stagecoach by Peter Pohl

In April of 1880, my partner Hawk and I sold our small, but profitable building materials store to a large corporation. They made us a cash offer that we could not refuse. Now I could travel in style and comfort by Stagecoach to San Francisco. I took the Seeley line from San Diego to Los Angeles because it went along the picturesque coast. I'll board Wells Fargo for my trip from Los Angeles to San Francisco.

As I boarded the stage in Old Town San Diego, I noticed the driver. He was an odd looking fellow, well over six feet tall, raw boned and skinny. His dark eyes were set deep in their sockets, accentuated by his high cheek bones and his pale skin. He wore black cloths except for a red bandana. There was no hair protruding from under his black felt hat. I assumed that he was bald. He looked old, but moved with the energy of a young man.

I heard the station master ask him, "Who are you? Where is Pedro, our regular Whip?" Drivers, I learned, were called "Whips".

"Pedro has the flu. He's running a high fever. I hired on as a temporary Whip," the strange looking man replied.

Five men and I filled the six seats in the Coach. All of them were well dressed. They looked like merchants. I was not interested in their conversation nor the bottle of Moonshine whiskey they passed around.

184

After riding twenty miles inside the coach, I got tired of my drunken companions. At Carlsbad, our first stop, we changed the team of four horses. I asked our Whip to let me ride with him in the box, even though I felt intimidated by this man.

"Suit yourself," was his curt answer.

It was a glorious spring morning. We were still close enough to the coast to see the blue Pacific Ocean while traveling through a sea of wildflowers. There were orange California poppies and white and yellow daisies. Now I had a 360 degree view and the smell of horses. God, that felt good.

I mustered the courage to break the silence. "What breed are these sturdy coach horses?" I asked.

"They're Mustangs," he replied dryly.

"They remind me of the Barb horses that were bred by Berber tribes around Morocco; their size, the convex face, the heavier neck, but most of all, they seem to be laterally gaited, which sets them apart from other breeds," I said.

He turned his head toward me, and there was a faint smile on his face. "You're a real horseman, aren't you? I like that. I like to talk about horses."

We were a few miles south of San Clemente, our next stop. The road ran alongside some cliffs. I noticed a large piece of paper. It looked like a blue kite lying in the grass. A sudden blast of wind blew the kite right in front of our lead horses. They spooked and took off at a dead run.

As they veered to the edge of the road, the left front wheel hit a large rock and broke instantly. I felt the coach tilting to the left, toward the cliff. The Whip grabbed a rope that was attached to the linchpin below and jerked it out, thus releasing the horses from the coach. He yelled at me to jump as he jumped.

In my late teens, I'd worked as an acrobat in a circus. Jumping from moving horses to the ground, rolling over and getting up on my feet had become routine. My reflexes were instantaneous as I jumped from the moving coach. I did not suffer any injuries. The Whip also survived without injuries.

The horses broke free before the coach tumbled down the cliff, about two hundred feet onto the rocks below. I found a narrow path that led from the road down to the beach. The coach was smashed into pieces. All five passengers were dead. I found my two leather suitcases among the other luggage strewn around, and carried them back up to the road.

We spotted the horses about two hundred yards ahead. They were too busy enjoying the abundant grass along the roadside to care about anything else. We bundled up the harness and loaded it onto one horse. Another horse carried my suitcases.

185

The Whip and I each jumped on the other horses and headed for San Clemente, leading the horses carrying our gear behind us. It was a three mile ride to the next stop.

The young station master was stunned by our appearance. He stood with his mouth open in disbelief before he asked us what happened. We told him the whole story, starting with the kite that spooked the horses and the large rock that crushed the wheel. "It was a freak accident," the Whip told him. "Contact the local Sheriff and tell him to take care of the dead and their belongings."

The station master went to talk to his wrangler, who promptly saddled a horse and took off to get the sheriff.

"I see that you have a fresh team of horses for us, and a large coach. We'll take them to complete our trip to Los Angeles. I'm sure there will be passengers along the way waiting for us," the Whip said.

The station master was obviously uncomfortable with this request, but after a few "hmms" he spit it out. "Are you sure that you can drive this stage safely all the way to Los Angeles?" he asked.

"Sonny," the Whip replied, "I've been driving coaches, wagons and carriages for decades." And under his breath he mumbled "centuries actually."

That didn't make any sense to me. Surely I heard wrong.

With the wrangler gone, the station master had no intention of hooking up the team for us. We helped ourselves. No passengers were waiting at San Clemente. Our next stop was San Juan Capistrano, about twenty miles to the north. Our schedule called for us to spend the night here. They fed us a good steak dinner, and gave us two cots for the night. After dinner, I bought us some drinks. This was a good time to relax and talk.

"What's your name," the Whip asked.

"Josef Raditsz."

"Does that name end with 'sz'?

"Yes"

"Names ending in sz are usually Hungarian. Are you Hungarian?"

"Yes. I was born and raised on the Puszta"

That explains how you know so much about horses. Ah, the Puszta, land of Gypsies, musicians, artists, poets, fast horses, and beautiful women; or is it beautiful horses and fast women? I forget."

"You were right the first time," I said and we both laughed.

"Now, tell me about yourself; your name and where you're from."

"I'm Hector Muertez."

"Whoa! Muerte means dead or death in Spanish"

"Yes, but my name is Muertez, with a "z" at the end. It has been an honored family name, going back to early 17th century Spain." He studied me. "Besides Hungary, have you been to other countries in Europe?"

"I fought at Custozza, on the Italian side," I said.

"Why were you fighting for the Italians?"

"Those days I was a Mercenary Soldier of Fortune, fighting for whoever paid me the most. In 1859, I fought with the French at Solferino. Without Radetzky, the Austrians took a terrible beating. Casualties were high on both sides. I recall corpses stacked like cords of wood. It was a terrible sight, no matter which side you were on."

"I too fought at Custozza and Solferino, for Austria, of course. I was a Lieutenant in a Hussar regiment."

"A Hussar!" This surprised me. "No wonder that you are an expert horseman."

Breakfast was at 5:00 AM. By 5:30 we were on our way with four passengers.

Hector and I talked about different breeds, and told stories of horses that we had been particularly fond of, like old cowboys do. Along the way we picked up four more passengers. Our new coach had seating for nine.

It was Saturday, mid-afternoon, the day before Easter, when we arrived at Los Angeles, or as it was formally named "El Pueblo de Nuestra Senora la Reyna de Los Angeles," the town of our Queen of Angels. After we turned the passengers, coach and horses over to the station master, Hector spoke to me.

"Well, my friend, this is good bye. I have things to do here, people to see before I return to San Diego. I hope you'll enjoy your trip to San Francisco." And with this he took my hand into his boney hand for a crushing handshake. Then he disappeared in the crowd.

Sunday morning, I attended Easter Services. Mass was held at the Plaza Church which was just completed in 1822. After mass I strode around the Plaza, admired the statue of Felipe de Neve, one of the city founders in 1781, and the statue of King Carlos, then the reigning monarch of Spain.

There was nothing to keep me in Los Angeles. I was anxious to get to Santa Barbara, Monterey, and finally San Francisco. The Wells Fargo Stage I boarded here had a team of six horses because we would cross some mountainous terrain. We also had a heavier load of passengers and gear. This coach, again, had three rows of seats, room for nine passengers, and it was full.

Our driver's name was Jim Miller. The station manager was occupied with some chores and the wrangler was busy putting passengers and their luggage on the stage, so Miller had to hook up his own team. I went over and gave him a hand, hoping that this would put me in his good graces. It worked. When I asked permission to ride in the box with him, he readily agreed. Jim was an old timer, one of the famous California Whips. Sitting there, high up in the box of the large coach, six horses responding to his reins, he was truly a "King of the Road."

A skilled Whip like Miller controlled each of six horses with six reins, three in each hand, interlaced between his fingers. He used these reins with the finesse of a violin virtuoso. I saw Miller use the whip to knock a fly off a horse's neck without ever touching the horse.

Once we were on our way we introduced ourselves. "Is Los Angeles the starting point of your trip?" he asked.

"No," I said, "I came up from San Diego—took the Seeley line so that I could travel along the coast."

"Was your Whip named Pedro?"

"No, Pedro was ill, they told me. We had a substitute named Hector Muertez."

"Whoa," Jim said, and he stopped the stage abruptly. He stared at me while the blood drained out of his face. Hesitating, he moved his hand toward me, finally touching my shoulder. "I had to touch you, to see that you're real, not a ghost. You rode with the 'Agent of Death', and lived to tell about it?"

It was my turn to feel faint as I recalled Hector mumbling, "Centuries actually." Now it made sense to me. Jim and I sat in silence for a moment, till some color returned to his cheeks. Then Jim got the team moving again.

"Whatever did you say to Hector that made him spare your life?" Jim asked.

"I talked to him about horses. You know how much cowboys love to talk about horses. This was just before the accident"

"Accident? What accident?" The Whip looked concerned.

"A few miles south of San Clemente the road runs close to some cliffs. The left front wheel of the coach hit a large rock and was smashed to bits.

Hector yelled at me to jump, just as he pulled on the rope to remove the pin to free the horses from the carriage. Then he too jumped."

"Hector had a rope up in the box, with the other end tied to the linchpin?" Jim asked in disbelieve. "In forty years of driving stages, I've never even heard of such a thing. Josef, that was no accident. That was planned. And if you had not gotten into Hector's good graces with your horse talk, you would have gone down the cliff with the coach."

This rocked me to the core.

Jim seemed to be engrossed in thought. After a while he said, "You know, a rope attached to the linchpin is not a bad idea. Not bad at all. I just may propose this idea to Wells Fargo."

Maybe the "Angel of Death's," Hector Muertez's invention will save future lives like he had saved mine.

~~*

About the Author. While attending Junior High School in Austria, Peter wrote essays and won awards for some of them. These were written in German, of course. His life changed on March 12, 1938 with the "Anschluss," the bloodless annexation of Austria to Germany. In August 1938, his mother and he stood on the deck of the Italian Cruise ship, REX. They hugged each other as tears of joy ran down their cheeks at the first glimpse of the Statue of Liberty. There followed a scenic train ride to their new home in California where he had to learn English, talk and read before he could write in English. He lived with his aunt, romance novel writer, Vicki Baum, best known for her novel and motion picture *Grand Hotel*. Six years after his marriage, he and his late wife, Florence and their two kids moved to Hidden Hills, a 'horsey" community in the West San Fernando Valley. He took his love for horses seriously, becoming a breeder of Quarter Horses and an expert rider. He went to the auction with a friend and bought a horse. That started his writing again. He called his story, "Sold at the Auction." *Equestrian Trails Inc.* and later *Canadian Equestrian* magazine published his story. Since then, almost every story or essay of his has horses in it. "Sometimes God Has A Plan B" has a horse in it. It was published in our earlier anthology, *Serendipity*.

★ *2012 Poetry Young Adult Honorable Mention Winner – Memorable Night by Carolyn Olsen*

We stared at the night sky
With wonder and amazement.
The burning beauty of the night sky
Took our breath away.
The stars were winking down
At us as if they knew what was going through our minds.
That night I was so sure
I had fallen for him.
I felt as though reality
Was a nightmare I woke
Up from.
Time was only a memory.
Other people were nonexistent.
We kissed. It was magical.
There was so much love behind it.
I'll remember it forever.
Just as I'll remember my first.
I wanted to tell him
How I felt.
How I hoped to
Spend eternity with him.
How I wanted to always be his.
If I could go
Back in time and
Tell him those things,
I would.

~~*

About the Author: Carolyn Olsen, or Carly, is a Ventura County native. She grew up in Moorpark, where she attended high school, and graduated in 2013. She has moved on to Southern Utah University where she is currently studying English with an emphasis in Literature. While at school, she has worked for the Utah Shakespeare Festival, and the English Department as a tutor. She writes within the genres of poetry, science fiction/fantasy, realistic fiction, and literary criticism. She is working on her first full-length novel, which she hopes to have published. She currently runs a literary criticism blog on tumblr.

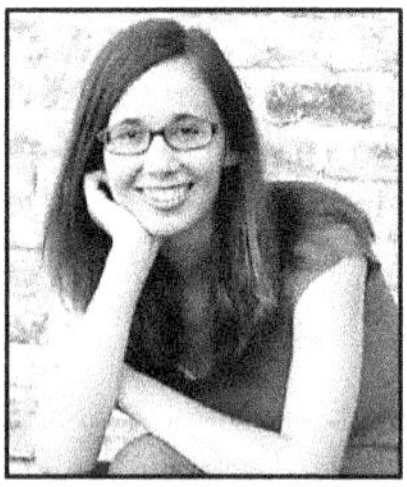

A dune buggy raced across the sand, spewing a rooster tail fan of sand in its tracks. The sun rose, introducing the new day. It was to be clear and hot with the morning temperature registering well above 100 degrees Fahrenheit. A cloud of dust on a nearby sand dune announced the presence of humankind—here to greet the day.

Chuck and Carl had spent the night on the sand, camping out by the roaring fire they had made, and downing a keg of beer. As the fire went to embers and then charcoal, they had curled up in their sleeping bags. At dawn, drowsy, but eager to set out for thrills, they were already doing spins and jumps across the desert floor. Cresting a dune, they spotted an almond shaped object a short distance away. They had been there yesterday, and that object hadn't been there then.

Carl said, "What the hell is that?"

He whirled the buggy in its tracks, and set out toward the object at a fast clip, dodging the boulders and larger plants in their course. They arrived at a point about fifty feet from the object, and came to an abrupt stop.

"Where did that thing come from?" Chuck said. "Let's get a closer look."

Carl killed the buggy's engine, and they got out. There were signs posted near the foot of the object: Private Property No Trespassing.

They decided it was an invitation to take a closer look. With their eyes fixed on the thing, they moved about ten yards toward it. Then, they heard the buggy's engine start. Turning around, they saw the buggy backing away.

"What the heck!" Chuck yelled, and "Whoa!" in the next breath.

The guys stared at the straying buggy. It spun around and accelerated away, spewing a sheet of sand in their faces. The guys fell on their knees in disbelief.

They looked up to find the buggy had stopped, and was facing them. Its engine speed was going from idle to super idle.

They jumped to their feet and ran after the wayward buggy. It turned and darted away as they gave chase. Both guys were used to strenuous exercise. They chased the buggy around in a circle trying to leap aboard, but they only managed to swing around and fly to the ground on every attempt. On the third miss, they slowly got to their feet.

Addressing the buggy, Carl said, "Okay, Devil Dog!" and motioned for Chuck to circle to the right, Carl moved around to the left. They walked slowly to intercept positions. The buggy had to come toward them. They had played defensive linebackers in high school. They knew how to run down a ball carrier—same drill they figured. If the buggy went between them, then both would have a shot at jumping aboard. Making an end run would give the other side a good shot at leaping on. They moved slowly converging on the buggy.

It began to bob up and down, and the lights flashed on and off. Then, it darted in a rush between them, like a playful dog. They both leaped; but it was too late, it passed just beyond their reach. They fell in the tracks as the buggy whizzed by. Amazed, the guys looked up to see the buggy facing away from them, the long whip antenna swaying like a tail from the back. They watched as the rear seemed to squat and gasoline began to stream out of the tank.

Carl yelled, "It's taking a leak!" They sprang to their feet and ran toward the buggy shouting, "Stop!"

The buggy wasn't moving, but the rear wheels began to spin faster and faster, spewing sand and showering the guys from head to toe. Wiping their faces, they were relieved to see the gasoline had stopped pouring from the tank.

"I hope that the damn tank isn't empty." Carl moaned.

Slowly, they walked toward the buggy. The engine wasn't running. The buggy didn't move. Cautiously, they boarded and took their seats.

The horn sounded. Beep! Beep!

The engine cranked and started. Carl looked at the dash and was relieved to see that the buggy still had enough gas to make it to the highway. He shifted into low and slowly let out the clutch. The buggy moved, rolled and steered in response to his motions.

He turned the buggy toward where their truck and trailer were parked. They climbed a hill. At the top, they looked back and saw the thing sweeping a blue light back-and-forth in their direction.

It seemed to be communicating. They felt compelled to reply, and both moaned, "Goodbye."

Chuck raised his right hand, doubled-up his fingers and shook his fist up and down, and through gritted teeth said, "Okay, Devil Dog, or whatever you are, you had some fun, but others will come and chase you down to earth!" Then, they turned and sped off, relieved there was enough gas to get off the sand.

When they reached their truck, they loaded the buggy on the trailer, and left exhausted and bewildered.

About the Author. John Caruthers is a scientist, engineer, and military aviator, who has observed and experienced how systems are developed and function on the planet Earth. From this background, he is interested in science and technology, and how these disciplines can help humans survive and progress toward a destiny that is largely unknown. He earned a Bachelor of Science Degree in Geology and a Master's Degree in Electrical Engineering, and graduated from the United States Air Force Navigation and Electronic Warfare Officer Training Schools. He served three years on a B-52 combat crew. And, over a span of three decades, he led the development of many military test programs. Science fiction deals with this aspect of the human condition; and therefore, his story delves into how we might meet an encounter with an extra-terrestrial alien. In this effort, he has written, and intends to self-publish, a sci-fi novel with the title *Earth Bound.*

Waves Crash on Rocks - Photo Courtesy of Gregg Miller, VCWC Photography Chair

"There are two ways to live a life either forget everything or, remember nothing."
~ Santosh Kalwar, *Quote Me Everyday*

Venice luggage handlers stranded in Frankfurt
It was their day to strike
Frankfurt lost my luggage and
Was rude and condescending
Berlin asked payment for my urine
Rome lost my reservations
Moscow refused to deplane the luggage
Wait I thought that was Venice
Yalta soldiers patrolled with AK 47's
Madrid frisked me between the legs
Mexico City charged extra for every little thing
Hawaii stole my jewelry
LAX ahh home sweet home
"Anything to declare?"
"No"
"What about these seeds?"
"They're a necklace"
"Can't bring seeds into the U.S."
"I bought it here at the Farmer's Market"
"Oh welcome home then"

~~*

About the Author. Danielle Brown is a poet and writer living in Ventura, California. She is a member of three poetry groups, the Ventura County Writers Club, the Society of Children's Book Writers and Illustrators, and Women Who Write. Danielle graduated from VCC with an A.S. in Library Science, from CSUN with a B.A. in Liberal Studies and a Multiple Subjects teaching credential, from the UCSB with a Master's Degree in Special Education. She retired from teaching in 2002 and now occupies herself with yoga, tai chi, water aerobics and traveling whenever the opportunity arises. The genres she favors are picture books and YA. She is currently working on a YA coming of age novel.

Robert tossed his bag on the bed and flipped his laptop open on the desk. He paused briefly and got up and pulled the curtains to a view of the proverbial babbling brook and cracked the window. He started back toward the laptop then turned away. As he unzipped his overnight bag, he took out the tiny notepad he had slipped in a side pocket. It was empty but for a few notes with some story titles, that he had made while driving up to the Writer's Retreat.

Robert sat on the bed and took a quick glance at the pad and placed it down next to his laptop. Finally, the retreat he never thought would happen was here. The novel that has been budding for half his life would now have a chance to bloom. And if not, he told himself that was fine, too. He will be out of excuses once and for all.

It seemed perfectly logical to him that in order to write, he had to get away from all distractions and give the idea some time to gel, at least get it on track. Then he could work on it daily as every writer everywhere says one must. He'd be driven by their mantra, "ass plus chair equals pages."

Those successful writers give the craft the respect it deserves by isolating a time and place. With two kids, a more than full time job, and a needy, unsupportive wife, it made that commitment impossible in the normal course of a day.

Robert heard someone walking outside his bedroom door which was cracked open. He noticed a woman carrying groceries. She dropped them on a countertop near the sink in the common area kitchen. She seemed attractive enough. But that kind of distraction is not what he needed. Hopefully, she will mind her own business.

However, now that she had been made aware that someone else was staying in the cottage for the weekend, the least he thought he must do was introduce himself.

Robert wandered out, somewhat reluctantly, and stuck out his hand, "Robert Marlowe, soon-to-be best-selling author."

"Veronica St –" she stopped herself, then continued, "yes, writer, hey if we don't call ourselves that, who else will, right?"

"Good point. Hmmm, looks like accomplished chef perhaps as well," Robert added as he observed all of the fresh vegetables and spices.

"Pleased to make your acquaintance, Robert," Veronica offered. "Actually, the ratatouille I am preparing will only be a first draft but you are welcome to join me. Can't write when hunger is gnawing away at us."

Robert acknowledged the sentiments and the invitation, but seemed hesitant, alluding to his desire to get back to writing his book.

"Go ahead and continue whatever you are composing, I'll let you know when it's time. I think I'll make enough for three just in case we have another guest," Veronica said, motioning toward the third, apparently empty room. "Besides, I might as well occupy myself while I wait for my muse to replace this knife with a pen."

Robert gave her a half smile, thinking to himself he had run across yet another looney writer, while graciously taking her up on her offer and went back into his room. This time he shut the door.

He sat down at his laptop and stared, then opened his notepad. While glancing, he started keyboarding. "The Camping Trips" by Robert Marlowe. Try as he may, that's as far as he got when he was distracted by what was probably a dog, but kinda looked like a fox. He rose and gazed out the window to see if he could get a better view.

Just then Veronica tapped on the door and said dinner was ready so he turned, mumbled acknowledgement and indicated he'd be right there.

Robert was a meat and potatoes kind of guy so the vegetable dish was unusual for him, but he enjoyed it and as Veronica pointed out, she had picked a few things from the organic garden saying it made her feel that she was bringing the retreat grounds into her body for a more consuming experience.

"So, Robert," Veronica began, "did you manage to make some progress while I was cooking? I didn't hear a lot of keystrokes."

Robert was a bit taken aback and a bit more uncomfortable thinking she was eavesdropping. But, "no, not really," he told her, "I am trying to get some notes organized first. How about you? What are you working on?"

Veronica smiled. "I'm not working on anything really. Did you want any more?" she asked. "It looks like there is no one in the third room. I'm glad."

"No. I'm satisfied, but thank you very much. I am curious, though. Didn't you come up here to write something?"

"Oh yes, that is my goal. But, I'm not here just to force out some mundane prose. I am searching for my muse. When she comes to me, her voice will flow through me with glorious enchantment and words filled with wonder."

Robert, thinking she really was certifiable, hesitated before speaking. "I'm kind of hoping for the same thing in a way. But, I am working on a novel about my youth. It's reminiscent of the first times my parents let me go anywhere without adult supervision. I went away to these monastery grounds where my friends and I would camp out in the woods and discover the meaning of life while surviving totally on our own. Actually, it's why I came to this place, to recreate that atmosphere. And on that note, do you want me to help with clean-up?'

"Not if you plan to go and wash dishes in the stream," Veronica gybed. "I've got this, no problem. Go back to your book."

"Thanks. I'd like to do a bit more before the sun sets," Robert said rising. He turned back and added, "Maybe tomorrow I can throw on a few steaks if you're game."

"Game on," Veronica replied.

Robert sat at the desk alternating between re-reading the title page on his laptop and looking out the window. By the time he glanced at his watch, it was ten o'clock. He thought to himself maybe it would be best to just get a good night's sleep and wake up early, feel refreshed and walk the grounds. He'd surely get inspired by sitting with his laptop in a place that reminded him of the carefree camping days of his youth.

As Robert was leaving his bathroom, he shook a bottle of over-the-counter sleeping pills and after hesitating, took two, shut off the light and went to bed. Almost as soon as his head hit the pillow, as he lay looking up at the ceiling, he heard the recognizable sound of an old typewriter being pounded. It was clicking in fury from what he had thought was the empty room next door. However, he managed to battle the intermittent tapping until his sleeping aids kicked in. The next thing he knew, the first light was peeking in through the window shade and he arose and allowed the light to flow in.

Robert was in the kitchen leaving a note for "Veronica and Guest" to feel free and have some coffee. He had his laptop case over his shoulder and quietly headed out of the cottage to find a place to write. As he got out front, he turned back toward his room from the outside contemplating whether to shut his curtains. He noticed that the third room shade was partially askew. He cautiously peered in out of curiosity and noted an old typewriter on the desk, but the room certainly looked like it was not occupied by anyone. He thought about going back and maybe talking to Veronica, but her curtains were still closed tight so he embarked on his journey toward fulfilling his mission.

The grounds were very engaging and nostalgic of the days Robert had remembered as a kid camping out. However, try as he may, taking his time, and moving from tree stump to rock, overlooking the water, to benches set up for meditation, each time Robert pulled out his laptop he couldn't seem to get any more than an opening sentence and then going back and hitting the delete key to erase. Ultimately, he gave up and went back to the cottage dejected.

When he returned, he noticed Veronica sitting out on the veranda with a coffee cup and a journal which was closed on the table nearby.

"Did you find your muse yet? Robert quipped.

"No, not yet. I was sure you must have kidnapped her," Veronica countered.

Robert didn't want to tell her what a failure his day was so he said it had been quite a productive morning but it was time to charge up his laptop again while he left for the country market to get a few steaks for dinner, assuming she was still on.

"Gosh," she said, "I'm barely awake. But sure, why not, just a small piece, though."

Robert was pleased but didn't show it much. "We gotta eat eventually," he said. "I'm thinking same time as last night. Oh—" he stopped for a moment, "did you wake up from that typewriter going in the third room half into the night?"

"What?" Veronica said with surprise and some definite doubt, "I didn't hear anything. I don't think anyone has checked in there."

Robert stopped himself deciding not to pursue it when he realized it would be awfully hard to explain and moved on about his business. He plugged in his laptop and went out to his car which was parked next to Veronica's. If the third guest was around, there was no car to indicate such. Robert headed down the winding, tree-lined road toward the country store more than a little frustrated with his lack of progress.

After unloading his groceries, Robert decided to try and write some more in his room. He soon got up and paced a bit, then tried a bit of meditation to get back into that head space when he was younger. He had the whole wide world ahead of him, away from his family, alone, even from friends, as he often chose to be in the afternoons, listening to the random words of nature in their own languages.

But thinking and dreaming was not writing. Perhaps a bit of nourishment would do the trick. The steaks were beckoning and maybe a little repartee with Veronica would pull some thoughts to the surface. She may be a little dingy he thought, but whatever he had been trying with solace was certainly coming up short.

Veronica and Robert sat out on the veranda eating silently until Veronica put her utensils back on the plate after only a few bites of meat.

"I feel bad Robert, but sitting out here eating beef, it kind of makes me feel uncomfortable, like I'm going against nature somehow."

"That's okay. You warned me. You think it is a barrier to your muse?"

"I wasn't thinking about that. Trying to draw my muse in doesn't work. I've accepted that after years of trying. She's awfully mysterious it seems, and really has her own timing."

"Well, you can say that again. And I've lost my patience. A few more hours is really all I've got here, and then it is back home to the rat race early tomorrow. I am going to force something out, even if it is just drivel." Robert paused. "My wife was right I guess. Not only is it probably pointless to be writing in the first place, I don't even have it in me. I think if a muse were to come it might just whisper something about cooking lessons instead."

Robert got tired of staring at the screen and started packing up his things. He picked up the copy of Thoreau's *Walden; or Life in the Woods*, he'd brought for inspiration, but thumbed through it and hesitated, fearful he'd end up just copying it in some way. But, before he knew it, he was drawn in and sat and read till he started to nod off. Then, it began again—the deliberate striking of the typewriter in earnest, just like the night before. He looked at his watch and it was after eleven.

The irony was not lost on him, having resigned himself to the realization that the answer to writing his novel was not in getting away from his daily routine at home. However, as disenchanted as he was, he did figure that much out after all. And wasn't that accomplishing something? He tried to convince himself again and went back to reading but the typing was irritating him more and more. Finally, he knocked on the wall and it stopped.

Just as he had undressed and gotten ready for bed, though, it started up again. This time he knocked and it stopped for a few seconds only. He decided to get up and go out and knock on the door. Before he did, he noticed through his window shade what appeared to be a light coming from that room. As he went up to his desk to get a better look, he banged into the corner and knocked his book to the floor. When he picked it up, the light was off. He grabbed his robe and thought he heard a door closing very quietly and deliberately.

He hustled out the door and before he could get any further, he saw Veronica putting her cup down on the kitchen table with her journal opened and a pen sitting on top.

"You had to have heard it this time," Robert blurted.

"Yes. I did," she stated and smiled and sat down. "Finally."

"What do you mean, finally? Isn't that typing driving you nuts?"

"I didn't hear any typing," she replied, "I meant I heard my muse. You must be hearing things yourself again, Robert?"

"Well, I am telling you I know I did." He went over to the third room and started knocking on the door. Then, he tried turning the door knob and it was locked. He headed over to some drawers in the kitchen. "There's got to be a flashlight," he said as he fumbled about and found one and turned it on. "Aha, come on, I'll show you."

Veronica seemed a bit disturbed, but got up and followed Robert around to the outside window. Robert crept to the side of the window he'd looked in earlier that day and again it was apparent that no one was in there. He tracked the light over far enough for Veronica to see the typewriter. Reaching across, he grabbed Veronica's arm, pulling her toward him. "See, there's the typewriter. And there's paper in it. Look."

Veronica did so and acknowledged that, but said, "I don't know what that means. It's a typewriter and there is paper in it. Maybe the owner of the cottage uses it or offers it to some of the guests who want that experience."

"But, there wasn't any paper in it when I looked last time."

"Are you sure, Robert? I'm sorry. I didn't hear anything and the room looks undisturbed to me. And sadly, your timing isn't real good for me. I am finally getting vibes from my muse. I need to get back to writing while it is flowing. I honestly think you should go back to bed and get some rest. You must have been dreaming or something."

Robert was confused, annoyed, and frustrated as he grabbed his sleeping pills and took three this time. He opened his book, started to read and dozed off quickly.

The light shown through his shade and he sat up. He opened the curtains and noticed that Veronica was already packed and out by her car apparently leaving. He pulled on his robe and took a quick look in the mirror, brushed his hair with his hand, and then hurried out to catch up to her and say farewell before she left.

As Robert approached her car she was turned away and just shutting the trunk when he noticed what looked like an old typewriter near Veronica's suitcase.

"Wait," Robert demanded. "There's the typewriter. What's going on?"

"Robert, please," Veronica replied quickly, "I do all of my writing in a journal." She opened it and showed him. "And look, my muse was very kind to me. I never went to sleep, in fact. So, I am very tired and I am going to go home and take a long nap. But, I'll be back again. You coming to the next retreat in the Fall?"

"Oh, I don't think so. No point really. But, thanks for keeping me company and I'm very happy for you and your muse. By the way, does she make house calls?"

"Oh, that's the thing, you never know."

As Veronica pulled away, Robert went back into the cottage. He headed toward his room, but when he passed the third room, he stopped, turned back, and tried the doorknob again. This time the door was unlocked. He opened it and saw that the typewriter was missing. Startled, he looked out the window and wanted to run after her, but Veronica was long gone. Robert shook his head and started back out, now somewhat amused, when he noticed there was a curled paper from the typewriter sitting on the desk. He picked it up and read what was written: "The secret to writing is rewriting and rewriting and rewriting ...."

Robert went back to his room carrying the paper. As he placed it on the desk he stared at the title page on his laptop. He sat down and made a quick alteration, "The 'LAST' Camping Trip." That was it. His story had to begin at the final camping trip. It needed to be about the culmination of all of the lessons he learned along the way and it changed the direction of his life. Robert was off and running. He began writing in a flurry. The muse had come to him at last. And checkout time wasn't for several more hours.

Robert took one more look around the cottage as he was leaving. The entire scene had a whole new feeling of illumination. He had discovered what he was searching for. He threw his things in the back seat of his car and got into the driver's seat. As he started up the engine, he glanced at the passenger seat and couldn't believe his eyes. How did that get there he thought? It was the typewriter.

Old Typewriter Courtesy of Carol Malone

About the Author. Billy Martin—three consecutive VCWC anthologies top the list of his publishing credits to date. He has been a member for ten years and lost every short story contest since he joined. He is currently published sporadically in the *Thousand Oaks Acorn* and has been a columnist for the *Community Link* for the past three months with BOOMERANG: *what goes around comes around.* He is writing a tongue-in-cheek look at dieting book called, *Liten-Up! - The 2yr. Diet.* He spent the last decade trying to write screenplays unsuccessfully and switched back to his sweet spot last summer. When he was twelve years old on Long Island, he'd run down the driveway to grab the afternoon, *Newsday,* as it was being thrown. He'd turn right to Erma Bombeck, then Ann Landers. He loves soft commentary, amusing rather than humorous. He loves the greats like Charles Osgood, Andy Rooney, Dave Barry, Art Buchwald, and Woody Allen. He's a tie-dyed in the wool, first generation, American Baby Boomer born in NY, and living in CA.

what do the dead know?

what do the dead know?
do they know that
we dream about them --
smouldering sometimes
awkward sexual dreams?

& the anger --
beating them with fists
pounding
making them dead again?

nobody alive knows

we can only hope that
their compassion
is a thousand times
greater

than when we dealt them
the dirty cards down
here -

when we lied to them with every other breath

~~*

About the Author. Mike Faran lives in Ventura, California as a retired candlestick maker. He served four years in the USAF and attended Cal State Fullerton where he received a BA in English. His poetry has been published in *Rattle, Atlantic Review, The Main Street Rad, The Comstock Review, The Haight Ashbury Literary Journal, Slant*, and others.

My Dad and His Fish by Jean Tufts

My dad liked to fish and sometimes he took me with him. He could fish without catching anything much longer than I could though. I already knew I shouldn't throw rocks in the water or make loud noises, because it would scare the fish he was trying to catch. Luckily, there were lots of other interesting things to do at a lake or stream, that didn't make noise.

I spent a lot of time at the edge with a cup trying to catch the little silvery minnows. Sneaking up and slowly dipping the cup into the water, I'd think I had them for sure. I'd raise it up slowly and carefully, but like pinched watermelon seeds, they always squirted away at the last instant.

There were also a lot more interesting bugs and worms than at home. I liked the dragon fly's brilliantly changing metallic colors. I marveled at their ability to stop in midair, hover then zip abruptly off in another direction. I studied the big black beetles that could walk on the surface of the water. There was a tiny ring of depressed water around each pointed foot and I wondered why it didn't poke through. Dad explained that water had a kind of "skin" on the surface that held them up.

When I did catch a fish, I loved the feel of it tugging on my line. But as much as I liked catching them, I didn't like to kill them. I felt bad as I watched them flopping and struggling, mouths gasping. Sometimes, when no one was looking, I eased them back into the water where they could breathe. Dad did not approve. He said fish were caught to be eaten. I didn't much like to eat them, so throwing them back worked out well for both me and the fish.

It wasn't that they didn't taste good, they just didn't seem worth the trouble. Little bits of meat, barely big enough for a bite, had to be carefully picked out from among the bones.

To make it even harder, all of those tiny needle-like bones were almost invisible because they were the same color as the meat. Children were warned about getting a bone caught in their throat. I visualized it lodged crosswise with the sharp points puncturing both sides. Mother said eating bread was supposed to dislodge the bones, but what if it didn't. Eating fish just seemed dangerous, like running with scissors.

Watching the dead fish being gutted and the scales scraped off wasn't very appetizing, but I really liked watching this operation. I had a great curiosity for what was inside of things and how they worked. When Dad slit the fish up the middle, all of those interesting little wet lumps, sacks and twisted tubes slid out. Pretending I was a scientist, I examined them closely, trying to figure out what they were and why they were different colors. I felt I'd made a major discovery when I saw how the food changed as it passed through the tubes, finally becoming droppings.

Someone told me fish scales had growth rings like trees and you could tell the fish's age by counting them. I held some tiny Bluegill scales up in the sun. I counted the rainbow colored rings. No matter how big or small, the fish all seemed to be the same age.

Dad was proud of his catch and eating the fish reminded him of past fishing trips and the taste and size of those fish. Liking fish the way he did, put me in contact with some other fishy delicacies that were surely an acquired taste. The worst were sardines. How could anybody willingly eat something that smelled like that?

One day, Dad and I seemed to be on our own at lunchtime. Mom always cooked and served our meals, so it was interesting to have Dad doing it. I watched as he poured me a glass of cold milk and made a peanut butter and jelly sandwich, folded over instead of cut. He warmed some of that morning's coffee in a little pan. It sputtered and sizzled as he poured it into his cup. Then putting a can of sardines and a box of crackers on the table, he sat down next to me.

"Oh, let me wind it, let me wind it," I begged. He nodded and I pulled the key from the bottom of the can. He helped me pull up the little metal tab and I put it through the key slot.

"I'll hold the can steady for you," he said, and I started to wind. "Now don't let it get going crooked." I carefully rolled the metal strip around the key until the end. "Wait now, those edges are sharp, I better pull it off the rest of the way." Then Dad lifted the lid, uncovering all of the shining little fish bodies. He speared a sardine with his fork, put it on a cracker and ate it.

We had been fishing the weekend before and I looked at the sardines with new interest. They were such tiny little things, all exactly the same size and so neatly lined up in there. "How do they catch sardines?" I asked. "It would have to be a really tiny hook and how would you ever get a worm that small stuck on it?"

Dad laughed, spraying some cracker crumbs onto the tablecloth. He chuckled again as he explained. "Big fishing boats catch them in nets by the millions."

"Oh." I looked at the shiny, silvery bodies. "Someone went to a lot of trouble fitting them in there so neatly." Then I thought about all those tiny insides. "It must be a big job to gut them, they're so small."

Dad laughed again. "No, no, they're cooked whole and preserved." When he saw the look on my face, he gave me a little hug. "Don't worry they're fine, just fine the way they are."

I poked one with the point of a knife. The tiny sunken eye stared up, shiny and blank. "But what about all those bugs and worms they ate, they're all still in there. They've still got scales and eyeballs and the fish poop—the fish poop is still in there, too!" Then another thought occurred to me. "The bones, Dad. Those dangerous bones—what about the bones and the teeth?"

"Everything is all cooked and preserved," he said. "The bones get soft. Besides, the bones are good for you, rich in calcium. Calcium gives you strong bones." He poked my arm playfully with his finger.

How could he believe something like that? Who in the world thought these things up anyway? Sardines did not have one single thing going for them as far as I was concerned. Stinky little dead fish with all of the stuff you were supposed to remove still in there and my dad was eating them. I think this was the first time I wondered if my dad was as smart as I had always thought he was.

~~*

About the Author. Forty-five years ago Jean Tufts, her husband, their two sons, a dog and two cats moved into their home in a rural area of Moorpark. Many animals came and went over the years, including a variety of wild creatures the boys brought home. A lot of Jean's short stories are about animals. She also has a good imagination and entertains herself with a bit of fiction. She is currently assembling a book of animal stories. Working in a library was a fun job for a book lover and it led to an even more enjoyable job as the Enrichment Librarian at an elementary school. There, Jean created special monthly programs, paired with related books and stories. Becoming a storyteller followed quite naturally and the tellers were encouraged to develop original stories. Jean still makes up stories, now written to be read.

"It's the journey that matters, soak it in.
Learn lessons out of it.
Impact positively so that if you never get to your destination,
at least you'd leave a legacy to be remembered."
~ Emem Uko

Inebriation *by Hildegard J. Blass*

Walter Baer was his true name
    He had no talent, had no fame,

But booze was taking times for now.
    His hair would grow, and so his brow.

His looks would fade, he needed care
    But he just drank in deep despair.

Thunderbird the drink of choice,
    Asking to stop, was only noise.

Headaches from the alcohol
    Registered deep in Walters soul.

Antabuse, the pills were taken
    Thunderbird for now forsaken.

It only took a week or two
    When thirst set in, what did he do?

With money back in shaking hands
    He bought more booze familiar brand.

Why he goes on and on this way?
    I do not know it's hard to say.

Excessive drinking made him choose
    The life he certainly will lose.

Or was there more to Walter Baer
    No one could see, just I did care.

He must have lost a certain will
    To live a life of goodness still.

One day he walked away real slow
    I called; come back please do not go,

But he kept going sad and bend
    Not thinking of a waiting end,

Now Walter is no longer here
    He rests on ice, not drinking beer.

About the Author: Hildegard J. Blass was born in Germany a long time ago. She made sure to learn the beautiful English language to express herself with poems, short stories, and essays. Her hobby is creating paintings of the things that interest her. She also loves to read inspirational books and *Time Magazine*. She is happy to have met people at the Ventura County Writers Club.

The Night is Near - Courtesy of Wendell Ward

When age chills the blood, when our pleasures are past--
For years fleet away with the wings of the dove--
The dearest remembrance will still be the last,
Our sweetest memorial the first kiss of love.
~ Lord (George Gordon) Byron

My crew and I
Are working hard
Pulling the boats upstream
We've left our families
Our homes for dreams
Of the Pacific Ocean view
Storms are hard on our boats
But no enough to knock us
So we keep going
With heads held high
And the ocean deep behind our eyes
It's winter now
Degrees below zero
I'm fearful that
We might not make it
But the ocean keeps us hoping
We've traveled through storms and snow
Hands sore
Feet aching
Ocean view behind our eyes
So we won't stop moving
It's finally near
My heart can feel it
One more step
I think it's there
I know it's there
Just one more step to victory
There's the ocean
Blue and green
No moment can be this great
We've traveled through storms and snow
Hands sore
Feet aching
The difference is
That image that lay behind our eyes
Has moved to
In front of us
For us to touch
For us to love
Now we rest our
Sore hands
Our aching feet
And our tiresome eyes

About the author: Olivia Adelman is driven by music and athletics, Olivia's love for writing introspective poetry is further inspired by her simple love for life itself. Olivia lives with her parents and three sisters in the beautiful Ojai Valley. Olivia is excited about the opportunity to share her writing and experience the world in front of her.

Sunset over Ventura Harbor – Courtesy of Wendell Ward

"...we should be remembered for the things we do.
The things we do are the most important things of all.
They are more important than what we say or what we look like.
The things we do outlast our mortality.
The things we do are like monuments that people build
to honour heroes after they've died.
They're like the pyramids that the Egyptians built to honour the Pharaohs.
Only instead of being made out of stone,
they're made out of the memories people have of you.
That's why your deeds are like your monuments.
Built with memories instead of with stone."
~ R.J. Palacio

**A Tribute to Marjorie L. Moore who passed away in 2014.
You'll always be in our remembrance, Marjorie.**

August 1939, 2:45 P.M., Studio City, California.

The lunch counter customers had vanished for the time being. Recalling the other waitress's words, "Keep busy, even if you have to re-do and re-do," Suzy did just that, polishing the shiny chrome napkin holders, the glass salt, pepper, and sugar containers for the second time within twenty minutes. Then she proceeded to wipe down the red leather stools. Glancing over her new domain, the auburn haired teenager smiled as she gazed at the spot free marble counter.

She was thrilled to earn money as the Great Depression held its grip over most of the country. With all the expenses from her mom's illness and death, money was in short supply. Suzy wanted to help her dad. She turned her head toward the low rumble coming from the rear of the building where the bowling lanes were located, then the crack of collision, ball against pins and the jubilant "Yeah". Someone had scored a needed strike. Suzy smiled.

One of the heavy wooden front doors of the lobby swung open. As Suzy glanced around a blinding blast of the late afternoon sunshine encompassed a tall, dark form. She closed her eyes, blinking several times to regain her vision as the shape sauntered toward the counter. When her focus cleared, it was like looking at a magazine cover. The man in his western shirt and bolo tie was trim and handsome. His long legs were in narrow western style pants, the toe of his boots barely peeking out. He sat down and smiled, Suzy handed him the menu as her heart did a flip-flop.

"Young lady, I'll take coffee black, bacon, lettuce and tomato on wheat toast, please." He spoke with a soft Texan drawl. His eyes were grey-green, his mustache perfectly trimmed, his dark hair had a slight wave, a little longer than most men. He handed the menu back to her.

She filled a mug with freshly brewed coffee and placed it before him before going into the kitchen to make his sandwich. The kitchen had a pick-up window which allowed customers to see the server and vice versa, but she tried not to stare.

The bacon-tom-sandwich was the best she had ever made. She added a generous scoop of potato salad, pickles and olives and took it to him.

"What's your name, young lady?"

"Suzy"

"You have a beautiful smile, Suzy," he said with a grin.

She blushed scarlet and thanked him before turning towards a second customer just arriving. It was one of the pinsetters; he ordered the same thing he had for the last two days.

"Chocolate malt, nice and thick." He repeated the word *thick* and winked at her. Suzy smiled and whirled around to grab a chilled canister. She measured out three and a half heaping scoops of ice cream, grabbed some milk from the fridge, a teaspoon of malt powder and a generous squirt of dark chocolate syrup before pushing it onto the milkshake mixer. The machine sprung to life, loudly churning the ingredients into a thick creamy mass as she selected a frosty tall glass to serve it in. He grinned as she set it down in front of him along with some cellophane wrapped cookies. "Don't ever lose that sparkle in your hazel eyes, Suzy," he said with a smile.

Suzy thanked him and turned toward the handsome vision of the cowboy, "We have some fresh apple pie. Would you like some?"

He smiled that slow smile and drawled, "Just coffee, little lady, thank you."

Suzy thought she would melt into the same frothy drink she had just prepared.

With Universal Studios situated in Studio City, it wasn't unusual to see stars, behind the scenes workers or extras in the bowling alley. She assumed the handsome man was a movie star not a wannabe. As Suzy refilled his mug, she noticed his long-fingered, strong tan hands. He wore an oblong silver and turquoise ring. The cuff of his shirt had silver-rimmed flat pearl buttons. Not only was he nice-looking, he was immaculate.

The Texan finished the coffee, pushed his lanky body to his feet. He was more than six feet tall. "I hope to see you again Suzy, my name is Joe."

"Bye Joe," she said, grinning from ear to ear. She knew she was blushing while he smiled and slowly turned to stroll toward the front door. As she cleared off the counter and scooped up his generous tip, she knew this man was special. She hoped to see him again, soon.

The last hour of her shift went quickly as Suzy took care of new coffee customers and a few supper ones. Bowlers arrived laughing and excited about the upcoming evening league action. A short time later, she was driving her brother's car home still thinking about the western, soft-spoken, kind-eyed customer. His image was still sharp in her mind. He must be a movie star. He was too handsome to work behind the scenes.

She drove carefully, knowing how lucky she was to have the car for the summer. Her brother was working with the Civil Conservation Corps for the summer, after dropping out of college. Their mother's death one year earlier had left him deeply depressed. The two had always been exceptionally close and Suzy knew being up in the Sierra Mountains working with the forest rangers would be good for her brother, but she really missed him. He offered the loan of his car, a generous gesture, even from the brother who always tried to take good care of her. He told her she could take it to the beach. On their last trip there together Tony showed her where to park to avoid dings, warning her, "Don't scratch it."

However, on her third solo visit to the beach, she returned to the car late in the day to find a six-inch scrape on the right fender. The lot was empty and there was no one in sight to tell her what had happened. Suzy was devastated and fought tears all the way home. She knew her brother would be furious with her, even though she had no control over it. Suzy reluctantly gave up going to the beach. Every time she used his car she saw the injury to his shiny old car.

Home seemed a dreary place when Dad was at work and her brother was away. She coasted into the driveway, then locked the car and walked around to the back door. She immediately changed and went into the kitchen to start dinner. She set the table before scrubbing the fresh carrots from their garden, carefully cut them into slices and added a pinch of salt and a fresh sage leaf to the pan along with a little water. Looking at the wall clock, she decided to wait ten minutes before cooking them, so they wouldn't be overdone.

Suzy pulled the leftover mashed potatoes from the fridge, added an egg and some seasoning then patted them into cakes for frying. She added a huge pat of butter to a cast iron skillet and turned on the burner. Removing the leftover beef pot roast from the ice-box, she sliced half of it and arranged the slices on a plate. They usually ate left over meats at room temperature in the summer, so she set the plate on the unlit burner where the heat from the vegetables would take the chill away.

She watched the golden butter lose its color as it melted and slightly sizzled. Lifting the handle to tilt the pan and coat the bottom with the now liquid butter, she carefully placed the potato pancakes into the pan. Her dad loved them fixed this way and the buttery smell chased the emptiness from the modest house. She heard Dad's car come into the driveway. She quickly mixed a green salad adding a cut up garden tomato and dressing to it.

As always, Dad walked in with a smile. "Hi, honey, do you need any help?"

"Thanks, Daddy, but I think I have it under control."

"Then I'll wash up, change and be right back. Smells good."
Suzy checked the carrots with the cooking fork, tender, but not soft … perfect. She turned off the burner and slid the lid part way off to stop their steaming. She turned over the potatoes for a minute or two before dishing them onto the plate she had warming. Dinner was always at six thirty and she had everything on the table just as her dad entered the kitchen.

"This smells wonderful. Suzy, you've become a really good cook," Dad said as he sat down.

"Thanks, Daddy."

A few days after Mom died, Dad told the fifteen-year-old she would have to do most of the cooking. Her mom had never taught her to cook, so her dad taught her what he knew and reminded her she could read, as he handed her a recipe book. He encouraged each attempt. Suzy knew her father loved her. She felt lucky to have him for a father, but she still missed her mother.

The following day was a busy one at work, which went by very fast. There wasn't much action going on the lanes, but the pool room across the lobby had several tables going. In addition, from the counter with the doorway open to the bar she could hear spontaneous laughter. Joe came in and took a seat. He glanced at the menu, "How's the roast turkey san?"

"The turkey is moist and fresh. Would you like it on wheat toast?"

A wide grin spread over his face. "Sounds good, Suzy."

He'd barely finished his words when one of a group of loud young men walked up to order sandwiches and cokes for all of them. Suzy explained she could fix the order, but wasn't allowed to leave the counter to deliver it into the poolroom as the man requested.

She knew who this young ruffian was. He played a tough New York gang member in a recent movie. He had given her a hard time before. "Then one of us will pick up the damn order. There goes your tip," he grumbled as he swaggered away.

Suzy looked at Joe, feeling very embarrassed. "Roast turkey san on wheat toast coming up."

He smiled. "And coffee, please. I'll be back in a minute." Joe got up and ambled across the lobby as she went into the kitchen to prepare his plate. A few minutes later, she looked across the lobby and saw Joe tower over the teenagers, talking quietly. When he returned to his seat, she slipped his coffee in front of him. "Your sandwich will be ready in a minute."

"Thank you, Suzy."

She finished preparing his plate and took it to him. Then she got busy with the tough kid's order. Within minutes, one of the young men came to pick up the tray. He was polite to her as he glanced at Joe.

After he left, she turned to Joe, "What did you say to those guys?"

He grinned, "I told them you're my kid sister and I didn't appreciate them treating you like that."

Suzy laughed. "I think I'd like to be your kid sister. Thanks. That was kind of you."

"There's no call for anyone to act that way. These young kids know they can't be rude just because they're actors. They would never get away with that in Texas."

"I thought maybe you're from Texas. How do you like it out here?"

"Well, both my Dad and I found work. That's a good thing. Work is scarce back home right now. My younger brother and I live with our folks in Van Nuys."

"Oh, I live in Van Nuys, too."

Joe smiled at her. "Oh, yeah. What pie is fresh tonight?"

"We have a great looking boysenberry one as well as a cherry one."

"I'll try the berry one."

Suzy refilled his coffee and sliced the berry pie, "Would you like a scoop of ice cream?"

"Yes, vanilla, please."

Joe finished his supper or whatever he called these odd hour meals and had a third cup of coffee before leaving. Suzy watched him leave and hoped he would come back soon, very soon. She could use a friend.

Joe continued to show up at the counter several times a week. By the time Suzy had worked there three weeks, her brother returned home and needed his car. She wasn't sure how she was going to get back and forth to her job. Traveling by bus was not an option in Van Nuys and taxis were expensive. Her brother gave her a ride Saturday morning and Dad was going to pick her up, even though it was out of his way. As it turned out, it didn't matter because the manager called her into the alcove between the counter and the bar area right after the noon rush.

"Suzy, how old are you?"

She glanced at his eyes and saw the accusation. She looked down, embarrassed by her deceit.

"You're not eighteen, are you? I just now noticed you left your age blank on the application."

"I'm sixteen. I'm sorry. I really wanted a job."

"I have to let you go. I hate to because you're a good worker and the customers like you. But, we could lose our liquor license by having an under-age person working here."

"I'm sorry, I didn't realize that."

"I'll have your pay ready in a few minutes." As Suzy listened to him, she heard the low rumble of balls whirling down the lanes. It was a sound she had grown to like and knew she would miss this place.

She walked back to the kitchen and told her co-worker, Debbie, what happened. She was the one who told Suzy to leave the age blank. "I'm sorry Suzy, I hoped that wouldn't happen."

Joe arrived as Suzy removed her smock and picked up her purse. He called to her as she rounded the front of the counter, patting the seat next to him he asked, "What's going on?"

"I've been let go, because I'm too young." Suzy said with a sigh, "I've got to call for a ride home."

"No need to do that. You said you live in Van Nuys, when I finish this coffee I'm headed home so I'll give you a ride."

"I live way out on the west side of Van Nuys."

"Doesn't matter. I'm glad to do it. I promised to stop by the house and get Mom's grocery list. Okay?"

Suzy suddenly felt better. She smiled up into his concerned looking face. "Thanks, Joe." Before he could answer, the manager showed up with her check.

"I added a little extra because it's such short notice. Good luck finding another job, Suzy"

"Thank you."

Joe and Suzy headed out to the parking area, giving them time to become better acquainted. "Joe, have you appeared in any of the westerns Universal is releasing?"

Joe looked down at her, his eyes twinkled with amusement. "I'm not an actor, I'm a carpenter."

She stopped walking and stammered out, "I thought … you're so handsome … and so western that you're surely an actor. You look far too clean to be a carpenter." It came out before she could stop it. This tended to happen occasionally, especially when she was flustered. Her cheeks turned scarlet. She bit her lip, wondering why she said such a stupid thing.

As they walked, Suzy glanced sideways at Joe, admiring his smooth gait and erect posture as he led the way to a light grey sedan with Texas plates then opened the passenger door for her.

She smiled, "Thanks, it's nice of you to give me a ride home." She giggled, adding, "You may be sorry, I do live out in the sticks."

"Doesn't matter. We're both in Van Nuys."

After they grinned at each other, he closed the door. Then Suzy's mind started questioning her action. Her Dad's words echoed through her head. *Never go anywhere with a man you don't know.* He had even given her a fifty-cent piece for a taxi in an emergency. She started to panic. Then she re-assured herself that she'd known Joe for weeks. Suddenly she realized Joe was telling her something. She tried to catch the rest of what he was saying.

"I make props and do alterations in backdrops."

"That sounds sort of like fun work. Do you enjoy it?"

"I appreciate the work and there is quite a bit of overtime. Many afternoons the director calls a two-hour break, after which we work well into the night." Joe turned right onto Van Nuys Blvd.

"I'd like to work at a studio, I think."

"Well, you'll probably have to wait until you're eighteen to apply," he said with a smile.

Joe turned right and then left on a residential street, parking in front of the third house on the left. "Come on in, I'd like you to meet my mom." Joe opened her car door and she followed him.

He opened the polished oak front door and called in as they entered, "Hi, Mom."

He led Suzy through the house as she heard a woman's voice call out, "I'm in the kitchen."

"She usually is." He said with a smile.

When they entered the kitchen, Suzy saw a tall woman with her hands covered in flour. Seeing Suzy, she withdrew them from a large bowl and wiped them on a towel. The woman smiled broadly at Suzy as Joe kissed his mom's cheek.

"Mom, this is Suzy. I'm giving her a ride home before I do the marketing." Then he turned to Suzy, "I'll be right back."

The smell of fresh yeast permeated the kitchen. It gave off a homey, wonderful odor. "Suzy, I'm happy to meet you. Joe mentioned you a couple of times. He has always wanted a kid sister." She smiled and extended her hand in greeting.

Suzy shook hands immediately liking the friendly woman. "Are you making bread?"

"Yes, I am."

"Isn't that hard to do?"

"I've been doing this for so many years it's kind of automatic now." She smiled again and went back to kneading the dough. Suzy watched in amazement as the woman deftly pushed and pulled the lump around on the floured board, punched the mass a few times before gathering it back into a ball. She returned the dough to the large pottery bowl, covered it with a clean dishtowel and set it at the back of the unlit stove.

"This takes a couple more hours of rising before it's ready to be shaped into loaves."

Joe walked back into the kitchen, picked up a list from the table his mom had been working at. "Is this all, Mom?"

"Yes, thank you, dear."

216

"Glad to help, see you later." Suzy watched him kiss his mom's cheek again. His mom turned toward Suzy. "Come by when you can stay and chat, dear. I'd be happy to teach you how to make bread."

"Thank you. I'd like that." Suzy smiled, blinking back a tear as she thought of her own mom for a moment.

They turned off the dirt road onto her gravel driveway, she could see her brother with his head stuck under the hood of his car. She opened the door and got out. "Tony, hi. I'm home."

Rising up from his car, Tony adjusted his glasses and stared at them. Then he walked over to Joe's car.

"Tony, this is Joe. He gave me a ride home. I lost my job today."

Joe smiled slightly, stepped out of the car and extended his hand to the younger man. "Hi, Joe Branson, glad to meet you, Tony."

Tony still stared at Joe. "Same here."

He was scrutinizing the tall stranger with his kid sister.

Joe got back into the car. "I'll be on my way."

After the car pulled out of the driveway, Tony turned to his sister with a scowl. "What the heck are you doing in the car with a total stranger?" He had both hands on his hips as he glared at her. "You're just too damn trusting. You can't ever do that again. He's too old to be giving you a ride."

Suzy knew she had pushed Tony too far. If he told their dad, she might never be able to leave the house. She never contacted Joe again.

In 1948, seven years later after World War II, Suzy and her husband went to a theater in Studio City. During the intermission, Suzy glanced around the auditorium. Not many people were present. About ten rows in front of them, a lone tall man stood and walked up the aisle. Suzy stared in amazement at him, his slow easy gait, his height, his face. It was Joe.

He recognized her at the same time. A smile spread over his face as he walked into the empty row of seats in front of them. Suzy was thrilled to see her old friend. His dark hair was softened by a generous sprinkling of grey, but other than that he looked the same. She introduced the two men then chatted up a storm with Joe. Leaning forward, she placed her hand on the back of the seat in front of her. Joe placed his hand over hers and gave it a squeeze. "Do you two have any children?"

"Yes, a two-and-a- half-year-old girl." Suzy answered.

"Wonderful," Joe answered as he smiled at Suzy's husband. "I'd better be on my way. Great to see you kids. Suzy, you grew up lovely. You haven't changed one bit." Joe patted her hand, pulled away, and stood up. He left before she could ask about his life.

You haven't changed either, Suzy thought as she silently reveled in the miracle of their meeting once again. A few minutes later, as the lights dimmed and the second feature began Suzy mulled over the rare

217

happenstance that brought them to the same place at the same time. *Fate meant for them to meet again after all these years.*

It happened only that one time.

Throughout the rest of her life, Joe remained a special recollection in her secret thoughts. She'd see his concerned grey-green eyes and remember his gentleness, and she knew she was a better person through their brief friendship.

~~*

About the Author: Marjorie Moore—Artistry, in one form or another was always a big part of Marjorie's life. She drew in pencil, pen and ink, pastels and painted in oils, acrylics and watercolors. She painted people, animals, landscapes, flowers and also took up china painting for a period. At about eighty years of age, she began to explore new outlets for her indomitable creative spirit and converted her writing journals and *Emblem Club* newsletter articles into short stories. Marjorie joined the Ventura County Writer's Club in 2009 and served as an assistant editor on the anthology committee. Then she joined a writing critique group to further hone her skills. She was a willing learner, supportive consort and a caring friend. In addition, may I say she was a wonderful wife, companion, mother, grandmother, and great-grand mother who continues to be a great loss, but also an inspiration to us all. In 2014, Marjorie was diagnosed with lung cancer shortly after her ninety-first birthday and chose to be admitted to a care facility where she continued to encourage and befriend others. She left us here July 2, 2014, and I can say she is most certainly smiling at the fact her "Joe" has been chosen to be included in this year's Anthology! *~ Diana Moore, daughter.*

~~*

As you go forward in your life, remember, what you do today will be the stuff of someone's remembrances tomorrow.

~ Carol Malone
VCWC Anthology Chair

www.ingramcontent.com/pod-product-compliance
Lightning Source LLC
Chambersburg PA
CBHW070108260626
47160CB00004B/1368